MAJOR CRISES
IN
WESTERN
CIVILIZATION

II

1745 to the Nuclear Age

New York Chicago Burlingame

HARCOURT, BRACE & WORLD, INC.

Library of Congress Catalog Card Number: 65–19790

PRINTED IN THE UNITED STATES OF AMERICA

CONTENTS

The French Revolution: Dynamics
of the Terror, 1793–94
DAVID H. PINKNEY

Contents

The Industrial Revolution in England:
The Chartist Movement, 1837–58

RICHARD W. LYMAN

Contents

British Imperialism: The Scramble
for Africa, 1870–1914
ROBIN W. WINKS

Crisis in Man's Self-knowledge: The Psychology of Sigmund Freud

MARGOT DREKMEIER

The Bolshevik Seizure of Power, November 1917

RICHARD PIPES

Contents

The Destruction of German Democracy: The Rise of Nazism, 1928–34

JAMES J. SHEEHAN

The Moral Dilemma of Nuclear Warfare
THEODORE ROSZAK

PREFACE

"HISTORY, to be above evasion or dispute," said Lord Acton, "must stand on documents, not on opinions." Though historians are today painfully aware that documents themselves are not above dispute or varying interpretations, they hold without exception that documents are the raw material of historical knowledge. Particularly for the beginning student, the smooth flow of a narrative text and the polished presentation of the finished lecture may be deceptive, lending history the appearance of a steady, even a predetermined and inevitable, flow that belies the uncertain course of nearly every historical sequence. The student who has wrestled with the primary sources in a problem context learns to appreciate that every sentence of history must be "forged in the teeth of irreducible and stubborn facts." Having leveled hills, brought down trees, and filled in gaps himself, he is in a better position to appreciate—and to evaluate—the smooth surface of a text account or the final product of the lecturer's art.

Major Crises in Western Civilization offers the student sixteen documentary problems focused on critical events and turning points in the experience of Western man. The two volumes ("The Greeks to 1660" and "1745 to the Nuclear Age") include a wide range of historical questions—political, diplomatic, economic, religious, social, intellectual, and scientific—and many different kinds of documents: state papers and letters, contemporary articles and essays, diary entries and poems. Guiding the student (gently) as he learns to analyze these different sources are the points of view, toward history and toward historical records, implicit in the contributing editors' selection and arrangement of their material.

The distinguished president of Harvard, Charles W. Eliot, once commented that "all true education is self-education with some assistance from the outside." In evaluating the material in *Major Crises in Western Civilization*, the student will discover for himself that history, far from being cut and dried, abounds with controversial issues that challenge his intelligence and call for his soundest and wisest judgments. The range of these issues—and therefore of the judgments they invite—is wide. Some may require a consideration of two contradictory statements concerning one event; others, a comparison of several widely separated documents and occurrences. For instance, do the documents reveal common characteristics in the downfalls of republican Athens, Rome, Florence, France, and Germany? Do they indicate why Luther held his ground but Galileo recanted? Do they suggest what Freud might have thought of Nazism?

Some direction for the student is naturally necessary, for the primary sources exist in a historical environment. The chronology that opens each chapter furnishes a simple guide to the sequence of events. The introduction supplies the background material and the immediate context of the problem, without prejudging or predigesting either the documents or the issues. The documents, many of them made available in English translation for the first time, are arranged in a logical sequence. Headnotes provide continuity between and particular facts about the individual documents. The conclusion, deliberately kept very brief, summarizes the denouement and points to subsequent developments. The study questions suggest further lines of inquiry, and they, with the recommended readings, may be of value to students preparing critical essays or term papers.

The general editors wish to express their deep appreciation to each of the participating editors for providing students with these contributions from the resources of their learning. We are also grateful to the instructors and undergraduate students in Stanford University's course in the History of Western Civilization for experimenting with trial chapters and for offering many helpful suggestions for the most effective presentation of these problems.

R.W.L.
L.W.S.

Stanford University

Encyclopédie and Enlightenment: "Changing the General Way of Thinking," 1745–64

PETER GAY

COLUMBIA UNIVERSITY

CONTENTS

CHRONOLOGY

1745

FEBRUARY 25   Le Breton takes out a license to publish an encyclopedia.

OCTOBER   Le Breton goes into partnership with three other
publishers to increase capital.

DECEMBER   The license to publish is renewed.

1746

FEBRUARY   Diderot goes on the publishers' payroll.

JUNE 27   The Abbé Gua de Malves is named editor-in-chief
of the *Encyclopédie*. He employs Diderot and
d'Alembert.

JULY 7   *Pensées philosophiques* (written that year by Diderot and published anonymously) is condemned by
parlement of Paris.

AUGUST 3   The publishers and the Abbé Gua de Malves part
amicably.

1747

OCTOBER 16   Diderot and d'Alembert are named editors-in-
chief.

1748

APRIL 30   The license is renewed, with Diderot listed as an
editor.

1749

JUNE 9   Diderot's *Lettres sur les aveugles* is published.

JULY 24   Diderot is arrested for *Lettres sur les aveugles* and
taken to solitary confinement at the fortress of
Vincennes.

AUGUST 21   Diderot is permitted to leave solitary confinement.
He works on the *Prospectus* to the *Encyclopédie*.

NOVEMBER 3   Diderot is freed.

1750

NOVEMBER   Diderot's *Prospectus* is circulated.

1751

JUNE 28   Volume I of the *Encyclopédie* is published.

NOVEMBER 17   The Abbé de Prades defends a heterodox thesis at
the Sorbonne.

1752

FEBRUARY Volume II of the *Encyclopédie* is published.

FEBRUARY 7 Partly because of the Prades scandal, the *Encyclopédie* is suppressed.

1753

NOVEMBER Volume III of the *Encyclopédie* is published.

1754

OCTOBER Volume IV of the *Encyclopédie* is published.

DECEMBER 20 Diderot signs a new, more generous contract with his publishers.

1755

NOVEMBER Volume V (including Diderot's article "Encyclopédie") is published.

1756

SUMMER Volume VI of the *Encyclopédie* is published.

1757

JANUARY 5 Damiens tries to murder King Louis XV, wounding him slightly.

APRIL 16 A royal proclamation announces the death sentence for irreligious and subversive writings.

NOVEMBER Volume VII (including d'Alembert's scandalous article "Genève") is published.

1758

JANUARY D'Alembert withdraws from his editorship.

JULY 27 Helvétius' *De l'esprit* appears and causes immediate scandal.

AUGUST 10 The Council of State rescinds its permission to publish *De l'esprit*.

NOVEMBER 22 The Archbishop of Paris condemns *De l'esprit*.

1759

JANUARY 23 Attorney General Omer Joly de Fleury denounces the *Encyclopédie* before the *parlement* of Paris.

JANUARY 31 Pope Clement VIII condemns *De l'esprit*.

MARCH 8 A royal decree suppresses the *Encyclopédie*.

JULY 21 A royal decree orders booksellers to return money to subscribers.

SEPTEMBER 3 Pope Clement VIII condemns the *Encyclopédie*.

1762

MARCH Voltaire hears of the execution of Jean Calas (a Toulouse Huguenot executed for supposedly mur-

dering his son) and begins to propagandize in behalf of his family.

AUGUST   The Jesuit Order is suppressed in France.

1764

DECEMBER   Volumes VIII to XVII of the *Encyclopédie* are
published.

INTRODUCTION

I D E A S have power, although rarely as much power as their advocates think. Generally, ideas are products; they depend on the fortunate encounter of men and circumstances. They are the mirrors of the times, and their epitomes. But they are not always passive: in making clear what has been obscure, in sharpening conflicts, they also act on their age. Diderot defined the task of a good encyclopedia as "changing the general way of thinking," and if any intellectual enterprise ever succeeded in this task, it was precisely his *Encyclopédie.*

The ideal of gathering all human knowledge into a single work goes back to antiquity. So does the word: as Diderot reminds his readers in his great article "Encyclopédie," the word signifies *"concatenation of knowledge;* it is made up of the Greek prefix EN, *in,* and the nouns KYKLOS, *circle,* and PAIDEIA, *knowledge."* It is the aim of an encyclopedia, he explains, "to assemble all the knowledge now scattered across the world, expound its general structure to the men among whom we live, and transmit it to those who will come after us, so that the labors of past ages may not have been useless to ages to come, that our offspring, as they become better educated, may at the same time become happier and more virtuous, and that we may not die without having deserved the thanks of mankind." This is a noble aim, and a grandiose one, surprising in our time of abundant and bland reference works. Diderot's *Encyclopédie* was different from the encyclopedias of today: it had precursors, but none so rich, none so complete, and it was tendentious. It brought out into the open the latent struggles between radical writers, the men of the Enlightenment who self-consciously called themselves *philosophes,* on the one hand, and the authorities of church and state on the other. In our century the troubles of an encyclopedia (except perhaps in the Soviet Union) are primarily technical and financial. In eighteenth-century France they produced a crisis that reverberated through Europe.

When the *Encyclopédie* was conceived by a combine of booksellers, no such startling consequences were anticipated, or desired, by anyone. The point was to make money as simply as possible. In early 1745, the publisher Le Breton undertook to provide the French reading public with the translation of a successful English venture, Ephraim Chambers' *Cyclopedia, or Universal Dictionary of the Arts and Sciences,* which had appeared in 1728. Le Breton planned some changes in format and detail (two volumes of text were to become four, and the illustrations were to be gathered together into a fifth volume), to correct errors and lengthen some of the articles, but for the rest he was content to stay with Chambers' articles and arrangement. He made an agreement with an Englishman, John Mills, to supervise the French edition, printed a prospectus soliciting subscriptions, and obtained a printing license from the government for the venture. But Le Breton and Mills quarreled almost immediately; their association was dissolved, leaving public demand widely aroused but unappeased.

Then (it is impossible to say when, but perhaps late in 1745, perhaps early in 1746, while Le Breton was attempting to associate himself with other publishers in order to command more capital) Diderot appeared upon the scene, and almost immediately the modest translation became a vast undertaking. There were months of complicated and tedious negotiations, a renewal of the license, and finally, on October 16, 1747, a group of publishers made a contract with Diderot and the mathematician d'Alembert: "Diderot was to get 7200 livres in all: 1200 of it to be paid in a lump sum upon publication of the first volume, and the remaining 6000 to be paid at the rate of 144 livres per month. D'Alembert was also to be paid at the rate of 144 livres per month, but the total was to be only 2400 livres." [1] The selection of editors for the venture was a supreme stroke of good luck: no two men could have been more intelligent, or more inventive, than Diderot and d'Alembert.

In 1747, when Diderot concluded this contract, he was a little-known journalist. He had been born on October 5, 1713, in the provincial town of Langres, the son of a skillful and prosperous cutler from whom he early acquired respect for the mechanical arts. He had been educated at Langres by the Jesuits, who conducted the best schools in France and inculcated in young Denis Diderot, as they did in so many other pupils, an abiding love and intimate knowledge of the classics. As an adolescent he wanted to be a priest, but he soon lost his vocation and went to Paris to become a writer. For a number of years he lived the life of an impecunious man of letters, haunting the cafes, picking up occasional income through translations, experimenting in life and with literature, and ceaselessly educating himself. He married unhappily and had mistresses. Like many other young men of his time, he brooded his way out of the Christianity of his fathers; in 1746, when he was thirty-three and on the verge of associating himself with the projected *Encyclopédie*, he published his first radical philosophical work, the *Pensées philosophiques*—anonymously, of course. It was a collection of aphorisms which betrayed the influence of deism. Diderot was still a religious man, trusting that through reason alone man may glimpse God and the ethical laws governing the universe. But he was no longer a Christian, and the *parlement* of Paris, the supreme judicial body in the land, accordingly ordered the book burned. Since its author was unknown, at least for the moment, the burning did not make Diderot famous, but the historian may see in the incidents a foretaste of the crisis to come.

Jean le Rond d'Alembert was in 1747 far better known than Diderot, his friend and fellow editor. He had been born on November 17, 1717, the illegitimate son of Madame de Tencin, a Parisian prominent in high society,

[1] Arthur M. Wilson, *Diderot: The Testing Years* (New York, Oxford University Press, 1957), p. 80.

and of Louis-Camus Destouches, an officer in the artillery. Madame de
Tencin, unwilling to bring up the unwanted baby, left him on the steps of
the Paris church of St. Jean le Rond, which was to supply part of the boy's
name. He was brought up by affectionate foster parents and showed his
brilliance when he was still very young; in the early 1740's, as a result of
his bold mathematical papers, he began his lifelong association with the
distinguished group of scientists making up the Académie des Sciences. By
1747 he was nationally known as an outstanding mathematician, a Newtonian
who was advancing the frontiers of dynamics and making contributions to
such diverse and difficult areas as the mathematics of vibrating strings and the
precession of the equinoxes. He was also an unbeliever and a fine stylist, and
thus the perfect associate for Diderot.

Between them, Diderot and d'Alembert rounded up a distinguished group
of collaborators, including Rousseau, Montesquieu, Holbach, and Voltaire,
who lent much luster, some notoriety, and (it must be admitted) relatively
little substance to the enterprise. Diderot himself wrote hundreds of articles,
long and short, including many articles on crafts and nearly all the articles
on the history of philosophy. D'Alembert (until he left his post in 1758)
contributed a variety of scientific articles and did not forget to strike out at
his old teachers, the Jansenists, for their supposed religious fanaticism. But
there were dozens of other encyclopedists, many quite prolific, who are for
us as admirable to watch and as hard to distinguish as worker bees. Diderot
was and always remained the soul of the enterprise; he worked on it to the
end, with enormous gusto and almost endless patience. But Diderot himself
emphasized in the article "Encyclopédie" (and quite justly) that the whole
could be brought to completion only by "a society of men of letters and of
skilled workmen."

The dramatic history of the *Encyclopédie*—the appearance of its first volume in 1751, its continuing and historically important troubles throughout
the 1750's, and its triumphant completion in 1772, when the last volume of
illustrations appeared—will unfold, step by step, in the documents that
follow and in the commentaries that accompany them. In this Introduction
it is necessary only to conclude with some general observations. First of all,
it is improper and indeed impossible to separate the articles on crafts or techniques from the articles on philosophy, politics, and religion. They belong
together, and not because the former are a screen for the latter: to change
the general way of thinking meant, for Diderot and his coworkers, to introduce his readers to scientific, empirical methods of thinking in all fields. It is
true that many of the articles made anti-religious propaganda—some adroitly,
some rather grossly—but this was not an end in itself. It was part of a
comprehensive movement toward a modern world view. It follows (secondly)
that the vehement reaction to the volumes, as they rapidly appeared in the
1750's, was quite understandable: irreligious polemics had been published
before, and dealt with before, but what the *Encyclopédie* did was to embed
those polemics in a general world view which was a real and serious threat

to a civilization still officially Christian. After all, Western Europe as a whole was experiencing a notable decline in religious fervor, and even in religious belief, among the educated. The *Encyclopédie* therefore was a powerful cultural force: perhaps it did not convert many people to the new scientific view of the world, but it sowed doubt, encouraged the half irreligious, and effectively preached modernity. Hence (finally) the *Encyclopédie* was a fateful venture for its editor-in-chief, as much as for its enemies. Diderot, the most versatile and most imaginative of literary men, read out his eyes for twenty years on manuscripts and galley proofs, wrote innumerable articles, tried to appease irate authorities, negotiated with greedy booksellers, kept a large, temperamental stable of contributors in line, and thought his time well spent. He knew that intellectual revolutions are made not by giant steps alone; they are also made in, and by, detail.

DOCUMENTS

1] The *Encyclopédie* Announced

> While Diderot had concluded his contract with the publishers in October 1747, his *Prospectus* did not appear until November 1750. One reason for the delay was that Diderot had been in prison: in July 1749 Diderot was arrested on a *lettre de cachet* and sent to the fortress at Vincennes for writing his *Lettres sur les aveugles,* which struck the authorities as a malicious materialist document. He was not released until November, upon the intervention of some influential acquaintances and the petition of the publishers, who were becoming frantic. The *Prospectus* made large claims for the forthcoming encyclopedia and aroused widespread expectations. By April 1751, about two months before the first volume appeared, a thousand subscribers had signed up for it.*

ENCYCLOPEDIA, OR ANALYTICAL DICTIONARY
OF THE ARTS, THE SCIENCES,
AND THE PROFESSIONS

Prospectus

The work we are announcing is not merely a proposed one. The manuscript and the drawings for it are complete. We can guarantee that there will be no fewer than eight volumes and six hundred plates, and that the volumes will follow each other without interruption.

Having informed the public of the current state of the *Encyclopédie,* and of the diligence which we will employ to publish it, we must satisfy the public about the nature of this work and the means we have taken to carry it to completion. We shall set these forth with the least possible ostentation.

It cannot be denied that, since the revival of letters among us, we owe partly to dictionaries the general enlightenment that has spread in society and the germ of science that is gradually preparing men's minds for more profound knowledge. How valuable would it not be, then, to have a book of this kind that one could consult on all subjects and that would serve as much to guide those who have the courage to work at the instruction of others as to enlighten those who only instruct themselves!

This is one advantage we thought of, but it is not the only one. In condensing to dictionary form all that concerns the arts and sciences, it remained necessary to make people aware of the assistance they lend each other; to make use of this assistance to render principles more certain and their con-

---

* Translated by Nina B. Gunzenhauser from Denis Diderot, *Prospectus* to the *Encyclopédie, ou Dictionnaire raisonné des sciences, des arts et des métiers,* in Diderot, *Oeuvres complètes,* eds. Jules Assézat and Maurice Tourneux, 20 vols. (Paris, 1875–77), Vol. XIII, pp. 129–31, 133–34, 140.

sequences clearer; to indicate the distant and close relationships of the beings that make up nature, which have occupied men; to show, by showing the interlacing both of roots and of branches, the impossibility of understanding thoroughly some parts of the whole without exploring many others; to produce a general picture of the efforts of the human spirit in all areas and in all centuries; to present these matters with clarity; to give to each the proper scope, and to prove, if possible, our epigraph by our success:

> *Tantum series juncturaque pollet,*
> *Tantum de medio sumptis accedit honoris!* [1]
> Horace, *Ars poetica*, v. 249

Up to now no one has conceived a work this large, or at least no one has carried one out. Leibnitz, of all scholars the one most capable of appreciating its difficulty, wanted it to be overcome. However, there were encyclopedias, and Leibnitz was not unaware of this when he asked for one.

The majority of these works appeared during the last century and were not completely scorned. It was found that if they did not show much talent, they at least bore the marks of labor and of knowledge. But what would these encyclopedias mean to us? What progress have we not made since then in the arts and sciences? How many truths discovered today, which were not foreseen then? True philosophy was in its cradle; the geometry of infinity did not yet exist; experimental physics was just appearing; there was no dialectic at all; the laws of sound criticism were entirely unknown. Descartes, Boyle, Huyghens, Newton, Leibnitz, the Bernoullis, Locke, Bayle, Pascal, Corneille, Racine, Bourdaloue, Bossuet, etc., either had not yet been born or had not yet written. The spirit of research and competition did not motivate the scholars: another spirit, less fecund perhaps, but rarer, that of precision and method, had not yet conquered the various divisions of literature; and the academies, whose efforts have advanced the arts and sciences to such an extent, were not yet established. . . . At the end of this project you will find the tree of human knowledge, indicating the connection of ideas, which has directed us in this vast operation. If we come out of it with success, we will be primarily indebted to Chancellor Bacon, who laid out the plan for a universal dictionary of the arts and sciences at a time when there were, so to speak, neither arts nor sciences. This extraordinary genius, faced with the impossibility of writing the history of what men knew, put down instead what they needed to learn. . . .

[In compiling this encyclopedia,] we have consulted the most competent people in Paris and in the kingdom. We took the trouble of going to their workshops, to question them, to write from their dictation, to develop their thoughts, to obtain from them the terms peculiar to their professions, to draw up tables of these and define them, to talk with those from whom

---

[1] The more that sequence and connection can do,
The more charm is added to everyday subjects.

reports were obtained, and (an almost indispensable precaution) to correct, in long and frequent interviews with some people, what others had imperfectly, obscurely, and sometimes inaccurately explained.

2] The *Encyclopédie* Introduced

Volume I of the *Encyclopédie*, covering the letter A, appeared on June 28, 1751. It opened with a rather cringing dedication to the comte d'Argenson, who (among other duties) supervised publications, and who had been responsible for Diderot's imprisonment. More nobly, it was prefaced by a lengthy preliminary discourse, written by d'Alembert. The "Discours préliminaire," reprinted below, surveyed in broad strokes the history of man's mind and outlined the method—empirical, scientific, anti-metaphysical and anti-scholastic —that the editors of the *Encyclopédie* intended to follow in their vast undertaking. The "Discours préliminaire" was lucidly written and brilliantly argued, and it was widely praised.*

The *Encyclopédie* is, as its title proclaims, the work of a company of men of letters. Were we not one of them, we might venture to claim that they have, or are worthy of having, a good reputation. But without wishing to anticipate a judgment which scholars alone may form, it is at least our duty to set aside, before everything else, the objection most capable of prejudicing the success of such a vast enterprise. We declare, therefore, that we have by no means had the temerity to take upon ourselves alone a burden so far beyond our capabilities, and that our role as editors consists principally in putting in order materials of which the greater part was supplied to us. We explicitly made the same statement in the body of the *Prospectus,* but it should perhaps have appeared at the beginning. With this precaution we would apparently have answered in advance a large number of fashionable people, and even some men of letters, who have asked us how two people could handle all the arts and all the sciences. They must have glanced at the *Prospectus,* since they have wanted to honor it with their praises. The only way of silencing their objections once and for all is to use, as we are doing here, the first lines of our work to demolish them. These opening lines are therefore reserved solely for those of our readers who do not see any point in reading further; we owe to the others a much more extensive account of the production of the *Encyclopédie:* they will find it in the continuation of this discourse; but this account, so important by virtue of its nature and its substance, must be prefaced by some philosophical reflections.

The work which we are beginning (and wish to complete) has two aims: as an *encyclopedia,* its purpose is to set forth, as well as possible, the order and continuity of human knowledge; as an *analytical dictionary of the*

* Translated by Nina B. Gunzenhauser from D'Alembert, "Discours préliminaire de l'Encyclopédie," in D'Alembert, *Oeuvres,* 5 vols. (Paris, 1821–22), Vol. I, pp. 17–19.

arts, the sciences, and the professions, its purpose is to contain, for each science and each art, whether liberal or mechanical, the general principles on which it is based and the most essential details which make up its body and substance. These two points of view, of *encyclopedia* and of *analytical dictionary,* will therefore dictate the outline and the division of this preliminary discourse. We will consider them, pursue them one after the other, and report on the means by which we have attempted to satisfy this double aim.

If one has ever reflected at all on the connections between discoveries, it is easy to realize that the arts and sciences lend each other mutual assistance, that there is consequently a chain which joins them. But it is often difficult to reduce to a small number of rules or general ideas each particular science or art; it is no less difficult to enclose in a unified system the infinitely varied branches of human knowledge.

The first step we have to take in this research is to examine, if we may be permitted that term, the genealogy of our knowledge and the relationships within it, the causes which must have led to its birth and the nature that distinguishes it—in brief, to go back to the origin and generation of our ideas. Aside from the benefits we will reap from examining this encyclopedic enumeration of the arts and sciences, this will not be out of place at the head of an analytical dictionary of human knowledge.

We can divide all our knowledge into direct knowledge and reasoned knowledge. Direct knowledge is that which we receive immediately without any operation of our will, which, finding open (if we may say so) all of the doors of our soul, enters it without resistance and without effort. Reasoned knowledge is that which the mind acquires in operating on direct knowledge, in uniting and combining it.

All of our direct knowledge can be reduced to that which we receive through the senses; from which it follows that we owe all our ideas to our sensations. This principle of the earliest philosophers was long regarded as an axiom by the Scholastics; for them to give it this honor, it needed only to be ancient, and they would have defended with equal heat substantial forms or occult qualities. Therefore, at the renaissance of philosophy this truth was treated in the same manner as the absurd opinions from which it should have been distinguished; it was proscribed along with them, for nothing is so dangerous to truth, and lays it open to such misjudgment, as mixture with or proximity to error. The system of innate ideas, tempting in many respects, and more striking perhaps because it was less known, succeeded the axiom of the Scholastics, and after having reigned for a long time, it still has some partisans; with such difficulty does truth regain its place when prejudices or sophism have driven it out. At last, quite recently, there has been almost universal consensus that the ancients were right; and that is not the only question on which we are beginning to draw near them again.

3] First Difficulties

Volume I was well received; however, with its vigorous "Discours préliminaire," its informative technical articles on agriculture, industrial processes,
and medicine, and its bold political article by Diderot, "Autorité poli-
tique," it aroused some suspicion as well as much applause. There were some
rumblings that the work smacked too much of Locke and seemed rather tepid
on religion. The Jesuit *Journal de Trévoux* began its attack. Then there occurred an unlucky incident—the first of many. On November 18, 1751,
shortly before Volume II of the *Encyclopédie*, from B to "Cézimbra," was to
appear, one Abbé de Prades defended a thesis at the Sorbonne which was first
passed, but was soon discovered to be filled with heterodox, blasphemous doctrine. De Prades was an Encyclopedist and a friend of Encyclopedists, and the
orthodox opposition took this opportunity to denounce the whole enterprise
as a threat to religion. De Prades was condemned and fled to Prussia; his
Sorbonne examiner, who had evidently not read the thesis he approved, was
deprived of his chair, and on February 7, 1752, the *Encyclopédie* was officially
suppressed.

A] A JESUIT ATTACK *

First, if we had had more erudition, more time, more books, we would have
made still further discoveries in the *Encyclopédie*; we would have engaged
in discussions which would have shown the depth of this great work.

Second, there are some matters that are well treated in it, and we believe
that we have taken this into consideration without partiality, without pre-
tense, without exposing ourselves to anyone's criticism.

Third, too much liberty has been taken in using a wealth of material contained in other books. There has been excessive borrowing, a practice which
could in the long run dim the glory of the enterprise and cast a shadow on
the authors' attainments.

Fourth, in many places, religion is accorded no respect at all, with regard
to which we earnestly entreat all who take this work in hand to be infinitely
wary on a point of such great importance.

B] A BISHOP'S CHARGE †

Up till now, Hell has vomited its venom, so to speak, drop by drop. Today
there are torrents of errors and impieties which tend toward nothing less
than the submerging of Faith, Religion, Virtues, the Church, Subordination,
the Laws, and Reason. Past centuries have witnessed the birth of sects that,
while attacking some Dogmas, have respected a great number of them; it

* Translated by Nina B. Gunzenhauser from Père Berthier, *Journal de Trévoux*, March
1752, pp. 467–68, in Marcel Hervier, *Le Dix-huitième Siècle (Les Écrivains français jugés
par leurs contemporains*, Vol. II) (Paris: Delaplane, 1931), p. 252.

† [Archbishop of Montauban, *Mandement*.] From *Diderot: The Testing Years* by Arthur
M. Wilson. © 1957 by Oxford University Press, Inc. Reprinted by Permission. [P. 156.]

was reserved to ours to see impiety forming a system that overturns all of them at one and the same time.

c] A Royal Prohibition *

His Majesty has recognized that in these two volumes the authors have frequently inserted maxims tending to undermine royal power, to establish the spirit of independence and revolt, and through obscure and equivocal wording to lay the foundations of error, of the corruption of morals, and of irreligion and disbelief.

4] First Difficulties Overcome

> This prohibition did not last. The Encyclopedists had friends at court, especially Chrétien-Guillaume de Lamoignon de Malesherbes, who had become *directeur de la librairie*, in general supervision of publications, in 1750. Largely at his instance the enterprise was permitted to continue, and Volume III of the *Encyclopédie* appeared in November 1753. In the following selection the journalist Friedrich Melchior Grimm, Diderot's close friend and publisher of an exclusive newssheet that circulated among the social elite and crowned heads of Europe, hailed its reappearance.†

Here at last is the third volume of the *Encyclopédie* undertaken by a company of men of letters under the direction of Mr. Diderot. All Europe has witnessed the harassment to which this important work has been subjected, and all decent men were shocked by it. Who indeed could watch calmly the hatreds, the jealousy, the execrable plots contrived by hypocritical bigots and cloaked by the mantle of religion? . . . Unfortunately for the Jesuits, it was not so easy to continue the *Encyclopédie* as it was to bring about the downfall of the philosophers, who had nothing in the world to support them but their love of truth and consciousness of their merits, poor resources beside those who have power in their hands and who, exposed to false insinuations, unforeseen events, headlong haste, innumerable obstacles, have a thousand ways of being unjust, while only one way of being right remains to them. Everything was well planned: the papers of Mr. Diderot were confiscated. In this way the Jesuits thought they could undo an encyclopedia which was already completed; in this way they thought they could have the glory of that whole enterprise, by arranging and putting in order the articles they considered ready. But they had forgotten to confiscate the mind and

* Translated by Nina B. Gunzenhauser from Conseil du Roi, "Arrêt," February 7, 1752, in Marcel Hervier, *Le Dix-huitième Siècle* (*Les Écrivains français jugés par leurs contemporains*, Vol. II) (Paris: Delaplane, 1931), p. 253.

† Translated by Nina B. Gunzenhauser from Grimm, Diderot, Raynal, Meister, etc., *Correspondance littéraire, philosophique et critique*, ed. Maurice Tourneux (Paris: 1877–82), Vol. II, p. 298.

the spirit of the philosopher, and to ask him for the key to a great many articles which, far from being able to understand, they tried in vain to decipher. This humiliation is the sole vengeance our philosophers have had on their enemies, as stupid as they are malicious, if indeed the humiliation of a pack of such contemptible enemies can be a satisfaction to philosophers. The government was obliged, not without a certain amount of embarrassment, to take steps to hire Mr. Diderot and Mr. d'Alembert to resume a work that had been fruitlessly attempted by people who for a long time have held last place in literature.

5] The *Encyclopédie* Reaffirmed

Permission to continue the *Encyclopédie* greatly improved the editors' morale, and in Volume III ("Cha" to "Consécration") they took the occasion to snap back at their critics and reaffirm their principles in a confident "Avertissement" by d'Alembert. And then, in Volume V, Diderot himself wrote his long, impressive article "Encyclopédie."

A] D'ALEMBERT'S REAFFIRMATION *

You will find in this work, as one journalist has cleverly observed, neither the *Life of the Saints*, which Mr. Baillet has written adequately and which is not at all our aim, nor the genealogy of the great houses, but the genealogy of the sciences, more precious to those who know how to think; not the uninteresting adventures of ancient and modern writers but the fruit of their labors and their discoveries; not the detailed description of each village that certain learned people take the trouble to write nowadays, but an account of the trade of the provinces and the principal cities, and the singular details of their natural history; not the conquerors who have devastated the earth but the immortal geniuses who have brought enlightenment to it; and finally, not a multitude of sovereigns whom history should have proscribed. The very names of princes and great men have the right to be found in the *Encyclopédie* only by virtue of the good that they did for the sciences, for the *Encyclopédie* owes everything to talents, nothing to titles, and it is the history of the human spirit and not of men's vanity.

B] DIDEROT'S REAFFIRMATION †

We saw that the *Encyclopédie* could only be the endeavor of a philosophical century; that that century had arrived; that fame, in raising to immortality

---

* Translated by Nina B. Gunzenhauser from "Avertissement des éditeurs," in the *Encyclopédie* (Paris, 1753), Vol. III, p. iv.

† Translated by Nina B. Gunzenhauser from Diderot, "Encyclopédie," in *Oeuvres complètes*, eds. Jules Assézat and Maurice Tourneux, 20 vols. (Paris, 1875–77), Vol. XIV, p. 474

the names of those who had achieved it, perhaps would not disdain to take on ours, and we have felt inspired by the idea, so consoling and pleasing, that people may still speak of us when we have ceased to be; by that murmur, so voluptuous, which makes us hear from the mouths of some of our contemporaries what the men for whose knowledge and happiness we are sacrificing ourselves will be saying, men whom we respect and love though they are yet to come. We have felt growing within us that seed of emulation which begrudges death the best part of ourselves and which saves from annihilation the only moments of our existence of which we are truly proud.

6] Orthodoxy Strikes Back

The continuing and growing popularity of the *Encyclopédie* worried alert Christians more and more as volume succeeded volume. Between 1754 and 1756, Volumes IV, V, and VI came out, carrying on from "Conseil" to "Fné." The atmosphere was growing tense: France was at war with Prussia and Britain, and the leading Encyclopedists were fond of British ideas and openly admired the Prussian king. Then, on January 5, 1757, a deranged man named Damiens tried to stab King Louis XV to death. He failed, but the attempt strengthened alarm at "subversive ideas" (which had no connection with Damiens' mad *attentat*), and on April 16, 1757, a savage Royal Proclamation announced the death sentence for all those convicted of "writing or of having had written or of printing any writing tending to attack religion, to rouse opinion, to impair Our authority, and to trouble the order and tranquillity of Our States." [2] Amid this tension, attacks on the *Encyclopédie* grew more virulent. The most effective assailants were three journalists, Elie Catherine Fréron (1718–76), skillful and biting; Jacob-Nicolas Moreau (1717–1804), little known until he likened the *philosophes* to an imaginary tribe, ludicrously and suggestively called the "Cacouacs"; and Charles Palissot de Montenoy (1730–1814), a playwright and polemicist who for a while—not for long—enjoyed Voltaire's friendship. Samples of the criticism by Palissot and Moreau appear below.

A] PALISSOT *

They announced the truth, or what they took to be the truth, with a pomp that truth has never known. One detected at the beginning of some philosophical productions a tone of authority and decision that up till now had only belonged to the Pope. They carried over to moral treatises, or to metaphysical speculations, a language which they condemned everywhere else as that of fanaticism. *I have lived,* said one; *I write of God,* said another pompously; *Young man, take this and read,* he continued. *O Man! hear, this is your story,* wrote a third. This tone of inspiration in some, of emphasis

---

[2] Wilson, *op. cit.*, p. 276.

* Translated by Nina B. Gunzenhauser from *Petites Lettres sur de grands philosophes,* 1st Letter (1757), in Marcel Hervier, *Le Dix-huitième Siècle* (*Les Écrivains français jugés par leurs contemporains,* Vol. II) (Paris: Delaplane, 1931), pp. 255–56. The writers criticized are, in order, Charles Pinot-Duclos (1704–72), novelist and social observer; Diderot; and Rousseau.

in the others, so far from being that of the reason that questions, or of the truth that persuades, aroused some sensible people. Examining closely the works that promised such great things, they found that some were slavishly copied from Bacon, though it had not been deemed relevant to forewarn the public about this, and that the others contained nothing but ideas that have been batted about a thousand times, simply given an air of novelty either with an epigrammatic twist in the bad taste that is currently fashionable or with a certain tone of audacity well suited to taking in simple-minded people.

B] MOREAU *

Their only weapon consists of a venom hidden in their tongue; at each word they pronounce, even in the most gentle and pleasant tone, this venom flows out, escapes, and spreads far and wide. With the aid of the magic they practice with care, they have the skill to cast it as far as they wish. Since they are no less lazy than they are evil, they attack directly only those from whom they have nothing to fear; most frequently they throw their poison from behind.

They are magnificent speakers: their language has something sublime and unintelligible about it that inspires respect and sustains admiration. Everything in their language is image, sentiment, even passion; for they discovered that enthusiasm was the surest way of knowing the essence of things. They are right, for if there is not one truth common to all men, to what fixed point could the Cacouacs cling in order to sway them? But their general inclination is to prevail through persuasion. They have therefore had to depend mainly on the surprise that is aroused by the clamor of their figures of speech, the energy of words, the rapidity of images succeeding and chasing each other—in brief, of that rapture that sometimes seized the Delphic Oracle on the sacred tripod, and that once possessed a Cacouac chief at the view of a torrent, a forest-covered mountain, a storm that thundered some leagues away. . . .

They would like all the peoples of the universe to become Cacouacs. It is certainly not for love of the native land, as I have said before; they have none at all. It is just that it is nice to be admired by a greater number of people.

. . .

[The Cacouacs proclaim:] We took care to collect precisely what was most ridiculous in a few customs and maxims of certain peoples. We began by seeking to win favor and respect for the grossest errors: we wanted to have them considered just as solidly based as principles whose truth either is

* Translated by Nina B. Gunzenhauser from "Avis utile," in *Mercure,* October 1757 and *Nouveau Mémoire pour servir à l'histoire des Cacouacs* (1757), 17, 73, both in Marcel Hervier, *Le Dix-huitième Siècle* (*Les Écrivains français jugés par leurs contemporains,* Vol. II) (Paris: Delaplane, 1931), pp. 256–58.

recognized by all men or is attested to by the most authentic documents. Alongside these maxims we ranged a host of apocryphal and despicable tales: we built them into a sort of edifice that we knew would be easy for us to knock down, convinced at the same time that it would in its fall bring down in ruins the principles on which men of all times and all places have set the foundations of their society. One noble enterprise especially intrigued our ambition, and that was to overturn with one blow all the religions of the Universe. The true religion gave us a good deal of trouble, but we flatter ourselves that we have lost it to view in the crowd of superstitions that characterize all the others—in this illustrious project the Cacouacs did not feel sure enough of their magic, and they plainly found it expedient to make use of lies and dishonesty.

7] Two Great Tactical Mistakes

Into this inflammable atmosphere the *philosophes* threw two lighted matches. In the fall of 1757 there appeared Volume VII of the *Encyclopédie* (from "Foang" to "Gythium"). In addition to the usual innocuous and interesting material, it contained d'Alembert's article "Genève," which created an immediate and immense scandal. D'Alembert had gathered material for it on a long visit to Voltaire (who had settled near Geneva), and in it he maladroitly said out loud what many thought was true: that the Genevan pastorate, cultivated and French in its tastes, professed a tepid and rationalist Christianity, which was closer to philosophy than to religion. In addition, d'Alembert urged the Calvinist republic to permit a theater within its borders—a most sensitive point. The Genevans protested loudly; Voltaire urged d'Alembert to stand by the truth. But in January 1758 d'Alembert, tired of the whole business, decided to withdraw from the *Encyclopédie*, to Diderot's intense disgust.

Then in July 1758 Claude-Adrien Helvétius (1715–71) published his *De l'esprit*, a treatise on ethics wholly materialist, utilitarian, secular in doctrine. Rich, and prominent at court, Helvétius had had no trouble getting permission to publish, but once the book was out the storm could not be contained. Helvétius was not an Encyclopedist, but he was the friend of Encyclopedists, and he seemed to be speaking their language. Consequently, the censor who had passed the book was fired, Helvétius lost his court connections, and *De l'esprit* was condemned by all conceivable authorities.

In what follows, a long selection from "Genève" is printed first, as a fine example of Encyclopedist tactics and style and as a sample of what aroused the pious in eighteenth-century France. Two condemnations of Helvétius' *De l'esprit* follow.

A] "Genève" *

GENEVA (*Hist.* & *Polit.*). This city is located on two hills, at the end of the lake which bears its name and which formerly was called Lake Leman. Its situation is highly agreeable. On one side one sees the lake, on the other

* Translated by Nina B. Gunzenhauser from *The* Encyclopédie *of Diderot and D'Alembert: Selected Articles* . . . , ed. John Lough (Cambridge: Cambridge University Press, 1954), pp. 83–97 *passim*.

the Rhone, around it a pleasant countryside, slopes covered with cottages all along the lake, and at some leagues' distance the ever icy summits of the Alps, which look like mountains of silver when they are lit by the sun on clear days. The port of Geneva, situated on the lake, with its jetties, small ships, markets, etc., and its location between France, Italy, and Germany, make it industrious, wealthy, and commercial. It has many beautiful buildings and pleasant walks; the streets are lighted at night, and on the Rhone a very simple pumping machine has been constructed that supplies water right up to the highest sections of town, which are at an elevation of a hundred feet. The lake is about forty-five miles long and ten or eleven miles across at its widest point. It is a kind of small sea which has its storms and which produces other curious phenomena. *See* WATERSPOUT, CUTTLE-FISH, etc., and *Hist. of Acad. of Sciences for the years 1741 and 1742*. The latitude of Geneva is 46°12′, its longitude 23°45′. . . .

Between the two gates of the city hall of Geneva one can still see a Latin inscription in memory of the abolition of the Catholic religion. The Pope is referred to as the Antichrist. This expression, which the fanaticism of liberty and novelty permitted itself in a century still half barbarian, appears to us today hardly worthy of a city so philosophical. We dare to invite the substitution, for this offensive and vulgar monument, of a truer, nobler, and simpler inscription. For Catholics the Pope is the head of the true Church; for sensible and moderate Protestants, he is a sovereign whom they respect as a prince without obeying him; but in a century such as ours there is no longer an Antichrist for anyone.

Geneva, in order to defend her liberty against the encroachments of the dukes of Savoy and their bishops, made herself still stronger by the alliance with Zurich and especially by the one with France. It was with this help that she resisted the arms of Charles Emmanuel and the treasures of Philip II, a prince whose ambition, despotism, cruelty, and superstition ensure his memory the execration of posterity. Henry IV, who had assisted Geneva with three hundred soldiers, was himself in need of her aid soon afterward; she was not useless in the time of the League and on other occasions. From that stem the privileges which the Genevans, like the Swiss, enjoy in France.

These people, wanting to bring fame to their city, summoned Calvin, who justly enjoyed a great reputation: a literary man of the first order, writing in Latin fully as well as one can in a dead language, and in French with a purity remarkable for his time. This purity, which our able grammarians still admire today, sets his writings well above almost all others of his century, just as the works of [the Jansenists of] Port-Royal still gain distinction today, for the same reason, from the barbarous rhapsodies of their rivals and their contemporaries. Calvin, an adroit jurist and as enlightened a theologian as a heretic can be, set up in collaboration with the magistrates a code of civil and ecclesiastical laws, which was approved by the people in 1543 and has become the fundamental law of the republic. The excess wealth of the church, which served before the reformation to nourish the extravagance of the bishops and their subalterns, was applied toward the foundation of a hospital, a college, and an academy; but the wars which Geneva had to endure for almost sixty years prevented commerce and the arts from flourishing there as much as the sciences did. Finally, the failure of the attempted scaling of the city walls in 1602 by the Duke of Savoy opened the period of tranquillity of this republic. The Genevans repulsed their enemies, who had attacked them by surprise; and, to spoil the taste of the Duke of Savoy for similar enterprises, they hanged thirteen of the principal enemy generals. They felt that they could treat as highway robbers men who had attacked their city without a declaration of war; for that peculiar new policy of making war without having declared it was not yet known in Europe, and if it has been practiced since then by the large states, it is too prejudicial to the small ones ever to be to their liking. . . .

It is a very singular thing that a city which has scarcely twenty-four thousand inhabitants and whose cut-up territory contains fewer than thirty villages nevertheless is a sovereign state and one of the most flourishing cities in Europe. Enriched by her liberty and her trade, she often sees everything around her in flames without feeling its effects. The events that shake Europe are for her only a spectacle, which she enjoys without taking part in it. Linked with the French by her treaties and her trade, to the English by her trade and by religion, she makes pronouncements on the justice of the wars which those two powerful nations wage against each other, although she is too wise to take any part in them, and judges all the sovereigns of Europe without flattering them, without hurting them, and without fearing them.

In Geneva there are four classes of people: the *citizens,* who are sons of bourgeois and born in the city; they alone can attain the magistracy; the *bourgeois,* who are sons of bourgeois or of citizens but born in a foreign country, or who, being foreigners, have acquired the rights of the citizenry, which the magistrate may confer; they may serve in the General Council and even in the Grand Council, known as *The Two Hundred.* The *residents* are the foreigners who have the permission of the magistrate to live in the city and who are nothing else. Finally, the *natives* are sons of residents; they have a few more privileges than their fathers, but they are excluded from the government.

At the head of the republic are four syndics, who hold office for only one year and may not become syndic again for four years. To the syndics is joined the Small Council, composed of twenty councilors, a treasurer and two secretaries of state, and another body called the Judiciary. Day-to-day affairs and those that require immediate action, whether they are criminal or civil, are the business of these two bodies.

The Grand Council is composed of 250 citizens or bourgeois; it is the judge of major civil cases, it grants pardons, it deliberates about what should be brought before the General Council. This General Council includes the entire body of citizens and bourgeois except those under twenty-five years of age, bankrupts, and those who have incurred some disgrace. To this assembly belong the legislative power, the right over war and peace, alliances, taxes, and the election of the principal magistrates, which is conducted in the Cathedral with great order and propriety, even though the voters number about 1500.

By this account it can be seen that the government of Geneva has all the advantages and none of the inconveniences of a democracy; everything is under the direction of the syndics, everything emanates from the Small Council for deliberation and everything returns to it for execution. Thus it would seem that the city of Geneva had taken for its model this very wise law of the government of the ancient Germans:

De minoribus rebus principes consultant, de majoribus omnes; ita tamen, ut ea quorum penes plebem arbitrium est, apud principes praetractentur.[3]
—Tacitus, *Germania*

Criminal justice is exercised with more exactitude than rigor. Torture, which has already been abolished in several states and should be abolished everywhere as a useless cruelty, is prohibited in Geneva; it is used only on criminals already condemned to death, to discover their accomplices if that is necessary. The accused may demand communication of the proceedings and may have the help of his family and a lawyer to plead his case in public. Criminal sentences are pronounced in the public square by the syndics, with much pomp.

Geneva knows nothing of hereditary dignity; the son of the first magistrate remains part of the crowd unless he emerges through his own merit. Nobility and wealth give neither rank nor prerogatives nor easy elevation to office; patronage is strictly prohibited. Government posts are so unprofitable that there is nothing in them to excite greed; they can tempt only noble souls by the compensation attached to them.

There are few lawsuits; most are settled by mutual friends, by the lawyers themselves, and by the judges.

Sumptuary laws prohibit the use of precious stones and gilding, limit expenditures for funerals, and require all citizens to go on foot in the streets; carriages are used only for the country. These laws, which in France would be regarded as too severe and almost barbarian and inhuman, are no obstacle to the true necessities of life, which can always be obtained at little expense; they only curtail display, which contributes nothing to happiness and brings ruin without being useful.

There is perhaps no other city that has more happy marriages; Geneva is in this respect two hundred years ahead of our ways. Because of the regula-

---

[3] The chiefs deliberate about minor matters, the people about greater ones, but in such a way that those things about which the people decide are discussed earlier among the chiefs.

tions against ostentation, people are not afraid to have a multitude of children. Thus luxury is not, as it is in France, one of the large obstacles to population growth.

The theater is not tolerated in Geneva. It is not that they disapprove of the performances themselves; they are afraid, they say, of the taste for ornament, dissipation, and libertinism that the troupes of actors might spread among the young people. But would it not be possible to remedy this drawback by strict and well-enforced laws concerning the conduct of actors? By this means Geneva would have the theater and morality too and enjoy the advantages of both; the theatrical performances would mold the taste of the citizens and give them a fineness of tact, a delicacy of feeling that it is difficult to acquire without this assistance. Literature would benefit without libertinism increasing, and Geneva would reunite the wisdom of Lacedaemon with the civility of Athens. Another consideration, worthy of such a sensible and enlightened republic, should perhaps induce her to permit theatrical performances. The barbarous prejudice against the profession of actor, the degraded status we have given to these men who are so necessary to the progress and support of the arts, is certainly one of the principal causes contributing to the licentiousness for which we reproach them; through wanton pleasure they try to make up for the esteem their position cannot bring them. Among us, an actor with good morals is doubly respectable, but he is scarcely appreciated. The tax-farmer who provokes public poverty and lives off it, the courtier who grovels and does not pay his debts—that is the sort of man whom we honor most. If actors were not merely tolerated in Geneva but were first controlled by sensible regulations, then protected, and even shown respect as soon as they were worthy of it, and finally placed on absolutely the same level as the other citizens, that city would soon have the advantage of possessing what is thought to be so rare and is rare only through our own fault—a troupe of estimable actors. Let us add that this troupe would soon be the best in Europe. Many people who had a taste for and inclination toward the theater and who were afraid of incurring shame by exposing themselves to our theater would flock to Geneva to cultivate, not only without shame but even with esteem, this talent, so agreeable and so uncommon. A stay in that city, which, since it has no theater, many Frenchmen consider dreary, would become one of honest pleasures, as it is now one of philosophy and liberty; and foreigners would not be surprised to see that in a city where decent and correct performances are forbidden, coarse and witless farces are permitted, as repugnant to good taste as they are to good morals. And that is not all. Little by little the example of the actors in Geneva, the regularity of their conduct and the respect they would enjoy because of it, would serve as a model for the actors of other countries and as a lesson to those who have until now treated them with such harshness and even inconsistency. One would not see them on the one hand pensioned by the government and on the other an object of anathema; our priests would break the habit of excommunicating them, and the bourgeois, of regarding them with contempt; and a tiny republic would have the glory of having reformed Europe on this point, which is more important than one might think.

After England, Geneva was the first to accept smallpox vaccination, which is being established with such difficulty in France, and which will be established, although some of our doctors are still fighting it, as their predecessors fought the circulation of the blood, emetics, and so many other incontestable truths or useful practices.

All the sciences and almost all the arts have been so thoroughly cultivated in Geneva that one would be surprised to see the list of scholars and artists in all fields this city has produced in the last two centuries. She has sometimes even had the advantage of possessing celebrated foreigners, who have been induced to move there by the pleasant location and the liberty that is to be enjoyed; Mr. Voltaire, who three years ago took up his abode there, finds among the republicans the same marks of esteem and consideration that he received from several monarchs.

The industry that prospers most in Geneva is that of watch-making; it employs more than five thousand persons, that is to say, more than a fifth of the citizens. The other trades are not neglected, including agriculture; the lack of fertility of the soil is remedied by care and hard work.

All of the houses are built of stone, which often prevents fires; fires that do occur, however, are attended to promptly because of an efficient system set up for putting them out.

The hospitals in Geneva are not, as elsewhere, a simple retreat for sick and infirm poor people. They extend hospitality to poor wayfarers, but what is more important they draw a multitude of small pensions which they distribute to poor families to help them live without being compelled to move or give up their work. The hospitals spend triple their income every year, so abundant are their alms of all kinds.

It remains for me only to speak of the religion of Geneva; it is this part of the article that will perhaps interest philosophers most. We now discuss this detail, but we ask our readers to remember that we are only historians here, not controversialists. Our articles on theology are intended to act as antidotes to this one, and recounting is not approving. We refer our readers therefore to the words EUCHARIST, HELL, FAITH, CHRISTIANITY, etc., to arm them in advance against what we are going to say.

The ecclesiastical constitution of Geneva is purely presbyterian: no bishops, much less canons. It is not that they disapprove of episcopacy, but since they do not believe it to have divine right, they felt that pastors less rich and less important than bishops were better suited to a small republic.

The ministers are either pastors, like our curés, or postulants, like our priests without benefices. The pastor's income never goes above 1200 livres, without any surplice fees; it is the state that gives it, for the church owns nothing. Ministers are ordained only at twenty-four years of age, after extremely rigorous examinations on science and morality; it might be wished that the majority of our Catholic churches would follow this example.

The clerics have nothing to do with funerals; these are a simple police function carried out without any pomp. The Genevans believe that it is ridiculous to be ostentatious after death. Burial is in a huge cemetery rather far from the city, a custom which should be followed everywhere. *See* EX-HALATION.

The clergy of Geneva have exemplary morals. The ministers live in great harmony; one never sees them, as in other countries, bitterly disputing among themselves on unintelligible matters, persecuting each other, indecently accusing each other before the magistrates. But they are far from thinking alike on all the articles which are regarded elsewhere as the most important to religion. Some no longer believe in the divinity of Jesus Christ, whom Calvin, their leader, so zealously defended and for whom he had Servet burned. When one speaks to them about this execution, which rather belies the charity and moderation of their patriarch, they do not undertake to justify it. They admit that Calvin committed a very blameworthy deed, and they are content (if it is a Catholic who is talking to them) to counter the execution of Servet with that abominable Saint Bartholomew's Day, which every good Frenchman would like to obliterate from our history with his blood, and the execution of John Huss, which the Catholics themselves, they say, no longer attempt to justify, in which humanity and good faith were equally violated, and which should cover the memory of the Emperor Sigismund with eternal opprobrium.

"It is," says Mr. Voltaire, "no small example of the progress of human reason that one was able to print in Geneva, with public approbation (in the *Essay on Universal History* by the same author) that Calvin had a monstrous soul as well as an enlightened spirit. The murder of Servet today seems abominable." We believe that the praises accorded to that noble freedom to think and write are to be shared equally by the author, his century, and Geneva. How many countries there are where philosophy has made no smaller progress, but where truth is still captive, where reason does not dare to raise its voice to blast what it condemns in silence, where too many faint-hearted writers, who are called *sensible,* respect the prejudices they could combat with as much propriety as certainty!

Hell, one of the main elements of our creed, no longer is one for some ministers in Geneva today. It would, according to them, be an injustice to the Divinity to imagine that that Being filled with goodness and justice could be capable of punishing our faults with an eternity of torment. They explain as best they can the explicit passages in the Scriptures which are contrary to their opinion, claiming that one must never take literally everything in Holy Writ that appears to offend humanity and reason. They believe, therefore, that there is suffering in the next life, but only for a time. Thus Purgatory, which was one of the principal causes of the separation of the Protestants from the Roman Church, is today the only suffering after death that some of them acknowledge: a new item to add to the history of human contradictions.

To put it briefly, some pastors in Geneva have no other religion than a perfect Socinianism, rejecting everything that is called a *mystery* and imagining that the first principle of a true religion is to propose no belief that offends reason. Thus when they are pressed on the *necessity* of revelation, that dogma so essential to Christianity, some substitute the word *utility*, which seems milder to them. In that respect, if they are not orthodox they are at least consistent with their principles. *See* SOCINIANISM.

A clergyman who thinks this way should be tolerant, and is in fact tolerant enough not to be looked upon favorably by the ministers of the other reformed churches. One can still say, without claiming to approve the religion of Geneva in other respects, that there are few countries in which theologians and clerics are greater enemies of superstition. But in return for this, since intolerance and superstition serve only to multiply disbelievers, there is less complaint in Geneva than elsewhere about the advance of disbelief, which should not be surprising. Religion there is almost reduced to the worship of a single God, at least among almost all who are not of the lower classes; the respect for Jesus Christ and for the Scriptures is perhaps the only thing that distinguishes the Christianity of Geneva from a pure deism.

The clerics in Geneva do better than just being tolerant; they confine themselves solely to their functions, by being the first to give the citizens an example of submission to the law. The Consistory, established to watch over morality, inflicts only spiritual suffering. The great quarrel between the priesthood and the empire which in the centuries of ignorance shook the crowns of so many emperors and which, as we know only too well, causes disagreeable problems in the most enlightened centuries, is completely unknown in Geneva; the clergy do nothing without the approval of the magistrates.

Worship is very simple; no images, no votive lights, no ornaments in the churches. They have, however, just given the cathedral a portal in rather good taste; perhaps they will little by little come to decorate the interior of temples. What in fact would be the objection to having pictures and statues, warning the people, if they wished, not to worship them in any way and to regard them only as monuments intended to retrace, in an effective and agreeable manner, the principal events of the religion? The arts would gain by it without superstition profiting from it. We speak here, as the reader must sense, starting from the principles of the pastors of Geneva and not from those of the Catholic Church.

The divine service is made up of two things: preaching and singing. The preaching is confined almost entirely to morality and is only the better for that. The singing is in rather bad taste, and the French verses they sing are even worse. One must hope that Geneva will reform on these two points. An organ has just been installed in the Cathedral, and perhaps they will arrive at praising God in better language and better music. Nevertheless, truth obliges us to say that the Supreme Being is honored in Geneva with a propriety and peaceful meditation that is not seen in our churches.

We will perhaps not give such long articles on larger monarchies; but in the eyes of the philosopher the Republic of Bees is no less interesting than the history of great empires; and it is perhaps only in small states that one can find the model for the perfect political administration. If religion does not permit us to think that the Genevans have worked efficaciously for their happiness in the other world, reason obliges us to believe that they are as happy as one can be in this one:

O fortunatos nimium, sua si bona norint! [4]
Vergil

B] *De l'esprit* Condemned by the Archbishop of Paris *

We were thus destined, my dear brethren, to be clouded by vapors escaping from the abyss. These pestilent vapors are the false philosophy of the century, the absurd doctrine of materialism, the abhorrence of all religion, innate as well as revealed, the sophisms against the distinction between good and evil, between the just and the unjust, the maxims of the most shameful ethics, the reckless discussions of the rights and the conduct of sovereigns, all the pride of spirit, all the corruption of heart, all the unleashing of passion against the Lord and against his Christ. . . . These are the black vapors of Hell; they are the works of the Prince of Darkness, and we have the sorrow to see all-too-evident traces of them in a book being widely circulated among the flocks entrusted to our care.

The author of the book that arouses our zeal today is an avowed partisan of the philosophy of the century. He frequently complains, with all the ardor of a personal interest, of what he calls declamations against philosophers. He accuses the devout of hating philosophy, and on these grounds he taxes them with bigotry and fanaticism. He is confident that today's philosophers are men of genius; he defends them, flatters them, heaps praise on them. He rises with force against those who hold back the progress of philosophy.

On all sides, books, speeches, examples are tending to establish the reign of disbelief. This capital in which you live, or which you visit, has become the center of perverse opinions, anti-Christian maxims, impious sophisms, open enterprises against the Gospel. Here reigns that proud and profane philosophy, a few of whose traits we have revealed. It insinuates itself in a

---

[4] Oh, only too fortunate if they but knew their own good fortune!

* Translated by Nina B. Gunzenhauser from Christophe de Beaumont, *Mandement portant-condamnation d'un livre qui a pour titre:* De l'esprit (November 22, 1758), in Marcel Hervier, *Le Dix-huitième Siècle* (*Les Écrivains français jugés par leurs contemporains,* Vol. II) (Paris: Delaplane, 1931), pp. 259–60.

thousand different ways, it spreads its poison in books on ethics, in nature studies, in political systems, in amusing pamphlets, in accounts of voyages, in theatrical plays, etc. . . . . Disbelief, disguised as philosophy, becomes a contagious evil.

These imperious men boast today about the number of their followers, and to hear them speak, one would think that this mob that follows them is a proof and a stamp of truth; as though it were difficult to win a great many people over to a cause that opens the door to all sorts of disorder, that abolishes all the bothersome laws of Christianity, that leaves all professions and all ages completely at liberty to gratify their desires!

c] *De l'esprit* Condemned by the Attorney General *

My lords, society, the state, and religion appear today before the tribunal of justice to proffer their suit. Their rights are being violated, their laws disregarded; impiety, which walks with head held high, appears in offending them to be promising impunity to the license that is gaining strength day by day.

Humanity trembles, the citizen is alarmed; from all sides ministers of the Church are heard lamenting at the sight of so many books that in spreading and multiplying could only be destined to shake, if that were possible, the foundations of our religion. . . .

It is with grief that we are forced to say it, but can one hide from the fact that a project has been conceived, a group formed to uphold materialism, to destroy religion, to inspire independence and nourish the corruption of morals?

Do excesses like these not require the most drastic remedies? . . .

. . . The book called *De l'esprit* is the code of the most odious and sordid passions, the apology for materialism and for all that irreligion can say to inspire hatred of Christianity and Catholicism. . . . You see, my lords, in the picture we have just drawn of the principal maxims of this work, nothing but the principles and detestable consequences of many other works which have appeared in the past, and in particular of the encyclopedic dictionary.

The book called *De l'esprit* is like an abridgment of that all-too-famous work, which in its true aim was to have been the book of all knowledge and which became the book of all error; they never ceased to boast of it to us as the most fitting monument to honor the genius of the nation, and today it is the country's disgrace. In the shadow of a dictionary that brings together an immense number of useful and surprising ideas on the arts and sciences, they included an alphabetical compilation of all the absurdities, all the impieties propagated by all the authors, embellished them, enlarged upon them,

* Translated by Nina B. Gunzenhauser from Omer Joly de Fleury, addressing the chambers of the *parlement* of Paris, January 23, 1759, in Marcel Hervier, *Le Dix-huitième Siècle* (*Les Écrivains français jugés par leurs contemporains*, Vol. II) (Paris: Delaplane, 1931), pp. 261–62.

put them in a more impressive light. This dictionary is composed in the taste of Bayle. They develop, according to the kind of articles, the *pro* and the *con*; but the *con*, when it is a matter of religion, of morals, of authority, is always presented clearly and given preference.

8] Second Suppression

Events now moved rapidly toward disaster for Diderot's great venture. D'Alembert's "desertion" (as Diderot grimly called it) delayed production on Volume VIII, and in any event the condemnations raining on Helvétius' *De l'esprit,* coupled with the feelings aroused by d'Alembert's ill-fated contribution to Volume VII, put the continuation of the *Encyclopédie* in danger. Diderot remained optimistic, but after Omer Joly de Fleury, the Attorney General, had addressed the *parlement* of Paris and bitterly denounced the *Encyclopédie,* the distribution of the work was suspended, and on March 8, 1759, a royal decree suppressed it—while Volume VIII was at the printer. On July 21, 1759, another royal decree ordered the booksellers to give the subscribers their money back on unpublished volumes. And on September 3, 1759, Pope Clement VIII in turn condemned the *Encyclopédie.* Everything seemed at an end.

A] THE *Encyclopédie* OFFICIALLY SUPPRESSED *

The king having granted a license on January 21, 1746, for a work to be published under the title of *Encyclopedia, or Analytical Dictionary of the Arts, the Sciences, and the Professions, by a Company of Men of Letters,* the authors of said dictionary released the first two volumes, the suppression of which His Majesty ordered by his decree of February 7, 1752, for reasons contained in said decree; but in consideration of the usefulness the work could have in some respects, His Majesty did not consider it fitting to revoke the license at that time and was content to give stricter orders regarding the review of subsequent volumes; in spite of these precautions, His Majesty has been informed that the authors of said work, abusing the indulgence they had been granted, gave out five new volumes that have caused no less scandal than the first, and that even aroused the zeal of the public minister of his parliament. His Majesty has judged that, after these repeated abuses, it is not possible to let said license remain in effect, that the advantages to be gained for the progress of the arts and sciences from a work of this kind could never balance the irreparable damage to morals and religion that is resulting from it; that in spite of new measures taken to prevent features as reprehensible as those in the first from slipping into the last volumes, there would always be an inevitable objection to permitting the continuation of the work, since it would assure the sale not only of the new volumes but also of those

* Translated by Nina B. Gunzenhauser from *Arrêt du conseil d'état du Roi, qui révoque les lettres de privilège obtenues pour le livre intitulé:* Encyclopédie . . . (March 8, 1759), in Diderot, *Oeuvres complètes,* eds. Jules Assézat and Maurice Tourneux, 20 vols. (Paris, 1875–77), Vol. XIII, pp. 118–19.

which have already appeared; that said *Encyclopédie,* having become a complete dictionary and a general treatise on all the sciences, would be in much greater demand by the public and consulted much more frequently, and that in this way the pernicious maxims with which the volumes already distributed are filled would be spread and would gain sanction. In consideration of which, THE KING BEING IN HIS COUNCIL, on the advice of the chancellor, has revoked and revokes the license obtained on January 21, 1746, for the work entitled *Encyclopedia,* or *Analytical Dictionary of the Arts, the Sciences, and the Professions, by a Company of Men of Letters,* and has forbidden all booksellers and others to sell, supply, or otherwise distribute the volumes that have already appeared, or to print new ones, under pain of exemplary punishment. His Majesty orders Mr. Bertin, Master of Ordinary Petitions of His Household, Lieutenant General of Police, to carry out the present decree, which shall be printed, published, and posted wherever appropriate. Done in the state council of the King, held at Versailles in the presence of His Majesty, the eighth day of March, one thousand seven hundred and fifty-nine.

Phélypeaux

B] THE PUBLISHERS ORDERED TO RETURN THE SUBSCRIBERS' MONEY *

The king being informed that the suppression of the work entitled *Encyclopedia,* or *Analytical Dictionary of the Arts, the Sciences, and the Professions, by a Company of Men of Letters,* ordered by the decree of March 8, 1759, has given rise to complaints on the part of subscribers who paid booksellers in advance the largest part of the price of said work, for which they have received only seven volumes, the value of which is not proportionate to the advance payments made, in the hope of having a complete work illustrated with a large number of plates; and considering at the same time that it would not be just to make the booksellers who took part in this enterprise return the full amounts that had been paid to them and that had been largely used for the preparation of said seven suppressed volumes, His Majesty has deemed it just to fix the sum which the booksellers are required to return to the subscribers. In consideration of which, the report having been heard, THE KING BEING IN HIS COUNCIL, on the advice of the Chancellor, has ordered and orders that the aforementioned Lebreton, David Senior, Briasson and Durand, booksellers, are required to return to all those who present to them a subscription signed by them for the work entitled *Encyclopedia,* or *Analytical Dictionary of the Arts, the Sciences, and the Professions, by a Company*

* Translated by Nina B. Gunzenhauser from *Arrêt du conseil d'état du Roi, qui ordonne aux libraires y dénommés de rendre la somme de soixante-douze livres à ceux qui ont souscrit pour le Dictionnaire des sciences* (July 21, 1759), in Diderot, *Oeuvres complètes,* eds. Jules Assézat and Maurice Tourneux, 20 vols. (Paris, 1875–77), Vol. XIII, pp. 119–20.

of Men of Letters, the sum of seventy-two livres; by means of which payment they will be discharged of their obligations to said subscribers. His Majesty orders Mr. Bertin, Master of Ordinary Petitions of His Household, Lieutenant General of Police, to carry out the present decree, which shall be printed, published, and posted wherever appropriate. Done in the state council of the King, held at Versailles in the presence of His Majesty, the twenty-first day of July, one thousand seven hundred and fifty-nine.

Phélypeaux

c] The *Encyclopédie* Condemned by the Pope *

Immediately upon the appearance of the large work, divided into several volumes, entitled *Encyclopédie* . . . we were informed, not only by the public clamor but by the opinions of it held by serious men filled with zeal for the Faith and Religion, that the book contained a number of things highly detrimental to Christian piety and moral order. . . .

We, therefore, whom God has made guardian and sentinel on the walls of Jerusalem . . . order each and every one of the faithful, under the same pain of excommunication and suspension respectively, who have said work in their homes, or into whose hands it may subsequently fall, that as soon as they are aware of the present writing, they are to take them to the local ordinaries, or else to the inquisitors of the faith or their vicars, who will take care to burn immediately the copies which have been delivered to them.

9] Final Victory

Harassment continued. In May 1760 Palissot's tasteless but popular lampoon of the radical party, *Les Philosophes,* was acted at the Théâtre Français. In the same month, Le Franc de Pompignan (1709–84), magistrate and undistinguished writer, used his acceptance speech at the Académie Française to add his word to the general condemnation of the Encyclopedists.

But Diderot found his champions. Malesherbes and other public officials winked at the clandestine printing of the remaining volumes; Voltaire, the most articulate and most formidable of *philosophes,* who had taken a rather mild interest in the *Encyclopédie,* came to its defense, directly by upholding its probity and its contribution to the public good, and indirectly by ridiculing its enemies. And general events shifted public opinion: the Jesuit order, a stout adversary, was in serious difficulties in France by the end of the 1750's, and in August 1762 it was officially suppressed. Then, too, a series of legal cases, including the famous Calas case, in which the *philosophes* appeared as the advocates of the innocent and the injured, focused attention on the failings of the old order and eased the task of the radicals.

In this improved climate, the printing of the *Encyclopédie* continued. On September 29, 1762, Diderot could write to Voltaire that he had galley proofs

* Translated by Nina B. Gunzenhauser from a pronouncement by Clement VIII, September 3, 1759, in Marcel Hervier, *Le Dix-huitième Siècle (Les Écrivains français jugés par leurs contemporains,* Vol. II) (Paris: Delaplane, 1931), pp. 262–63.

in his hands. There was one more trial, and that a severe one. Late in 1764, Diderot discovered that the chief publisher, Le Breton, had mutilated a number of articles and struck out some of Diderot's most cherished passages after Diderot had approved the galleys. Diderot could barely be persuaded to complete the work, but he did, and in December 1764, Volumes VIII to XVII (H to Z) came out with a false Neuchâtel imprint. The plates, indispensable especially for the articles on crafts and industry, came out soon after.

A] ANOTHER ATTACK: DE POMPIGNAN'S ACCEPTANCE SPEECH *

However fashionable philosophy and literature are today, truly literate men and true philosophers are as rare as ever. Pretensions are not qualifications. It is by the fruit of their studies that we must judge their success. One is not a man of letters just because he has read a great deal and written a great deal, knows languages, or has excavated the ruins of antiquity, or finally because he is an orator, poet, or historian. One is not always a philosopher for having written treatises on ethics, plumbed the depths of metaphysics, reached the heights of the most sublime geometry, revealed the secrets of natural history, divined the system of the universe. The scholar who has been educated and made better by his books—that is the man of letters. The wise man, virtuous and Christian—that is the philosopher.

B] VOLTAIRE DEFENDS HIS BRETHREN AGAINST PALISSOT †

It is up to you to examine your conscience and see if you are just in portraying Messrs d'Alembert, Duclos, Diderot, Helvétius, de Jaucourt, and *tutti quanti* as scoundrels who are teaching how to pick pockets. . . . If they were as you depict them, they would have to be sent to the galleys, which would have no place at all in comedy. I am speaking to you frankly; those whom you want to dishonor are considered the most honest people in the world; and I am not even sure that their integrity is not superior to their philosophy. . . .

I do not know Mr. Diderot at all; I have never seen him; I only know that he has been wretched and persecuted; that reason alone should make you drop your pen.

Moreover I regard the undertaking of the *Encyclopédie* as the most noble monument one could erect to the honor of the sciences; there are admirable articles, not only by Mr. d'Alembert, Mr. Diderot, and de Jaucourt, but by

---

* Translated by Nina B. Gunzenhauser from Le Franc de Pompignan, *Discours de réception à l'Académie française* (March 10, 1760), in Marcel Hervier, *Le Dix-huitième Siècle* (*Les Écrivains français jugés par leurs contemporains*, Vol. II) (Paris: Delaplane, 1931), pp. 263–64.

† Translated by Nina B. Gunzenhauser from Voltaire, *Correspondance*, ed. Theodore Besterman (Geneva, 1953–   ), Vol. XLII, p. 91.

many other people, who without any motive of glory or self-interest were delighted to take part in this work.

There are without question some sorry articles, and mine could very well be among them; but the good so prodigiously outweighs the bad that all Europe desires the continuation of the *Encyclopédie*. The first volumes have already been translated into several languages; why then ridicule in the theater a work that has become necessary to the education of men and to the glory of the nation?

c] DIDEROT: THE LAST WORD *

When we began to apply ourselves to this enterprise, we expected only the difficulties that would be created by the extent and the variety of its purposes; but that was a passing illusion, and we were not long in seeing the multitude of physical obstacles we had anticipated augmented by an infinitude of moral obstacles for which we were completely unprepared. The world can get older, but it does not change; an individual may improve himself, but the masses of the species get neither better nor worse; the sum of malevolent passions is constant, and the enemies of everything that is good and useful are as innumerable as ever.

Of all the persecutions that have been suffered in all ages and among all peoples by those who have yielded to the tempting and dangerous ambition of inscribing their names in the list of mankind's benefactors, there is almost none that we have not undergone. We have experienced everything that history has told us of foul deeds of envy, falsehood, ignorance and fanaticism. In the course of twenty consecutive years we have been able to count scarcely a few moments of peace. After days consumed in ungrateful and unrelieved labor, how many nights we spent awaiting the evils that spitefulness tried to draw us into! How many times have we not arisen uncertain whether, giving in to the slanderous cries, we should not tear ourselves away from our families, our friends, our fellow citizens, to seek under a foreign sky the peace we needed and the protection it offered us! But our homeland was dear to us, and we always expected that prejudice would yield to justice. Moreover, such is the character of the man whose intentions are good, and who gives himself up to the evidence, that his courage is inflamed by the obstacles with which he is opposed, while his innocence shelters him or makes him scorn the perils that menace him. The good man is capable of an enthusiasm the evil man does not know.

The honest and courageous feeling that has sustained us we have also encountered in others. All of our colleagues hastened to support us, and it was

---

* Translated by Nina B. Gunzenhauser from Diderot, "Avertissement" to the eighth volume of the *Encyclopédie* (December 1764), in Diderot, *Oeuvres complètes*, eds. Jules Assézat and Maurice Tourneux, 20 vols. (Paris, 1875–77), Vol. XIII, pp. 171–75.

when our enemies were congratulating themselves on having crushed us that we saw men of letters and fashionable people, who had until then been content to encourage us and commiserate with us, come to our aid and associate themselves with our work. If only we were permitted to give public acknowledgment to all of those capable and courageous assistants! But since there is only one whom we are free to name, let us at least attempt to thank him in a suitable manner: that is de Jaucourt.

If we have cried out with joy like the sailor when he spies land after a dark night that kept him erring between sky and sea, it is to de Jaucourt that we are indebted. What has he not done for us, lately in particular! With what steadfastness has he not refused the tender and powerful entreaties that sought to take him away from us! Never was the sacrifice of peace, of self-interest and of health more complete and more absolute; the most laborious and thankless research failed to daunt him; he applied himself to it relentlessly, content if he could spare others the distastefulness of it; but it is for each page of this work to supply what is missing in our praise: there is not one that does not attest to the diversity of his knowledge and the extent of his help.

The public has judged the first seven volumes; we ask for the current batch only the same indulgence. If one does not want to consider this dictionary a great and noble work, we would be in agreement, provided we are not envied the privilege of having prepared the materials. From the point where we started to the point we have reached the distance was tremendous. . . . Thanks to our labors, those who come after us will be able to go further. Without declaring what they have yet to do, we will turn over to them at least the best book on tools and machines that has ever existed, with the plates on the mechanical arts, the most complete description that has ever been given, and an infinite number of precious morsels concerning all the sciences. O compatriots and contemporaries! With whatever severity you judge this work, remember that it was undertaken, continued, completed by a small number of isolated men, thwarted in their views, shown in the worst light, slandered and insulted in the most atrocious manner, having no other encouragement than the love of the good, no other support than several commendations, no other help but that which they found in the confidence of three or four tradesmen!

Our main purpose was to collect the discoveries of preceding centuries; without having neglected this first design, we will not exaggerate at all in attributing to many volumes *in folio* the new riches that we have borne to the depository of ancient knowledge. Should a revolution, the germ of which is forming perhaps in some unknown canton of the earth or incubating secretly in the very center of the civilized world, break out in time, destroy the cities, scatter the nations once again, and bring back ignorance and darkness; if one single complete set of this work survives, all will not be lost.

At least it cannot be contested, I think, that our work is on a level with our century, and that is something. The most enlightened man will find in it ideas that were unfamiliar to him and facts he did not know. If only general education could advance at such a rapid rate that twenty years from now there would be, out of a thousand of our pages, scarcely a single line that was not popular knowledge! It is up to the rulers of the world to hasten that happy revolution; it is they who expand or contract the sphere of enlightenment. Happy the time when they will all have understood that their security consists in commanding educated men! The major crimes have never been attempted by any except blinded fanatics. Would we venture to murmur about our troubles and regret our years of labor if we could flatter ourselves that we weakened that spirit of madness so contrary to the peace of societies and that we led our fellow men to love each other, to tolerate each other and to recognize at last the superiority of universal ethics over all the particular morals that inspire hatred and disorder and that break or relax the general and common bond?

Such was our aim throughout. The great and rare honor which our enemies will have reaped from the obstacles they set up for us! The enterprise they thwarted so mercilessly is completed. If there is anything good in it, it is not they who will be praised for it, and perhaps they will be blamed for its defects. Be that as it may, we invite them to leaf through these last volumes. Should they use up all the severity of their criticism on them, and should they pour out on us all the bitterness of their spleen, we are ready to pardon a hundred injuries for one good observation. If they recognize that they have seen us constantly prostrated before the two things that make the welfare of societies and the only ones that are really worthy of homage—virtue and truth—they will find us indifferent to all their imputations.

As for our colleagues, we ask them to take into consideration that the materials of these last volumes were gathered in haste and prepared amid turmoil; that the printing was done with unprecedented speed, that it was impossible for one man, whoever he might be, to maintain throughout such a long process of revision all the presence of mind required by an infinitude of diverse subjects, the majority of them highly abstract; and if it has happened that errors, even stupid ones, have disfigured their articles, they can be neither offended nor surprised. But, to make sure that the esteem they enjoy, which must be precious to them, does not find itself compromised in any way, we agree that all the mistakes in this edition are to be unreservedly ascribed to us. After a declaration as unlimited and precise as this, if some of them forget that we had to work far from their eyes and their advice, it could only be the effect of a dissatisfaction that we never intended to give them and that was unavoidable. Well, what better could we have done than to call to our aid all those whose friendship and enlightenment had served us so well? Had we not been warned a hundred times of our inadequacy? Did we refuse to recognize it? Is there a single one of our colleagues to whom in happier times we would not have given every possible mark of deference? Will we be accused of having been unaware of how essential their cooperation was to the completion of this work? If we are accused of that, it will be one final grief saved for us, to which we will still have to resign ourselves.

If one adds to the years of our life that had passed at the time we planned this work those we have given to its accomplishment, one will easily realize that we have lived more years than we have left. But we shall have received the compensation that we look for from our contemporaries and our descendants if we make them say one day that we did not live entirely in vain.

CONCLUSION

THE DRAMATIC history of the *Encyclopédie* is characteristic of the Old Regime; it helps to explain both the intellectual background of the French Revolution and the inglorious collapse of time-honored institutions in the face of financial ruin and public pressure. The authorities were too bigoted and too insecure to allow the *philosophes* to publish their views in peace, but they were also too humane and too divided to repress them effectively. The *Encyclopédie* was thus both cause and effect; both the reflection and the precipitant of a crisis. When it was completed, it had done its job: to help "change the general way of thinking." But it succeeded at least in part because that way of thinking was changing anyway.

STUDY QUESTIONS

1] Do you think it would have been possible for the Encyclopedists and orthodox Christians to reach a peaceful accommodation?

2] In what way were the ideals of the Enlightenment reflected in such articles as "Genève"?

3] Did the journalists who censured and the officials who suppressed the *Encyclopédie* have any kind of rational case? If so, what was it?

4] How does Diderot's *Encyclopédie* differ from the encyclopedias of our day, judging from the documents you have read?

RECOMMENDED READINGS

PRIMARY

DIDEROT, DENIS. *Rameau's Nephew and Other Writings*, trans. by Jacques Barzun and Ralph H. Bowen (includes long extracts from the article "Encyclopedia") (New York, 1956).

LOUGH, JOHN, ed. *The* Encyclopédie *of Diderot and D'Alembert: Selected Articles Edited with an Introduction* (Cambridge, 1954).

ROTH, GEORGES, ed., *Denis Diderot: Correspondance*, 10 vols. to date (Paris, 1955–   ).

SECONDARY

CASSIRER, ERNST. *The Philosophy of the Enlightenment* (Princeton, 1951).

COBBAN, ALFRED. *In Search of Humanity: The Role of the Enlightenment in Modern History* (London, 1960).

DIECKMANN, HERBERT. *Cinq leçons sur Diderot* (Geneva and Paris, 1959).

GAY, PETER. *The Party of Humanity: Essays in the French Enlightenment* (New York, 1964).

GORDON, DOUGLAS H. AND NORMAN L. TORREY. *The Censoring of Diderot's Encyclopédie and the Re-established Text* (New York, 1947).

GRIMSLEY, RONALD. *Jean d'Alembert, 1717–83* (Oxford, 1963).

PROUST, JACQUES. *Diderot et l'Encyclopédie* (Paris, 1962).

THOMAS, JEAN. *L'Humanisme de Diderot*, 2nd ed. (Paris, 1938).

WILSON, ARTHUR M. *Diderot: The Testing Years* (New York, 1957).

The French Revolution: Dynamics of the Terror, 1793–94

DAVID H. PINKNEY

UNIVERSITY OF MISSOURI

CONTENTS

CHRONOLOGY

1789

MAY 5   Meeting of the Estates-General at Versailles.

JUNE 20   The deputies of the Third Estate take an oath not to separate until they have given France a constitution.

JUNE 27   Louis XVI orders the First and Second Estates to join the Third in the National Constituent Assembly.

JULY 14   Storming of the Bastille.

1791

OCTOBER 1   Meeting of the Legislative Assembly.

1792

APRIL 20   France declares war on Austria.

MAY 1   Prussia declares war on France.

AUGUST 10   A Parisian crowd attacks the Tuileries Palace; the Legislative Assembly suspends Louis XVI from office.

AUGUST 11   The Legislative Assembly orders an election of a constituent assembly, the National Convention.

SEPTEMBER 2–5   The massacre of suspects in the prisons of Paris.

SEPTEMBER 21   The Convention meets and abolishes the monarchy.

1793

JANUARY 21   The execution of Louis XVI.

JANUARY–MARCH   The formation of the First Coalition of European powers against the French Republic.

MARCH 10   The establishment of the Revolutionary Criminal Tribunal

MARCH 16   The outbreak of the revolt in the Vendée.

APRIL 6   The establishment of the Committee of Public Safety.

JUNE 2   The Convention orders the arrest of thirty-one Girondin deputies.

JULY–SEPTEMBER   Border fortresses fall to Austrians and Prussians; the British seize Toulon; Spanish cross the Pyrenees frontier; Federalists revolt in the provinces; food becomes scarce in cities and towns.

AUGUST 23   The Convention decrees the levy *en masse*.

SEPTEMBER 29	The Convention passes the Law of the Maximum.
OCTOBER 9	Government forces occupy Lyons.
OCTOBER 16	Execution of Marie Antoinette.
OCTOBER 30	Execution of twenty-one Girondin leaders.
DECEMBER	Toulon is recovered; organized resistance in the Vendée ends; Allied armies retreat across the Rhine.

1794

FEBRUARY 26 AND MARCH 3	The Convention approves the Ventôse Decrees.
MARCH 24	Execution of the leaders of the Ultra-Revolutionaries.
APRIL 6	Execution of the leaders of the Indulgents.
JUNE 10	Law of 22 Prairial increases the powers of the Revolutionary Criminal Tribunal.
JUNE 10–JULY 28	The Great Terror.
JULY 27	The Convention orders the arrest of Robespierre, Saint-Just, and Couthon.
JULY 28	Robespierre and twenty-one supporters are executed.
JULY–DECEMBER	The end of the Terror.

INTRODUCTION

FEW EVENTS in modern European history have shaken the world as did the French Revolution. Although it was part of a great revolutionary movement that touched all the West in the late eighteenth century, the Revolution in France was more violent and, simply because it occurred in France, more shocking. The spectacle of the wealthiest, the most powerful, and presumably the most stable and secure of all the nations of Europe summarily discarding its ancient institutions and replacing them with the rational creations of a representative assembly enthralled a world already stirred by the revolutionary ideas of the French *philosophes*. When the French embarked on a crusade to carry the revolution to their neighbors, deposed and executed their "Most Christian King," and made terror "the order of the day," it became clear that the French Revolution threatened to overturn the whole structure of European government and society.

Here the focus is on the most intense, the most dramatic, and to contemporaries the most frightening period of the Revolution—the Reign of Terror of 1793–94. The Revolution had begun in 1787–88 as an aristocratic defiance of the crown's efforts to reduce the state's large budgetary deficit and to forestall bankruptcy by levying taxes on privileged land. The opposition of the Assembly of Notables and of the Parlement of Paris forced Louis XVI to summon the Estates-General, the representative assembly of the clergy, the nobility, and the commoners, which had not met since 1614. Because it involved the whole nation, this move began the transformation of a conflict between crown and aristocracy into a prolonged struggle between the crown and the nobility on the one hand and, on the other, the bourgeoisie supported by an immense peasant revolt and by urban insurrection.

The deputies of the Third Estate, the commoners who came to Versailles in May 1789, had little sympathy with the royal view that they should approve new taxes and disperse. They wanted to end the regime of privilege, write a constitution, and relieve the economy of burdensome mercantilist restrictions. When Louis and his ministers, supported by most of the aristocracy, made clear their opposition, the deputies of the Third Estate declared themselves the National Assembly of France, invited the other estates to join with them, and took an oath not to separate until they had given France a constitution. Louis hesitated, considered resistance, then gave in. On June 27 he ordered the two upper estates to join the Third and, in effect, gave his approval to the new National Constituent Assembly.

The Assembly's first months were stormy. Movement of royal troops to Versailles raised fears among the Third Estate that the King was about to dissolve the Assembly and punish the deputies. The Revolution spread to Paris and the provinces. On July 14 the citizens of Paris, fearful of an attack on the city and resentful of economic privation, seized the royal fortress of the Bastille and organized a revolutionary municipal government and a municipal guard to defend it. Other cities, following the capital's example, installed new municipal authorities and established local militias. In rural areas peasants refused to pay their feudal dues and invaded chateaux to destroy records of their obligations, sometimes burning the chateaux with the records. In Versailles the deputies had to abandon their deliberate consideration of a constitution in order to deal with spreading violence and its implied threat to property. In a dramatic all-night session on August 4–5, 1789, they voted the end of noble and clerical privileges and other remaining vestiges of the feudal system. Later in the month they adopted a Declaration of the Rights of Man and of the Citizen that proclaimed the principles on which they intended to build the new France—liberty, equality, popular sovereignty, and respect for private property.

Through the next two years the Assembly was occupied embodying these principles into laws and institutions. It gave the country new administrative institutions, a new system of judicial courts, a new system of taxation. It confiscated the lands of the Church, issued money on the security of these lands, and used this currency to pay the state's debts and running expenses. It abolished internal customs barriers and suppressed guilds. By the Civil Constitution of the Clergy it subordinated the Roman Catholic Church to the state and reduced the clergy to elected employees of the civil government. Finally the Assembly fulfilled its vow to give France a constitution. The Declaration of the Rights of Man and of the Citizen stood at its head, but the constitution stopped far short of true popular sovereignty. It established a regime in which the sovereign power was shared by the King and a single-house legislature; furthermore, indirect elections and property qualifications for voting and for office-holding assured that the legislature would be less than democratic.

On September 30, 1791, the National Assembly met for the last time, and on the following day the new Legislative Assembly convened. Nominally the Revolution was now completed, the *ancien régime* forever buried. But France in the autumn of 1791 was a dangerously divided nation. Not all Frenchmen accepted the new regime, and many were determined to destroy it. The King himself never fully acceded to the role of a constitutional monarch, and he worked secretly to undermine the constitution he had sworn to uphold. The aristocracy resented the loss of their privileges and the income from feudal rights. Some of them had emigrated and, settled in neighboring states, busied themselves with plans to "liberate" France and with efforts to induce foreign rulers to help them do so. At the opposite end of the political spectrum were determined men who saw the new constitutional monarchy as a travesty of popular sovereignty and demanded its replacement by a democratic republic. The urban poor, ever fearful of hunger, were disturbed by the ending of traditional controls on prices and of regulation of the grain trade.

Most serious of all was the split of the nation over the revolutionary church settlement. The Pope had condemned the Civil Constitution of the Clergy, and about half of the clergy refused to take the prescribed oath that implied acceptance of the constitution. Henceforth, France had two churches —the constitutional church supported by the state, and the Roman Church, hostile to the Revolution and in rebellion against the state. Thousands of the faithful who had otherwise accepted the Revolution followed their priests into opposition.

Already in 1791 the Revolution had become embroiled in international complications. Its successes in France had revived the hopes and activities of liberals in neighboring countries. This spread of its principles alarmed foreign rulers and disposed them to listen to appeals of *émigrés* and of the French court for assistance in stopping the spreading infection. Within France in the winter and spring of 1791–92 were at least two powerful groups who believed that they would benefit from France's involvement in a war with the Austrian Hapsburgs, who were bound to the royal family of France by ties of family and common fears of revolution. The Girondins, a party of republican deputies in the Legislative Assembly, thought that a war would strengthen their hand against the monarchists, and they preached a crusade of peoples against kings. Louis XVI and the court foresaw in the event of war the country quickly overrun by Austrian troops, who would deliver the King from his bondage to the Revolution. On April 20, 1792, Louis proposed a declaration of war on Austria, and the Assembly voted it with only seven dissenting votes. Prussia soon came to the support of Austria.

From the beginning the war went badly for France. The army, demoralized by the defection of noble officers who resented the revolutionary government for its ending of noble privileges, offered no effective resistance to the invaders. Some regiments deserted to the enemy; others fled in disorder, killing their officers. Rumor spread of an aristocratic conspiracy among nobles and priests within France and the advancing foreign enemy to overthrow the Assembly. Louis was suspected of being in communication with the invader and of plotting a *coup d'état*. Among the Jacobins, the popular political clubs, and the National Guardsmen called up to help defend the country, the demand grew for deposition of this King, and on August 10, 1792, an armed crowd of Parisian artisans, shopkeepers, and working men—the *sans-culottes*—and National Guardsmen, directed by the Revolutionary Commune of Paris, attacked the Tuileries Palace and forced the royal family to flee to the Assembly. Under popular pressure the Assembly voted to suspend the King from office and ordered the election—by universal manhood suffrage— of a new constituent assembly, the National Convention.

The foreign threat grew more ominous, the fear of internal conspiracy mounted, and in September Paris had its first taste of the Terror in its crudest form—the violent elimination of suspected enemies of the Revolution. On September 2 word reached the capital that the Prussians had be-

sieged Verdun, the last fortress covering the road to Paris from the eastern
frontier. The tocsin was rung; the city gates closed. Rumor spread that aris-
tocrats and priests confined as suspects in the city's prisons would, as soon
as patriots left for the front, break out and massacre families of departed
volunteers. Groups of excited men rushed to the prisons and in the course
of four days killed some 1,300 persons, many of them completely innocent
of any hostility to the regime. The government made no effective effort to
stop the executioners, and a few weeks later Robespierre in a speech before
the Convention defended them for their patriotic work.

On September 21 the Convention met and in its first session abolished the
monarchy; the next day it indirectly proclaimed the establishment of the
Republic. On September 20 French troops had repulsed the Prussians at
Valmy, and this reverse, combined with bad weather and faltering supplies,
induced the Prussians to withdraw across the Rhine. Other French victories
soon ended the Austrian threat on the northern frontier. Through the fall
and winter months France enjoyed a respite, but the Convention, far from
making any gesture of appeasement to neighboring rulers, defied them by
promising aid to all peoples who wished "to recover their liberty" and then
shocked the crowned heads of Europe by trying Louis XVI on charges of
treason and condemning him to death. The King was executed on January
21, 1793, and soon a new and more formidable coalition, including Britain
and most of the countries of the Continent, was formed against the infant
Republic. In March invading armies again moved across the frontiers. At the
same time several departments in the west flared into revolt against the government in Paris and demanded restoration of the monarchy. Insurrection
spread to Normandy, to Bordeaux, to Lyons, to Toulon and the southeast.
By summer two-thirds of the departments were in revolt against the Republic. The desertion to the enemy of France's ablest general, Dumouriez, raised
the cry that there was treason within the government itself. In Paris the
sans-culottes, working through the popular clubs, put increasing pressure on
the government for more rigorous repressive measures against enemies of the
Republic, foreign and domestic. In June they forced the Convention to vote
the arrest of the Girondin leaders, moderates in the new, more radical assembly, on the grounds that they were traitorously hindering the war effort.

During that summer the plight of the Republic grew desperate. Attacked
by the coalesced kings of Europe, assailed by counterrevolutionaries at home,
betrayed, it seemed, by a myriad of secret enemies, its very survival hung in
the balance. On September 5, 1793, the Jacobin Club of Paris demanded
that the Convention decree Terror "the order of the day." The principal instruments of the Terror were already established: the Committee of Public
Safety to direct and coordinate all the activities of government, the Committee of General Security to administer the police, the Revolutionary Criminal Tribunal to dispense revolutionary justice, the deputies on mission, and
the committees of surveillance. These were now supplemented by the Law

of Suspects, which permitted the arrest of anyone even suspected of opposition, and the Revolutionary Army, established to enforce laws regulating
prices and the distribution of food.

The "Reign of Terror" began in earnest. Its manifest purposes were to
eliminate the enemies and suspected enemies of the Republic and to intim-
idate their accomplices. It differed from the Terror of September 1792 in
being a legal, organized, and deliberate instrument of government. The first
prominent victims were the Queen, Marie Antoinette, and twenty-one Girondin leaders. Following them to the guillotine, the firing squad, or "patriotic
baptism" were the Duke of Orleans, head of the younger branch of the
Bourbon family who had aspired to succeed Louis XVI; Bailly, former mayor
of Paris; and hundreds of nobles, priests, army officers, and common men
and women. Before its end in July 1794 the Terror had formally condemned
some 17,000 victims and executed without trial or let die in prison probably
an equal number. Between 300,000 and 400,000 suspects had been arrested
and imprisoned. During the final six weeks, the so-called Great Terror of
June and July 1794, the Revolutionary Tribunal in Paris, following the sim-
plified procedure prescribed by the Law of 22 Prairial, sent 1,515 men and
women to their deaths.

The Reign of Terror was not, however, simply a succession of wholesale
executions. In a broader sense it was also the whole regime of coercion under which Frenchmen lived in 1793–94. Although all Frenchmen were not
terrified or terrorized, most of them were being coerced by their government
into certain actions that they would not have performed under a regime
based on persuasion and consent. They were forced to refrain from criticiz-
ing the government, to sell grain at fixed prices, to work for fixed wages, to
serve in the army. In this sense the Terror involved not only trials and executions and imprisonment but also conscription of men and materials, price-
fixing, rent controls, and censorship. The coercion mounted gradually from
the first conscription decree of February 23, 1793, and it continued to function until the regime was dismantled, along with the instruments of the violent Terror, after the fall of Robespierre in July 1794.

Viewed either way, as a terrorization of the opposition or as a regime of
coercion, the Terror provides fascinating examples of human behavior in time
of crisis. Historians have studied it with exemplary thoroughness, but they
have not agreed on a single explanation of the purposes it was intended to
serve.

Probably most commonly accepted is the orthodox republican view that
the Terror was essentially political and repressive, an element in a government of national defense, organized under the menace of invasion, insurrection, and treason to defend France and the Republic. In self-defense the nation, led by the Committee of Public Safety and pushed by the patriot *sans-
culottes* of Paris, undertook measures to mobilize the country's resources, to
exterminate or at least to silence those who tried to use the crisis of war to
overthrow the Republic and to restore the monarchy. Once the crisis had

passed, this emergency regime of coercion was no longer necessary, and the Convention abolished it.

Some historians, the most influential among whom is Albert Mathiez, reject this purely political explanation of the Terror. They see it instead as part of an effort by Robespierre and a group of Jacobins around him to establish a measure of socialism in France. They point to the government's price-fixing and rationing, intended to assure necessities to all at prices all could pay; to the Ventôse Decrees of 1794, which provided for the distribution among indigent persons of property confiscated from "enemies of the Revolution"; and to efforts in the spring of 1794 to eliminate poverty by a national system of social security. The Committee of Public Safety used its coercive powers during the Terror to impose these measures on France. More recent historians, notably Georges Lefebvre and Ernest Labrousse, have modified this judgment of the Terror as a kind of premature socialist dictatorship. While still emphasizing the economic motivation of the Terror, they see pressure for economic controls and relief measures coming from the *sans-culottes* of Paris, who sought protection against soaring prices and continuing shortages of essential food and clothing. The *sans-culottes* were not socialists before their time, these historians hold, but reactionaries who wanted a return to the familiar economic controls of the old regime. The Jacobins and others in the Committee of Public Safety and the Convention agreed to impose controls, Mathiez's critics contend, only to meet the emergency of war and insurrection, and they never intended to make them permanent institutions of the Republic. The Ventôse Decrees, far from being an assault on private property, were only measures to facilitate the disposition into private hands of property temporarily in the possession of the state.

A third interpretation of the Terror is suggested by the discrepancy in time between the height of the foreign and internal crisis and the height of the Terror. The domestic insurrections were vanquished, and the foreign invaders were stopped, before the end of 1793. The danger that justified the political terror was past, but the Terror continued. In the spring of 1794 the factions of the republicans turned on each other with accusations of treason and counterrevolution. In March nineteen Ultra-Revolutionaries, too radical for the dominant groups, were sent to the guillotine. In April thirteen Indulgents, including Danton himself, accused of being too conciliatory with enemies of the Republic, lost their heads to the machine on the Place de la Révolution. Later in the spring, when the armies of the Republic were everywhere on the offensive, the Terror became even more intense. The Law of 22 Prairial (June 10, 1794) accelerated the procedure of the Revolutionary Tribunal, and for the next six weeks "heads fell like slates from the roofs." The court condemned men, women, and even children in wholesale lots on preposterously vague charges. In Paris more victims of the Terror died in those six weeks than in all the preceding eight or nine months. Crane Brinton has suggested that this last upsurge of the Terror can be explained only as the work of men with a fanatical belief in their possession of the truth. Convinced that they were of the elect, chosen to establish the Republic of Virtue in France, they undertook to eliminate the damned who refused or were unable to meet the standards of virtuous civic conduct demanded by Robespierre and his little band of prophets. "Virtue without terror," he declared, "is powerless."

The three groups of readings that follow illustrate the documentary foundations of each of these three interpretations of the Terror.

DOCUMENTS

1] The Terror as the Defense of France and the Revolution

a] DANTON'S SPEECH OF MARCH 10, 1793

In early March 1793 the Convention, already concerned over growing disaffection at home and the expanding coalition of the Republic's enemies abroad, was alarmed by news of French defeats in the Netherlands, and it began considering emergency measures to meet the impending crisis. On March 10 the Assembly, which had been discussing the creation of a new revolutionary court, was about to adjourn for the day when the fiery Danton rushed to the tribune and delivered the following warning.*

I summon all good citizens not to desert their posts. (All members resume their seats, profound silence reigns over all the assembly.) Really! citizens, at the moment when our position is such that if Miranda [French general in the Low Countries] were beaten—and that is not impossible—Dumouriez, surrounded, would have to stop fighting, you could leave without taking the great measures required for the good of the public cause! I feel how very important it is to take judicial measures which may punish the counter-revolutionaries, because it is for them that this court is necessary; it is for them that this court must take the place of the supreme court of the people's vengeance. The enemies of liberty show an impudent face; confounded everywhere, they are provocators everywhere. Seeing the honest citizen busy in his home, the craftsman busy in his workshop, they have the stupidity to believe that they are in the majority; well! tear them away yourselves from popular vengeance, humanity orders you to do so.

Nothing is more difficult than to define a political crime. But if a man of the lowest social class receives immediate punishment for a particular crime, if it is difficult to get at a political crime, should not extraordinary laws, formulated outside the established institutions of government, terrorize the rebels and reach the guilty? Here the salvation of the people demands great means and terrible measures. I do not see any middle course between the ordinary forms and a Revolutionary Tribunal.

· · ·

* Translated by Marguerite Greene from *Reimpression de l'ancien moniteur* (Paris), XV (March 13, 1793), 683.

Therefore I am asking that the Revolutionary Tribunal be organized forthwith, that the executive power in the new organization be endowed with the necessary means of action and energy.

.   .   .

I am asking that as soon as the measures of general security are taken, your commissioners leave immediately. . . . Let them go into the departments so that they may excite the citizens, that they may revive the love of liberty.

B] DECREES ESTABLISHING EMERGENCY INSTRUMENTS OF GOVERNMENT

The first of the three decrees given below (March 10, 1793) created an Extraordinary Criminal Tribunal; the second (April 6, 1793), a Committee of Public Safety; and the third (April 30, 1793), representatives on mission to each army.*

EXTRAORDINARY CRIMINAL TRIBUNAL

1. There shall be established in Paris an extraordinary criminal tribunal, which shall have jurisdiction over every counter-revolutionary enterprise, over all attacks against liberty, equality, unity, and the indivisibility of the Republic, the internal and external security of the state, and over all conspiracies tending to reestablish any other authority which makes an attack on liberty, equality, and sovereignty of the people, whether the accused be civil or military functionaries or simple citizens.

2. The tribunal shall be composed of a jury and of five judges, who shall direct the examination and shall apply the law after the declaration of the jurors upon the facts.

.   .   .

13. The judgments shall be executed without appeal.

COMMITTEE OF PUBLIC SAFETY

1. There shall be formed, by voice vote, a committee of public safety, composed of nine members of the National Convention.

2. The committee shall deliberate in secret; it shall be charged with supervising and accelerating the action of the administration entrusted to the provisional executive council, whose orders it may suspend when it shall

---

* From Frank Maloy Anderson, ed., *The Constitutions and Other Select Documents Illustrative of the History of France, 1789–1907*, 2nd ed. rev. (Minneapolis, 1908), pp. 152–54, 159–60.

Recueil général des lois, décrêts, ordonnances, etc., depuis le mois de juin 1789 jusqu'au mois d'août 1830 (Paris, 1837), Vol. IV, pp. 132–34, 170–73.

believe them contrary to the national interest, subject to informing the Convention thereof without delay.

3. It is authorized to take, under urgent circumstances, measures of external and internal defense; and the orders signed by the majority of its members present . . . shall be executed without delay by the provisional executive council. It shall not in any case issue warrants of capture or of arrest, except against executive agents and subject to rendering an account thereof to the Convention without delay.

REPRESENTATIVES ON MISSION

1. There shall be at all times three deputies as representatives of the people with each of the armies of the Republic. One shall be replaced each month.

2. They shall exercise the most active surveillance over the operations of the executive council, over the conduct of generals, officers, and soldiers of the army; they shall make a daily accounting of the situation of the supply depots, of all kinds of supplies, food and munitions; they shall exercise the most severe examination over the operations and conduct of all suppliers and contractors of the armies of the Republic.

3. They shall take all the measures that they deem suitable to accelerate the reorganization of the armies, the incorporation of volunteers and recruits into the existing cadres: to this end they shall work in cooperation with the commanding generals of divisions and other agents of the executive council.

4. The representatives with the armies are invested with unlimited powers for the exercise of the functions which are delegated to them by the present decree. . . .

5. The representatives of the people with the armies shall take without delay all measures necessary to discover, to have arrested and brought before the Revolutionary Tribunal, every military man, every civil agent and other citizens who aided, advised, or favored in any way whatsoever the treason of Dumouriez or any other plot against the security of the nation, or who secretly worked for the disorganization of the armies and attempted the ruin of the Republic.

c] Petition to the Convention, August 18, 1793

During the summer of 1793, with invading armies on French soil and two-thirds of the departments in revolt against the Republic, the Convention came under pressure from the political clubs and the Parisian activists to mobilize all the manpower of the nation for war. On August 18, 1793, a deputation from the forty-eight electoral districts of Paris presented the following address to the assembly.*

* Translated by Marguerite Greene from *Archives parlementaires de 1787 à 1860* (Paris, 1867–1913), First Series, Vol. LXXII, p. 251.

Representatives,

The delegates of the French people once again appear before you, led by the great interest of saving France.

Representatives, convince yourselves of these truths: in time of extreme danger half measures are always fatal; it is easier to shake the whole nation than a mere part of the citizens. If you ask for 100,000 soldiers, you will not find them; but millions of men will answer a general call.

.   .   .

Therefore decree immediately that the tocsin of liberty ring on an appointed day in all the communes of the Republic. Let the cohorts of the despots tremble! a countless multitude of arms moved by vengeance and justice will rise up against them; in an inevitable death they will see that it is impossible to enslave a free people.

Let there be no exemption for the man physically capable of bearing arms, regardless of what his functions may be; let only agriculture keep the indispensable arms to grow the essential foods; let the course of commerce momentarily be stopped; let all business stop; so that the great, the unique and universal business of the French be that of saving the Republic!

d] Decree for the Levy *en Masse,* August 23, 1793

The Convention embodied the demands of the petition of August 18 and other similar demands for national mobilization into law by decreeing all Frenchmen subject to conscription for service in the nation's defense.*

Art. 1. From this moment until the enemy shall have been driven from the soil of France, all Frenchmen are in permanent requisition for the service of the armies. The young men will go to battle; the married men shall forge arms and transport provisions; the women shall make tents and clothing and shall serve in hospitals; the children shall turn old linen into lint; the old men shall betake themselves to the public places to arouse the courage of warriors, to preach the hatred of kings and the unity of the Republic.

2. The national buildings shall be converted into barracks, the public places into workshops for arms; the soil of cellars shall be scrubbed to extract saltpetre.

3. Arms of regulation calibre shall be reserved exclusively for those who shall march against the enemy; the service of the interior shall be performed with hunting pieces and swords.

* From Frank Maloy Anderson, ed., *The Constitutions and Other Select Documents Illustrative of the History of France, 1789–1907,* 2nd ed. rev. (Minneapolis, 1908), pp. 184–85.

Recueil général des lois, décrêts, ordonnances, etc., depuis le mois de juin 1789 jusqu'au mois d'août 1830 (Paris, 1837), Vol. IV, pp. 372–73.

4. Saddle horses are requisitioned to complete the cavalry corps; the draft horses, except those employed in agriculture, shall haul artillery and provisions.

5. The Committee of Public Safety is directed to take all the measures necessary to establish, without delay, an emergency production of arms of all types, which expresses the ardor and the energy of the French people. It is accordingly authorized to organize all the establishments, factories, shops, and mills that shall be deemed necessary for the execution of this work as well as to requisition for this purpose, through the Republic, the artisans and workers who can contribute to their success.

. . .

8. The levy shall be general. Unmarried citizens and widowers without children from eighteen to twenty-five years, shall march first; they shall assemble without delay at the chief-town of their districts, where they shall practice every day at the manual of arms, while awaiting the hour of departure.

E] PETITION TO THE CONVENTION, SEPTEMBER 5, 1793

In the session of September 5, excited by news of ominous reverses on both home and foreign fronts, the Convention received many petitions for the increased use of terror. The spokesman for a deputation from the Jacobin Club and from the forty eight sections of Paris put the demand in the following words.*

Representatives of the people,

The dangers of the fatherland are extreme, the remedies must be equally extreme. You have decreed that the French would rise *en masse* to push back from our borders the hordes of bandits who devastate them, but . . . these tigers of the north who bring devastation everywhere are less to be feared by us than the traitors who agitate within, who divide us, who arm Frenchman against Frenchman; the impunity of the great culprits makes them bold; the people grumble, lose courage, seeing the boldest conspirators always escape the national executioner's axe; all the friends of liberty, of equality, wonder, become indignant at seeing the upholders of federalism not yet brought to trial. . . .

It is time, finally, for all the Frenchmen to enjoy this holy equality assured them by the Constitution; it is time to instill awe in the traitors and conspirators by striking acts of justice. Make terror the order of the day.

Representatives of the people, let the blade swing without distinction above all heads.

* Translated by Marguerite Greene from *Archives parlementaires de 1787 à 1860* (Paris, 1867–1913), First Series, Vol. LXXIII, p. 419.

F] Barère's Speech of September 5, 1793

Barère responded for the Committee of Public Safety to the pleas for more terror.*

For several days everything seemed to foreshadow a demonstration in Paris. Intercepted letters . . . revealed the constant efforts that the agents of the aristocracy were increasingly making to stir up trouble in what they call "the great city." Well! they will have this last trouble . . . (loud applause), but they will have it organized, regularized by a Revolutionary Army which will finally put into action this great word that we owe to the Commune of Paris: "Let us make terror the order of the day." Thus in an instant the royalists and the moderates and the counterrevolutionary rabble that agitates against you will disappear. The royalists want blood; well, they shall have the blood of conspirators of the Brissots, of the Marie Antoinettes. They want to prepare an insurrection; well, they will feel the effects of it; these are not illegal vengeances—they will be put into action by extraordinary tribunals. You will not be surprised about the means which we shall present to you when you know that from the bottom of their cells these villains still conspire and that they are the rallying point of our enemies. Brissot declared and printed that before his head would fall the heads of a number of members of the Convention would be gone and that the Mountain would be annihilated; it is thus that they seek through terror to stop you in your revolutionary march.

The royalists want to disturb the work of the Convention. . . . Conspirators! it will disturb yours (loud applause).

They want the Mountain to perish . . . ! Well! the Mountain will crush you!

G] Robespierre's Speech of December 25, 1793

On Christmas Day 1793 Robespierre expounded the principles of revolutionary government before the Convention and justified the use of terror in defense of the Republic.†

First we shall develop the principles and the necessity of the revolutionary government; we shall then show the true cause which tends to paralyze it at its birth.

．　　　．　　　．

* Translated by Marguerite Greene from *Reimpression de l'ancien moniteur* (Paris), XVII (September 8, 1793), 531.

† Translated by Marguerite Greene from *Reimpression de l'ancien moniteur* (Paris), XX (December 27, 1793), 51–53.

The function of the government is to lead the moral and physical forces of the nation toward the goal for which it is instituted.

The goal of constitutional government is to preserve the republic; that of revolutionary government is to found it.

The revolution is the war of liberty against its enemies; the constitution is the regime of victorious and peaceful liberty.

The revolutionary government needs an extraordinary action, precisely because it is at war. It submits to less uniform and less strict rules because of the stormy and changing circumstances in which it finds itself, and especially because it is forced to furnish continuously new and rapid resources for new and pressing dangers.

The constitutional government is concerned primarily with civil liberty, the revolutionary government with public liberty. Under the constitutional regime it is nearly sufficient to protect the individuals against the abuse of public power. Under the revolutionary regime the public power itself has to defend itself against all the factions that attack it.

The revolutionary government owes to the good citizens full national protection; to the enemies of the people it owes only death.

. . .

The impious cohorts of the foreign emissaries are recruited every day, France is inundated by them; they are waiting, and will be waiting eternally for a favorable moment for their sinister schemes.

. . .

Yes, the treacherous emissaries who speak to us, who caress us, are the brothers, are the accomplices of ferocious satellites who destroy our harvests . . . who massacred our brothers, slew without pity our prisoners, our women, our children. . . . What am I saying! The monsters who committed these heinous crimes are a thousand times less atrocious than the wretches who secretly tear our entrails apart, and they breathe, they conspire with impunity!

It is not in the hearts of patriots or of the poor that terror must be instilled; it is in the haunts of the foreign bandits, where the spoils are shared and where the blood of the French people is drunk.

H] THE TERROR IN PRACTICE *

THE TRIAL OF THE WIDOW CAPET

Revolutionary Criminal Tribunal: The end of the trial of Marie Antoinette de Lorraine-d'Autriche, widow Capet, 23rd of the first month, Year 2 [October 14, 1793]

* Translated by Marguerite Greene from *Reimpression de l'ancien moniteur* (Paris), XVIII (October 28, 1793), 218–19; XVIII (October 27, 1793), 268 (Supplement); XIX (December 28, 1793), 57; XIX (January 2, 1794), 101.
Translated by D. H. Pinkney from *Reimpression de l'ancien moniteur* (Paris), XVIII (November 18, 1793) 442 (Supplement).

The President of the Tribunal made the following charge to the jury.
Here are the questions which the court has decided to submit to you:

1. Is it an established fact that scheming and intelligence have existed with
foreign powers and other external enemies of the republic, the said scheming
and intelligence aiming at providing them with monetary help, giving them
entry to the French territory, and thereby facilitating the progress of their
arms?

2. Is Marie Antoinette of Austria, widow of Louis Capet, convicted of
having cooperated in these schemes and of having been associated with this
intelligence?

3. Is it an established fact that a plot and a conspiracy existed aiming at
inciting civil war inside the republic?

4. Is Marie Antoinette of Austria, widow of Louis Capet, convicted of
having participated in this plot and this conspiracy?

The jurors, after having stayed out approximately an hour for deliberation,
reenter the court and make an affirmative declaration on all the questions
submitted to them.

.   .   .

The accused is brought back into court.

.   .   .

The president pronounces the following judgment:
"The court, according to the unanimous declaration of the jury, condemns
the aforesaid Marie Antoinette, otherwise known as Lorraine-d'Autriche,
widow of Louis Capet, to death. . . ."

THE TRIAL OF THE GIRONDIN LEADERS

Revolutionary Criminal Tribunal, Session of 9 Brumaire [October 30, 1793]

After three hours of deliberation, the jurors came back into court. The
deepest silence reigns among all present.

The president polls the jurors on the following questions:

"Is it an established fact that a conspiracy existed against the unity and
the indivisibility of the republic, against the liberty and the security of the
French people?

"Jean-Pierre Brissot, etc., are they convicted of having been the authors or
accomplices of it?"

The unanimous response of the jurors is affirmative. Consequently, the
court condemns to death Jean Brissot and the others named at the head
of this trial.

.   .   .

The hall reverberates with the citizens' shouts of "Hail the Republic! Perish the traitors."

THE TRIAL OF GENERAL HOUCHARD

Revolutionary Criminal Tribunal, 26 Brumaire [November 16, 1703]

Jean-Nicolas Houchard, age fifty-three years, native of Forbach, commanding general of the Army of the Moselle, later of that of the North, convicted of being one of the authors or accomplices of scheming and intelligence practiced and arranged with the enemies of the Republic to facilitate their entry into France and to favor the progress of their arms, notably in the months of June and July 1793 in the Army of the Moselle then under orders to relieve Mayence and, in the month of September last, to relieve Dunkirk, was condemned to death and his property declared acquired and confiscated to the benefit of the Republic. He was executed the same evening on the Place de la Révolution.

REPORTS FROM NANTES, A CENTER OF THE REVOLT IN THE WEST

Carrier, representative of the people, with the Army of the West, to the National Convention, Nantes, 30 Frimaire, Year 2 [December 20, 1793]

Citizens,

My colleagues, you have decreed that the *Vendée* no longer exists, you will soon decree that not one single brigand exists.

The incident at Le Mans has been so bloody, so murderous for them that from that commune up to Laval the ground is strewn with corpses.

.   .   .

On the twenty-ninth Westermann marched on Nort; at 10:00 P.M. he seized the village of Touche . . . ; there he found approximately three or four hundred brigands; he massacred them all.

.   .   .

The defeat of the bandits is so complete that our posts kill them, take them and bring them to Nantes by the hundreds; the guillotine cannot keep up with them; I decided to have them shot; they are brought here and to Angers by the hundreds. To these I guarantee the same fate as to the others. I invite my colleague Francastel not to deviate from this wholesome and expeditious method. It is in the name of humanity that I purge this land of liberty of these monsters.

.   .   .

Greetings and fraternity.

Carrier

Commune of Paris, General Council, 11 Nivose [December 31, 1793]

The citizen Minier reads the following letter, written to him by a friend from Nantes.

Right bank of the Loire

"My friend, . . .

The number of brigands brought here in the last week is incalculable; more are arriving every moment.

"The guillotine being too slow, and since shooting them is also too slow and furthermore requires gunpowder and bullets, it has been decided to put a certain number of them in big boats, to tow them to the middle of the river, half a mile from the town, and there to sink the boat; this procedure is continuous.

.   .   .

"Ancenis, Saint-Florent and other localities are full of prisoners; but they will not stay there for a long time, since they perhaps too will receive the patriotic baptism."

2] The Terror as a Drive for Economic Equality and Social Justice

a] ADDRESS PRESENTED TO THE CONVENTION BY JACQUES ROUX, JUNE 25, 1793

The pressure on the Convention and the Committee of Public Safety for economic controls came chiefly from the popular societies and the assemblies of the sections of Paris, moved to action by high prices, scarcity of foods and other essentials, and by the belief that the common man was the victim of speculators, hoarders, and profiteers. On June 25, 1793, Jacques Roux presented this address to the Convention in the name of the Cordeliers Club and of two sections.*

Delegates of the French People,

One hundred times this sacred precinct has echoed the crimes of egoists and swindlers; every time you have promised to strike down the bloodsuckers of the people. The Constitution is going to be presented for the sanction of the sovereign people; in it have you proscribed speculation? No. Have you pronounced the death penalty against monopolists? No. Have you determined what the liberty of commerce consists of? No. Have you forbidden the sale of hard money? No. Well! We declare to you that you have not done enough for the happiness of the people.

Liberty is only a vain phantom if one class of men can starve the other

* Translated by D. H. Pinkney from *Annales révolutionnaires* (Paris), VII (1914), 548.

with impunity. Equality is only a vain phantom if the rich, by monopoly, exercise the right of life and death over their fellow men. The Republic is only a vain phantom if the counterrevolution can operate through the price of food that three-fourths of the population cannot pay except with tears.

.   .   .

Deputies of the Mountain, if you climbed from the fourth to the tenth floor of the houses of this revolutionary city, you would be moved by the tears and the moans of an immense population without bread and without clothing, reduced to that state of distress and misfortune by speculation and monopolies, because the laws have been cruel for the poor, because they have been made only by the rich and for the rich.

B] PETITION TO THE CONVENTION, AUGUST 20, 1793

On August 20, 1793, a delegation from the sections of Paris and the Jacobin Club made the following appeal to the Convention.*

Felix Lepelletier, spokesman of the delegation, asks that the alarms of the *sans-culottes* be calmed by fixing at three sous a pound the price of bread, which is now sold at fifteen or sixteen sous in several departments of the republic; he asks that the properties of the *émigrés* be sold in small parcels. . . .

The president of the Convention, Hérault-Séchelles, replied to the delegation.

It is not enough for the French Republic to be founded on equality; the laws, the morals of its citizens must also, by a happy agreement, tend to make the inequalities of wealth disappear. A happy existence must be guaranteed for all Frenchmen; henceforth the love of wealth must yield to the supreme love of the fatherland, the rich man must be less the owner than the happy beneficiary of a surplus of wealth that is dedicated to the happiness of his fellow citizens. This must be the spirit of the laws of a people of equals and brothers.

C] REPORT OF THE CONVENTION'S COMMITTEE ON SUPPLIES, SEPTEMBER 23, 1793 †

I hasten to present to the National Convention the results of the discussions of your commission concerning the maximum price to be fixed for the different merchandise of first necessity.

---

* Translated by Marguerite Greene from *Reimpression de l'ancien moniteur* (Paris), XVII (August 21, 1793), 441.

† Translated by Marguerite Greene from *Archives parlementaires de 1787 à 1860* (Paris, 1867–1913), First Series, Vol. LXXV, pp. 14–15.

This law is awaited with the greatest impatience, and the malevolence, the cupidity together with the detestable operations of our enemies on the outside do not allow us to postpone it any longer.

. . .

In ordinary times the price of things determines and fixes itself naturally from the mutual interest of the buyers and the consumers: this balance is infallible. It is useless even for the best government to get involved in it. No matter how wise, no matter how good its intentions may be, the government never achieves anything as just and it always risks harming the balance by putting a hand to it.

But when a general conspiracy of malevolence, of treachery, of furor for which there is no precedent, combines to break that natural equilibrium in order to starve us, to rob us, the good of the people becomes the supreme rule.

Society has the right . . . to reestablish and stabilize with a firm hand the balance which must exist between our production and our needs.

Then, however, an intelligent calculation is needed; one must, by fixing a ceiling, be content to establish wholesome and just limits that should not be exceeded.

D] LAW OF THE MAXIMUM, SEPTEMBER 29, 1793 [*]

Article 1. The articles which the Convention has decided to be of prime necessity and for which it has believed that it ought to fix the *maximum* or highest price are: fresh meat and bacon, butter, sweet-oil, cattle, salt fish, wine, brandy, vinegar, cider, beer, firewood, charcoal, mineral coal, candles, combustible oil, salt, soda, sugar, honey, white paper, skins, iron, brass, lead, steel, copper, hemp, linen, wool, woolens, fabrics, the raw materials used for fabrics, sabots, shoes, cabbages, and turnips, soap, potash, and tobacco. [The maximum prices of grain, flour, and forage had been fixed by the Decree of September 11, 1793.]

2. Among the articles included in the above list, the *maximum* price for firewood of the first quality, that of charcoal and of mineral coal, are the same as in 1790, plus a twentieth of the price.

. . .

The *maximum* or highest price of tobacco in rolls is twenty sous per pound . . . that of smoking tobacco is ten sous; that of salt per pound is two sous; that of soap is twenty-five sous.

[*] From Frank Maloy Anderson, ed., *The Constitutions and Other Select Documents Illustrative of the History of France, 1789–1907*, 2nd ed. rev. (Minneapolis, 1908), pp. 187–89.
Reimpression de l'ancien moniteur (Paris), XVIII (October 1, 1793), 5–6.

3. The *maximum* of the price of all the other commodities and articles of merchandise included in article 1 for the whole extent of the Republic, until the month of September next, shall be the price which each of them had in 1790 . . . and a third over and above that price.

. . .

7. All persons who may sell or purchase the articles of merchandise included in article 1 above the *maximum* of the price fixed and posted in each department shall pay through the municipal police a fine . . . of double the value of the article sold and payable to the informer; they shall be enrolled upon the list of suspected persons and treated as such. The purchaser shall not be subject to the penalties provided above, if he denounces the offense of the seller; each merchant shall be required to have a list displayed in his shop, bearing the *maximum* or highest price of his merchandise.

8. The *maximum* or highest price of salaries, wages, and manual labor by the day in each place shall be fixed . . . at the same amount as in 1790, to which shall be added half of that price in addition.

9. The municipalities shall requisition and punish, according to the circumstances, with three days imprisonment the workingmen, factory operatives and various laboring persons who may refuse without legitimate reasons to engage in their accustomed labors.

E] PETITION OF THE CITIZENS OF PARIS,
SEPTEMBER 4, 1793

In the session of September 4, Chaumette, Procurator of the Commune of Paris, presented a petition from citizens of the capital for the establishment of a Revolutionary Army to enforce the laws on requisitioning food.*

THE MAYOR OF PARIS: Citizen representatives, Paris has not yet been without provisions; for six weeks, however, the fear of the lack of them has made the citizens gather every night at the baker's door. The fear is based upon the fact that Paris nourishes itself only by daily arrivals. The lack of provisions is owing to the fact that the laws on provisions are not carried out; it stems from the egoism and the ill will of the rich grain-holders, and this evil is common to all great cities. The people, tired of these actions, come to present to you their wish. The procurator of the commune is requested to read to you the petition of the citizens of Paris.

CHAUMETTE: Citizen legislators. . . . The tyrants of Europe, the domestic enemies of the state persist atrociously in their frightful system of starving the French people to overcome them and to force them to exchange shame-

* Translated by Marguerite Greene from *Reimpression de l'ancien moniteur* (Paris), XVII (September 7, 1793), 520.

fully their liberty, their sovereignty, for a piece of bread, which assuredly they will never do.

New lords, no less cruel, no less greedy, no less insolent than the former ones have risen upon the ruins of feudalism; they have leased the farms or bought the land of their former masters and continue to walk the beaten path of crime, to speculate on public misery, to exhaust the sources of abundance, and to tyrannize the destroyers of tyranny.

. . .

You have made wise laws; they promise happiness, but they are not carried out for lack of executive power.

. . .

Legislators, the huge crowd of citizens assembled yesterday and this morning on the square and inside the city hall expressed only one wish, and a delegation brings it to you; here it is: (1) *Provisions* (2) *to have some* (3) *power to the law.* Consequently, we are charged with the mission of asking you for the formation of the Revolutionary Army that you have already decreed, and which the intrigue and the intimidation of the guilty have caused to be abortive. (Unanimous applause is heard several times.) Let this army immediately form its nucleus in Paris, and in all the departments through which it will pass let it grow in size by the addition of all men who desire the Republic one and indivisible; let this army be followed by an incorruptible and formidable court of law and by the fatal instrument that ends with a single stroke the plots and the lives of their authors.

F] ADDRESS TO THE CONVENTION FROM THE SECTION DES SANS-CULOTTES, SEPTEMBER 2, 1793 *

This address, probably never actually presented to the Convention, reveals the wishes of one group of Parisians for state intervention that went well beyond economic mobilization for war. After first appealing for the fixing of maximum prices and rents, the petitioner asked,

. . . that the maximum of private fortunes be limited, that any one individual be permitted to possess only this maximum, and that no one be permitted to rent more land than is required for a fixed number of plows, and that any one citizen be permitted only one workshop or store.

* Translated by D. H. Pinkney from Albert Soboul, *Les Sans-Culottes parisiens en l'an II; mouvement populaire et gouvernement révolutionnaire, 2 juin 1793–9 thermidor 1794* (Paris, 1958), p. 163.

G] Saint-Just's Speech of February 26, 1794

Advocates of the interpretation of the Terror as an instrument of social revolution point to the Ventôse Decrees as evidence of the government's intention to achieve a more equitable society by the redistribution of private property. In presenting them to the Convention Saint-Just made the following comments.*

The Revolution leads us to recognize this principle that whoever showed himself to be the enemy of his country cannot therein be a property owner. You will acknowledge this principle that only he who has cooperated in liberating the fatherland may have rights in it. Abolish mendicity, which dishonors a free state; the properties of the patriots are sacred, but the properties of the conspirators are there for all the poor. The poor are the powerful of the earth; they have the right to speak as masters to the government that neglects them.

. . .

As for you, destroy the rebel party, gild liberty, avenge the patriots who are victims of intrigue; make common sense and modesty the order of the day; do not tolerate the existence of a wretched or poor person in the state who would have to thank you for the misfortune of the good people and the happiness of the bad.

H] The Ventôse Decrees, February 26 and March 3, 1794

The first Ventôse Decree declared that the property of patriots was "inviolable and sacred," but that the property of "enemies of the revolution" would be confiscated for the benefit of the Republic. The second decree provided for redistribution of the confiscated property.†

Decree of 13 Ventôse, Year 2 [March 3, 1794]

The National Convention, after having heard the report of the Committee of Public Safety, decrees:

Art. 1. All the communes of the republic shall prepare a register of indigent patriots in their territory, with their names, their age, their occupation, the number and age of their children.

The district directorates shall forward these registers, with the briefest delay, to the Committee of Public Safety.

* Translated by Marguerite Greene from *Reimpression de l'ancien moniteur* (Paris), XIX (February 27, 1794), 568–69.
† Translated by D. H. Pinkney from *Reimpression de l'ancien moniteur* (Paris), XIX (March 4, 1794), 611.

2. When the Committee of Public Safety shall have received these registers, it shall make a report on the means to indemnify all the poor with the property of enemies of the revolution included on the list that the Committee of General Security shall have persented to it.

I] INSTRUCTIONS OF THE COMMITTEE OF PUBLIC SAFETY, MARCH 20, 1794 *

Circular of the Committee of Public Safety to the Representatives in the Departments, Paris, 30 Ventôse, Year 2 [March 20, 1794]

A great blow was necessary to kill the aristocracy; the Convention has struck it.

The unfortunate poor should regain the properties that crime has usurped from them; the Convention proclaimed their rights.

A general report on all prisoners must be sent to the Committee of General Security in charge of deciding their fates.

The Committee of Public Safety will receive the list of the indigents of each commune in order to determine the indemnity owed to them.

The two operations require the greatest speed; they must go forward together; terror and justice must be exercised on all points.

.   .   .

The Revolution is the work of the people: it is time that they enjoy its benefits.

J] REPORT OF THE COMMITTEE OF PUBLIC SAFETY, MAY 11, 1794

The Declaration of the Rights of Man and the Citizen of 1793 recognized the right of every man to a living, and in May 1794 Barère, speaking for the Committee of Public Safety, presented to the Convention a proposal to guarantee this right.†

Wherever the heart of the citizen beats for a fatherland, the cries of the abandoned child call for the help of this same fatherland; a man, he asks for work; an invalid, he implores national charity; an old man, he has a right to rest, consideration, and public assistance; they must embrace the generations that start and those that end.

It is not enough for the people to cut down the factions, to bleed rich

---

* Translated by Marguerite Greene from François Alphonse Aulard, *Recueil des actes du Comité du Salut public* (Paris, 1889–1955), Vol. XII, pp. 73–74.

† Translated by Marguerite Greene from *Reimpression de l'ancien moniteur* (Paris), XX (May 13, 1794), 445, 446, 453.

business, to destroy great fortunes; it is not enough to destroy the foreign hordes, to recall the reign of justice and of virtue; it is necessary to eliminate from the soil of the Republic the bondage of first necessities, the servitude of misery and this too hideous inequality among men, which allows one to have all the intemperance of fortune and gives the other all the anguish of want.

.   .   .

It is toward the humble cottage that you must especially turn your eyes today; it is on the poor and industrious inhabitants of the fields, who find work only after work is done, disdain in their infirmity, and oblivion in their old age, that the republican dew must fall.

What have the legislators done so far for the misery of the rural areas? What institutions have they established for these domestic laborers, these agricultural workers, these rustic craftsmen who have reached old age? What debt did the republic pay to these creditors of nature and of society who have fertilized the former to enrich the latter? The sad silence of the countryside and the rare tears of a few old people give us the answer.

Citizens, the public fortune has never been as high as it is at present. Rich with liberty, rich in population, rich in estates, the Republic plans to use for the betterment of its more unfortunate citizens the billions which the rich give to the counterrevolution. Those who wanted to assassinate liberty have enriched it; it is up to the Convention to repair the injustices of the monarchial laws, to have the great inequality of fortunes disappear, to erase the name *poor* from the annals of the Republic, to banish mendicity through welfare, and strongly to recall all citizens to the rights of humanity and to the duties of work.

.   .   .

Casting eyes upon the state of the Republic torn from the hands of despotism, you will easily see that there are two means of having despotism forgotten: the first is to sweep away the ruins of royalty by aiding the indigents it has created; the second is to prepare the measures that must prevent the reappearance of poverty on the soil of the Republic.

K] DECREES ON THE RELIEF OF POVERTY, MAY 11 AND 24, 1794 *

The National Convention, after having heard the report of the Committee of Public Safety, decrees:

In every department a register will be established whose title will be: *Book of National Welfare.*

.   .   .

* Translated by Marguerite Greene from *Reimpression de l'ancien moniteur* (Paris), XX (May 13, 1794), 453–54; XX (May 31, 1794), 597.

Title I.

Article 1. The registration in this book, of which a certificate will be issued by the administration of the department to the old or invalid farmer who will have obtained it, will give him the right to receive a yearly aid of 160 livres, to be paid in two installments, every six months and in advance.

.   .   .

Title II.

Article 1. The craftsmen who, in the rural areas, are involved with the mechanical arts, will also have a right to national welfare and to registration.

2. Their registration on this book . . . will entitle them to receive yearly a sum of 120 livres, to be paid every six months and in advance.

.   .   .

Title III.

Article 1. The mothers and the widows with children and living in the country also have a right to national welfare and to registration.

3. The registered mothers and widows will receive annually a sum of 60 livres and a supplement of 25 livres.

.   .   .

Title IV.

Article 1. Male and female citizens being registered in the book of national welfare mentioned above will receive free aid at home in case of sickness.

.   .   .

The committee of public safety . . . in execution of the decree of 16 Ventôse last [March 6], temporarily orders. . . .

1. That the invalid beggars, incapable of working, who have been or will be registered in their respective sections [of Paris], will receive as a relief payment . . . 15 sous [75 centimes] a day, 25 if married, and 5 sous for each child under twelve.

.   .   .

3. With the help of this aid there will be no more invalid beggars in the streets of Paris, and those who will be found begging will be arrested and taken to their sections in order to be identified; the necessary security measures will be taken on their behalf.

4. As for the beggars who are healthy and capable of working, and who therefore have no reason for begging, they too will be arrested and taken to their sections, which will make the proper inquiries about them and take such measures as they judge feasible.

3] The Terror as a Crusade for the Republic of Virtue

A] ROBESPIERRE'S SPEECH OF FEBRUARY 5, 1794

In a major speech before the Convention early in February 1794 Robespierre defined the aims of the Revolution.*

It is time to state clearly the goal of the revolution and the ends we want to attain; it is time for us to become aware ourselves both of the obstacles which still keep us from reaching that goal and of the means which we must adopt to achieve it.

. . .

What is the aim we want to achieve? The peaceful enjoyment of liberty and equality, the reign of that eternal justice whose laws have been engraved, not in stone and marble, but in the hearts of all men, even in the heart of the slave who forgets them or of the tyrant who denies them.

We want a state of affairs where all despicable and cruel passions are unknown and all kind and generous passions are aroused by the laws; where ambition is the desire to deserve glory and to serve the fatherland; where distinctions arise only from equality itself; where the citizen submits to the magistrate, the magistrate to the people and the people to justice; where the fatherland guarantees the well-being of each individual, and where each individual enjoys with pride the prosperity and the glory of the fatherland; where all souls elevate themselves through constant communication of republican sentiments and through the need to deserve the esteem of a great people; where the arts are the decorations of liberty that ennobles them, where commerce is the source of public wealth and not only of the monstrous opulence of a few houses.

In our country we want to substitute morality for egoism, honesty for honor, principles for customs, duties for decorum, the rule of reason for the tyranny of custom, the contempt of vice for the contempt of misfortune, pride for insolence, magnanimity for vanity, love of glory for love of money, good people for well-bred people, merit for intrigue, genius for wit, truth for pompous action, warmth of happiness for boredom of sensuality, greatness of man for pettiness of the great; a magnanimous, powerful, happy people for a polite, frivolous, despicable people—that is to say, all the virtues and all the miracles of the Republic for all the vices and all the absurdities of the monarchy.

In one word, we want to fulfill the wishes of nature, accomplish the

* Translated by Marguerite Greene from *Reimpression de l'ancien moniteur* (Paris), XIX (February 7, 1794), 401–04.

destiny of humanity, keep the promises of philosophy, absolve Providence from the long reign of crime and tyranny.

.   .   .

What kind of government can realize these marvels? Only a democratic or republican government.

.   .   .

But what is the fundamental principle of the democratic or popular government, that is to say, the essential strength that sustains it and makes it move? It is virtue: I am speaking of the public virtue which brought about so many marvels in Greece and Rome and which must bring about much more astonishing ones yet in republican France; of that virtue which is nothing more than love of fatherland and of its laws.

.   .   .

If the strength of popular government in peacetime is virtue, the strength of popular government in revolution is both virtue and terror; terror without virtue is disastrous, virtue without terror is powerless. Terror is nothing but prompt, severe, and inflexible justice; it is thus an emanation of virtue; it is less a particular principle than a consequence of the general principle of democracy applied to the most urgent needs of the fatherland. It is said that terror is the strength of despotic government. Does ours then resemble despotism? Yes, as the sword that shines in the hands of the heroes of liberty resemble the one with which the satellites of tyranny are armed. Let the despot govern his brutalized subjects through terror; he is right as a despot. Subdue the enemies of liberty through terror and you will be right as founders of the Republic. The government of revolution is the despotism of liberty against tyranny.

b] Saint-Just's Presentation of a Decree Against Conspiracies, March 13, 1794

In the spring of 1794, after the revolts in the West and the South had been suppressed, the foreign invaders driven back, and the royalists and Girondins purged, the Committee of Public Safety moved on to eliminate rival republicans who had deviant conceptions of the Republic. On March 13 Saint-Just, speaking for the committee, proposed a decree to facilitate action against conspiracies.*

In a few days you will receive a report on the persons who have plotted against the fatherland. The public interest and the interest of justice do not permit

* Translated by Marguerite Greene from *Reimpression de l'ancien moniteur* (Paris), XIX (March 14, 1794), 692.

that you be told more and did not permit that you be told less, because the law that I am going to propose to you was urgent and had to be justified.

After this report Saint-Just reads a proposed decree that is adopted unanimously . . . as follows:

.   .   .

The National Convention being invested by the French people with national authority, whoever usurps its power, whoever makes an attack on its security or its dignity, directly or indirectly, is an enemy of the people and will be punished by death.

Resistance to the revolutionary and republican government, of which the National Convention is the center, is an outrage upon the public liberty; whoever will be guilty of it, whoever will attempt by whatever act to debase the government, to destroy or to thwart it, will be punished by death.

c] THE ELIMINATION OF THE FACTIONS, MARCH–APRIL 1794

Late in March leaders of the faction of Ultra-Revolutionaries, headed by Hébert, were brought before the Revolutionary Tribunal, condemned to death, and executed—as reported in the first selection below. Within a week of their dispatch the Committee of Public Safety and the Committee of General Security turned against the more moderate Indulgents. In a speech before the Convention on March 31 (the second selection), Saint-Just brought the committees' charges against Danton and other Indulgents; on April 5, as the third selection reports, they were condemned and executed.*

THE ULTRA-REVOLUTIONARIES

Revolutionary Criminal Tribunal, 4 Germinal [March 24]

Hébert, Momoro, Ronsin, Vincent, Mazuel and other accomplices of the conspiracy, nineteen in number, have been condemned to death.

The execution took place in the afternoon, about five o'clock on the Place de la Révolution. A tremendous number of citizens were in all the streets and on all the squares through which they passed. Repeated cries of *Vive la République!* and applause were heard everywhere. . . . The public satisfaction, which was mixed with . . . profound indignation, was a renewed proof of the citizens' love for the Republic, saved by the punishment of these great culprits. Thus perishes whoever dares to attempt the reestablishment of tyranny!

* Translated by Marguerite Greene from *Reimpression de l'ancien moniteur* (Paris), XX (March 25, 1794), 40.
    Translated by Marguerite Greene and D. H. Pinkney from *Reimpression de l'ancien moniteur* (Paris), XX (April 1, 1794), 92–104.
    Translated by D. H. Pinkney from *Reimpression de l'ancien moniteur* (Paris), XX (April 6, 1794), 138.

The woman Quetineau, who was among the condemned, having declared herself pregnant, obtained a reprieve.

SAINT-JUST'S ACCUSATION OF THE INDULGENTS

Your Committees of Public Safety and General Security . . . charged me to ask of you justice, in the name of the fatherland, against men who for a long time have betrayed the popular cause, who have made war on you with all the conspirators, with Orléans, with Brissot, with Hébert, with Hérault and their accomplices, and at this moment conspire with kings leagued against the republic, who supported the plot to destroy you and to confound the republican government, were the defenders of traitors and your avowed enemies, and who, to escape justice, claim that you are attacked through them.

.   .   .

Those whom I have denounced have never known the fatherland; they have enriched themselves by crime. . . . There is no enemy whom they have not protected, there are no traitors whom they have not excused. Misers, egoists, apologists for vices, rhetoricians, and no friends of liberty, the republic is incompatible with them; they seek enjoyment of possessions at the expense of equality; their desire for influence is insatiable; the kings count on them to destroy you.

.   .   .

We believe that we ought no longer temporize with the guilty men, for you declared that we would destroy all the factions; they can revive and gain new strength: Europe seems now to count only on them. The time is here to destroy them. . . .

Here is the proposed decree.

The National Convention, after having heard the reports of the Committees of General Security and Public Safety, decrees the accusation of Camille Desmoulins, Hérault, Danton, Phélippeaux, Lacroix, accused of complicity with d'Orléans and Dumouriez, with Fabre d'Eglantine and the enemies of the republic; of having participated in the conspiracy attempting to reestablish the monarchy, of destroying the national representation and the republican government. Consequently, it orders that they be brought to trial along with Fabre d'Eglantine.

The decree is adopted unanimously amid the most vigorous applause.

THE EXECUTION OF THE INDULGENTS

Revolutionary Criminal Tribunal, 16 Germinal [April 5, 1794]

After three days of debate, Danton, Fabre, Lacroix, Phélippeaux, Desmoulins, Chabot, Bazire, Delaunay, Hérault, Westermann, Gusman, Espagnac, the brothers Frey, and Diedericksen were condemned to the penalty of death. They were executed the same day at five-thirty on the Place de la Révolution.

d] COUTHON'S SPEECH OF JUNE 10, 1794

On 22 Prairial, Couthon, a member of the Committee of Public Safety, presented to the Convention the draft of a law that "simply has no place," Crane Brinton has commented, "in the bread-and-butter world men are agreed in calling normal." *

The regime of despotism [the monarchy before 1789] had created a judiciary truth which was not the moral and natural truth.

The magistracy was a sort of priesthood founded upon error, and justice a false religion which consisted entirely of dogma, of rites and mysteries, from which morals were banished. The indulgent counterrevolutionaries wanted to subordinate national justice and the course of the Revolution to these rules of justice. The moral proofs were counted for nothing, as if another rule could determine human judgments, as if the most material proofs themselves could have value other than as moral proofs. The counterrevolutionary treachery hid under the veil of hypocritical refinement the design to assure the impunity of the conspirators.

. . .

A revolution like ours is but a rapid succession of conspiracies, because it is the war of tyranny against liberty, of crime against virtue. There is no question of giving some examples, but to exterminate the implacable satellites of tyranny or to perish with the Republic. Indulgence toward them is atrocious, clemency is parricidal.

He who wants to subordinate the public good to the prejudices of law courts, to the inversions of the jurists, is a fool or a criminal who wants to kill juridically the fatherland and humanity.

. . .

The Republic, attacked at its birth by enemies who are as treacherous as they are numerous, must strike them with lightning speed, while taking the necessary precautions to save the slandered patriots. It is only by putting the exercise of national justice in pure and republican hands that it can fulfill its twofold objective.

The natural defenders and the necessary friends of the accused patriots are the patriotic juries; the conspirators must not find a single defender. How much blood of good citizens could be saved, how many misfortunes

* Translated by Marguerite Greene from *Reimpression de l'ancien moniteur* (Paris), XX (June 12, 1794), 695–96.

could be spared the fatherland if one could get out of the rut of routine to follow the principles of reason and to apply them to our political situation.

.　　　.　　　.

You felt both the inadequacy of a single Revolutionary Tribunal to deliver the Republic from the perfidious and ferocious enemies within its bosom and the dangers of multiplying that institution excessively. You wanted at least to perfect it and rid it of the absurd or disastrous obstacles which can stop the march of national justice. Consequently you had ordered your Committee of Public Safety, two months ago, to present to you a draft of a decree capable of fulfilling this view.

Until today kept from this objective by no less pressing matters, we shall today try to realize your wishes.

E] THE LAW OF 22 PRAIRIAL, YEAR 2 (JUNE 10, 1794) *

Art. 4. The revolutionary tribunal is instituted in order to punish the enemies of the people.

.　　　.　　　.

6. Those are reputed enemies of the people who shall have promoted the reestablishment of the monarchy or sought to disparage or dissolve the National Convention and the revolutionary and republican government of which it is the center:

Those who shall have betrayed the Republic in the command of places and armies, or in any other military function; carried on correspondence with the enemies of the Republic; labored to make the supplies or service of the armies fail;

Those who shall have sought to impede the supplies for Paris or to cause scarcity within the Republic;

Those who shall have seconded the projects of the enemies of France, either by aiding conspirators and the aristocracy to hide and to escape justice or by persecuting and calumniating patriotism, or by corrupting the servants of the people, or by abusing the principles of the revolution. . . ;

Those who shall have deceived the people or the representatives of the people, in order to lead them into operations contrary to the interests of liberty;

Those who have sought to promote discouragement, in order to favor the enterprises of the tyrants leagued against the Republic;

---

* From Frank Maloy Anderson, ed., *The Constitutions and Other Select Documents Illustrative of the History of France, 1789–1907*, 2nd ed. rev. (Minneapolis, 1908), pp. 154–56.

Recueil général des lois, décrêts, ordonnances, etc., depuis le mois de juin 1789 jusqu'au mois d'août 1830 (Paris, 1837), Vol. V, pp. 283–85.

Those who shall have spread false news in order to divide and disturb the people;

Those who shall have sought to mislead opinion and to prevent the instruction of the people, to deprave morals and to corrupt the public conscience, to impair the energy and the purity of the revolutionary and republican principles. . . ;

Finally, all those who are designated in the preceding laws relative to the punishment of the conspirators and counter-revolutionaries, and who, whatever the means or the appearances with which they cover themselves, shall have made an attack upon the liberty, unity, and security of the Republic, or labored to prevent the strengthening of them.

7. The penalty for all offenses under the jurisdiction of the revolutionary tribunal is death.

8. The proof necessary to convict the enemies of the people is every kind of evidence, either material or moral or verbal or written, which can naturally secure the approval of every just and reasonable spirit; the rule of judgment is the conscience of the jurors enlightened by love of the country; their aim, the triumph of the Republic and the ruin of its enemies. . . .

9. Every citizen has the right to seize and to arraign before the magistrates conspirators and counter-revolutionaries. He is required to denounce them when he knows of them.

. . .

16. The law provides sworn patriots as counsel for calumniated patriots; it does not grant them to conspirators.

F] The Report of the Revolutionary Criminal Tribunal, June 29, 1794

With the adoption and application of the Law of 22 Prairial began the Great Terror in Paris. Suspects were no longer judged as individuals but in groups, as the following report of a typical day's work of the Tribunal illustrates.*

Revolutionary Criminal Tribunal, 11 Messidor [June 29, 1794]

F. Lallier, age fifty, wood merchant, ex-member of the Constituent Assembly, at Rambouillet;

S.-F. Brou, age forty, inspector of the Forest of Rambouillet;

M.-V. Corteuil, age fifty-four, inspector of the Forest of Rambouillet;

L. Huart, age forty, ex-vicar of Rambouillet;

E. Hocquemel, age fifty-nine, ex-tax magistrate, commissioner of the tyrant in the district court of Dourdan;

* Translated by D. H. Pinkney from *Reimpression de l'ancien moniteur* (Paris), XXI (July 3, 1794), 119–20.

E. Doublon, age twenty, embroiderer;

J.-F. Vaurs, age thirty-four, ex-curate of Gramont, student of the Military School of Alfort near Paris;

B. Darriot, age thirty-four, physician, ex-judge of the district court of Mont l'Unité, Department of the Haute-Garonne;

M. Derrey, age forty-two, ex-mayor of Toulouse;

J. Douziech, age forty-eight, ex-commandant of the National Guard of the Haute-Garonne, ex-soldier of the former Petite Gendarmerie;

J.-B. Ruffat, age forty, physician;

J. Louvet, age forty, ex-lawyer of Toulouse;

T. Sevenne, age twenty-six, wholesale merchant;

Convicted of having made themselves enemies of the people, in supporting protests against liberty; in preventing the payment of taxes; in participating in the plots of Capet; in weakening the unity and the indivisibility of the republic; in furnishing intelligence to the enemies of the state; in seeking to corrupt public officials through the system devised by the foreign faction, etc., were condemned to death.

J.-B. Bouthrin, age thirty-seven, gendarme at Vanvilliers, Department of the Haute-Saône;

Co-accused, was acquitted and freed.

C.-A. Dupuis-Lajaroux, age sixty-two, ex-noble;

G. Trouiller, age fifty-four, ex-curate of Beaucire, Department of the Haute-Loire;

J. Notaire, age twenty-six, cook of the émigré Juigné, ex-archbishop of Paris;

C.-A. Buron, age forty, wife of J. Notaire;

P.-J. Pregaux, age twenty-five, deserter from the former regiment of Castries, ex-domestic of an émigré;

P. Rodier, age forty-nine, farmer;

G. Piedonat, shoemaker.

Convicted of having made themselves enemies of the people in deserting the flags of liberty, in furnishing intelligence to the enemy, in wearing the black cockade, in serving as spies for the Austrians, in insulting the symbols of liberty, in provoking civil war by fanaticism, in seeking to disturb the fidelity of citizens to the nation, in concealing funds belonging to émigrés, etc., were condemned to death.

L. Rabeux, age sixty-one, laborer;

F. Leclerc, age sixty-one, gardener, rat poisoner, traveling without passport;

J.-L. Grenier, age twenty-six, self-styled sergeant of the Revolutionary Army at Cormeaux;

J. Boire, called Briard, age fifty, domestic;

Co-accused, acquitted and freed, except Grenier, who, accused of forgery, will be sent before the court which has jurisdiction over that offense.

G] ROBESPIERRE'S SPEECH OF JULY 26, 1794

On 8 Thermidor (July 26, 1794), the evening before his arrest, Robespierre repeated at the Jacobin Club a long and discursive speech he had made that day before the Convention.*

Citizens,

The revolutions that until our time have altered the face of empires have had for their object only a change of dynasty, or the shift from the power of a single person to that of several. The French Revolution is the first that has been founded on the theory of the rights of humanity and on the principles of justice. The other revolutions have required only ambition; ours imposes virtues. The others were absorbed by ignorance and forced into a new despotism; ours, emanating from justice, can repose only in its bosom. The Republic, led unconsciously by the force of things and by the struggle of the friends of liberty against ever-renewed conspiracies, managed to establish itself despite all the factions; but it has found their power organized around it, and all the means of influence in their hands; also it has been unceasingly persecuted since its birth in the persons of all men of good faith who fight for it.

. . .

Here I must let the truth escape and expose the real sickness of the Republic. Public affairs again take a perfidious and alarming course; the combined system of the Hébertists and the Fabre d'Eglantines is now pursued with an unheard of audacity; the counterrevolutionaries are protected. . . . Patriotism and liberty are proscribed. . . . Is that the revolutionary government that we have established and defended? No, that government is the quick and sure march of justice, it is the lightning thrown by the hand of liberty against crime. . . .

Watching the multitude of vices that the torrent of the Revolution rolled up pell-mell with the civic virtues, I have sometimes trembled at being dishonored in the eyes of posterity by the impure proximity of those perverse men who have mixed in the ranks of the defenders of humanity. . . . I have promised . . . to leave to my fellow citizens a redoubtable testament on the oppressors of the people, and from this moment I leave to them opprobrium and death! I know that it is easy for the league of tyrants of the world to crush a single man; but I also know the duties of a man who can die in defense of the cause of the human race.

* Translated by D. H. Pinkney from François Alphonse Aulard, *La Société des Jacobins; recueil des documents pour l'histoire du Club des Jacobins de Paris* (Paris, 1889–97), Vol. VI, pp. 246–80.

CONCLUSION

W I T H the threat to the Republic past or at least no longer as great as it had been in the crisis of the spring, summer, and autumn of 1793, the Terror grew intolerable for more and more Frenchmen. Robespierre became the focus of the opposition, and on 9 Thermidor, Year 2 (July 27, 1794), in a stormy session the Convention ordered his arrest and outlawed him. On the following day Robespierre, his close associates Saint-Just and Couthon, and nineteen of their followers were executed. The Terror did not long survive them. The Convention took back the powers it had delegated to the Committee of Public Safety and the Committee of General Security. It reorganized and restricted the authority of the Revolutionary Tribunal and soon abolished it. The Jacobin Club was suppressed in November, and the more radical clubs had already ceased to exist. Price controls were ended in December 1794. The social legislation of the spring was shelved. The Terror, whether an institution of national defense, a socialist experiment, or a prelude to the true Republic of Virtue, was over.

History tells much about the Terror. It records laws and describes institutions, defines economic fluctuations and reports their consequences, identifies the leaders, the heroes, and the victims. But some important questions are still unanswered. Why did the Terrorists act as they did? What motives, what visions of the future, what fears of the present, what conditioning of the past drove them to the extremes of human behavior revealed in this upheaval? Historians have produced many conflicting answers, and they will surely continue to do so—an illustration of the unending vitality of the history of the French Revolution. But this does not mean that better answers, perhaps definitive ones, will not be found. New methods, even new data, will bring new insights and new understanding. Historians have in recent years used techniques of the behavioral sciences to illuminate long-obscured corners of revolutionary history, and these techniques may help unearth more meaningful explanations of the behavior of the men of 1793 and 1794 than any we now possess.

Whatever their motives, the French had given to a world heretofore familiar in modern history only with coercion by kings and emperors an example of the potentialities and the dangers of coercion by a democracy. The example has remained a potent influence on the thinking of revolutionaries and reactionaries for more than a century and a half.

STUDY QUESTIONS

1] Was the Reign of Terror inevitable? How might it have been prevented? In what other way might the crisis of 1793–94 have been handled?

2] What important considerations does the explanation of the Terror solely as an instrument of national defense fail to take into account?

3] Were the actions of the Revolutionary Criminal Tribunal and of deputies on mission such as Carrier consistent with the principles of revolutionary government enunciated by Robespierre?

4] Do the economic and social measures adopted by the Convention presage nineteenth-century socialism? Do they have any affinity with social legislation of capitalist states of the nineteenth and twentieth centuries?

5] What threats to personal freedom do you see in Robespierre's Republic of Virtue? Could a twentieth-century Fascist dictator have used Robespierre's arguments justifying revolutionary government and terror in France to justify his own rule?

RECOMMENDED READINGS

PRIMARY

ANDERSON, FRANK MALOY, ed. *The Constitutions and Other Select Documents Illustrative of the History of France, 1789–1901*, 2nd rev. ed. (Minneapolis, 1908).

HIGGINS, E. L., ed. *The French Revolution as Told by Contemporaries* (Boston, 1938).

ROBINSON, JAMES HARVEY, ed. *The Eighteenth Century, the French Revolution and the Napoleonic Empire* (*Readings in Modern European History . . . ,* Vol. I) (Boston, 1908).

STEWART, JOHN HALL, ed. *A Documentary Survey of the French Revolution* (New York, 1951).

THOMPSON, J. M., ed. *English Witnesses of the French Revolution* (Oxford, 1938).

SECONDARY

AULARD, ALPHONSE. *The French Revolution: A Political History*, 4 vols. (New York, 1910).

BELLOC, HILAIRE. *Danton* (New York, 1899).

BRINTON, CRANE. *A Decade of Revolution, 1789–1799* (New York, 1934).

———. *The Jacobins: An Essay in the New History* (New York, 1930).

BRUUN, GEOFFREY. *Saint-Just, Apostle of the Terror* (Boston, 1932).

GAXOTTE, PIERRE. *The French Revolution* (New York, 1932).

GERSHOY, LEO. *Bertrand Barère, Reluctant Terrorist* (Princeton, 1962).

————. *The French Revolution and Napoleon* (New York, 1933).

GODFREY, JAMES L. *Revolutionary Justice: A Study of the Organization, Personnel, and Procedure of the Paris Tribunal, 1793–1795* (Chapel Hill, N.C., 1951).

GREER, DONALD M. *The Incidence of the Terror During the French Revolution: A Statistical Interpretation* (Cambridge, Mass., 1935).

HAMPSON, NORMAN. *A Social History of the French Revolution* (Toronto, 1963).

KERR, WILFRID B. *The Reign of Terror, 1793–1794* (Toronto, 1927).

LEFEBVRE, GEORGES. *The French Revolution from Its Origins to 1793* (New York, 1962).

————. *The French Revolution from 1793 to 1799* (New York, 1964).

MATHIEZ, ALBERT. *The French Revolution* (New York, 1928).

PALMER, ROBERT R. *Twelve Who Ruled: The Committee of Public Safety During the Terror* (Princeton, 1941).

RUDÉ, GEORGE. *The Crowd in the French Revolution* (Oxford, 1959).

SIRICH, JOHN B. *The Revolutionary Committees in the Departments of France, 1793–1794* (Cambridge, Mass., 1943).

SOBOUL, ALBERT. *The Parisian Sans-Culottes and the French Revolution, 1793–94* (New York, 1964).

SYDENHAM, M. J. *The Girondins* (London, 1961).

TALMON, J. L. *The Origins of Totalitarian Democracy* (Boston, 1952).

THOMPSON, JAMES H. *The French Revolution* (New York, 1945).

————. *Robespierre*, 2 vols. (Oxford, 1935).

The Industrial Revolution
in England:
The Chartist Movement,
1837–58

RICHARD W. LYMAN

STANFORD UNIVERSITY

CONTENTS

B] The Chartist Land Scheme
("First Report from the Select Committee on the National Land Company," 1847–48)

C] Democracy for What? The Conflict over Objectives
(The *London Democrat*, June 1, 1839; a contemporary pamphlet; the *Northern Star*, July 3, 1847)

CHRONOLOGY

1832
JUNE   Reform Act passed.

1833
AUGUST   Factory Act passed.

1834
FEBRUARY–AUGUST   The Grand National Consolidated Trades Union is founded, grows, and dies.
JULY   New Poor Law passed.

1836
APRIL   Beginnings of economic distress.
JUNE   London Working Men's Association founded.

1837
JANUARY   East London Democratic Association (later London Democratic Association) founded, in rivalry to L.W.M.A.
Agitation grows against the New Poor Law, as government attempts to apply it in the industrial north of England.
MAY   Birmingham Political Union reestablished (it had played a great part in the Reform Bill agitation of 1830–32).
MAY–JUNE   L.W.M.A. and Radical M.P.'s meet.

1838
MAY   The People's Charter published in London; the National Petition in Birmingham.
AUTUMN   Elections of Chartist delegates to forthcoming National Convention.

1839
FEBRUARY   National Convention meets in London.
APRIL   General Sir Charles Napier appointed to command Northern District to maintain order against threat of Chartist disturbances.
MAY   Convention moves to Birmingham.
JULY   Convention returns to London; National Petition rejected by House of Commons.

SEPTEMBER After arrests of many Chartist leaders and desertion of some others, the Convention disbands.

NOVEMBER Newport rising.

1841

DECEMBER Joseph Sturge moves to form the Complete Suffrage Union.

1842

APRIL Complete Suffrage Union Birmingham Conference; a second Convention meets in London.

MAY Second Chartist Petition rejected by House of Commons.

AUGUST–SEPTEMBER "Plug Plot" Strikes.

DECEMBER Second Birmingham Conference of Complete Suffrage Union fails to agree; the Union dissolves.

1845

Another Chartist Convention in London; origins of the Chartist Land scheme.

1848

FEBRUARY Revolution in France; publication of the *Communist Manifesto*.

APRIL Chartist Convention in London; the Kennington Common meeting; and the third and last great Chartist Petition is derisively rejected by the House of Commons.

AUGUST Select Committee of Commons recommends the winding up of the National Land Company.

1850

JUNE Harney founds a new Chartist paper, the *Red Republican*; the movement turns leftward, while losing support.

1858

FEBRUARY The last Chartist Convention meets.

JUNE Property qualification for Members of Parliament abolished—the first of the six points of the Charter to be enacted.

INTRODUCTION

W HATEVER may be said of the difficulties of assigning dates to the Industrial Revolution, and however many earlier "industrial revolutions" scholars may find in the records of previous economic history, understanding the essential differences between the world of the early 1700's and that of our own day requires a grasp of the drastic change of pace in economic development which has borne that traditional label so long. Today people speak of automation as "a second industrial revolution," but in fact the first has never stopped. Not only has it spread so far that we call countries it has thus far missed "underdeveloped," but it has continued to work transformations in the older industrial nations. To many, industrialization has come to be nearly synonymous with progress. Yet it has never lacked critics, and, if it has solved some problems, it has created others. In its early manifestations, principally in Great Britain in the late eighteenth and early nineteenth centuries, the conflicts raised by industrialization were the more severe for being unprecedented. Nations moving along the path toward industrialization today have at least the comfort of knowing that others have been there before them. Not so the British, factory owner and worker alike, a century and a half ago; for them the path ahead was unknown, and its pitfalls were strange and baffling.

What, for instance, was to become of the people who found themselves displaced by the coming of the machine and the factory? The phrase "technological unemployment" was not yet known, but the fact was familiar enough. What was to be done about the problems of the cities, catapulted by industrialization into a growth which was unplanned and all but ungoverned? How was society to meet the vastly expanded needs for policing, for sanitation, for decent standards in working-class housing? How was a race of peasants, attuned to a slow rhythm of life based on the weather and the seasons, to learn the new disciplines of the urban industrial work force, ruled by the factory whistle and the rush of power-driven machinery?

Even where a beginning was made in the solution of these problems, there remained others more difficult still. Must an industrial society be subject to the wild fluctuations between good times and bad, boom and depression, that made the early nineteenth-century worker's life a constant trial by uncertainty? The factory worker dreaded unemployment as a kind of social plague which, though not new, had never before been so sweeping in its devastations. Nor was his employer secure, as the appalling nineteenth-century bankruptcy rates attest. An employer might regard such insecurity as the price of progress in a competitive world. But, like other property-holders, he could not escape concern when periodic slumps swelled the number of paupers to be fed out of the local rates (taxes).

How was government to respond to these and related problems? Could it remain the virtually exclusive preserve of the landed aristocracy? Ought it not now be broadened at the base to include the newer forms of property, the factory owner, the railway entrepreneur? Ought representation go further still and include the propertyless industrial work force, or (as working-class leaders preferred to put it) those whose property consisted of their capacity to labor? Among them literacy and social discipline were increasing. It could be argued that they were no longer the turbulent and unruly "mob" of the eighteenth century, but were becoming capable of sustained and intelligent interest in politics.

Such questions arose in different countries at different periods. The example chosen here is that of the first major industrial nation, Britain, in its period of greatest travail over industrialization, the 1830's and 1840's. British industrialization began early, and the rate of change had become rapid by the 1780's. Through the wars of the French Revolution and Napoleon (1792–1815), the process went on apace, stimulated by the needs of national defense. Protest arose in those decades, too, notably the outbreaks known as Luddism, in which small bands of men went about, generally at night, carrying out industrial sabotage at the behest of a mysterious leader (perhaps several leaders) who called himself King Lud. When the war was over, there ensued a feverish period of postwar unrest, in which orators whipped working-class audiences into a frenzy (though seldom into any real violence) with demands for a variety of sweeping reforms, especially an extension of the suffrage to give workers a vote for Parliament.

To this the government's answer was stern repression; all reforms were held suspect as likely to provide the entering wedge for a revolution such as the French had endured. But so purely negative a response could not long suffice, given the presence of such powerful economic forces for change. By the 1820's governments still calling themselves Tory began to make tentative reforms. They opened the way to freer trade, for example, and toward the end of the decade they reluctantly abolished the most significant of the civil disabilities of religious minorities, Dissenters and Roman Catholics. By 1830 the stage was set for the protracted crisis that produced the 1832 Reform Bill. This ensured that the parliamentary franchise, though still rather narrowly restricted, would henceforth be uniform across the country; no longer would it constitute a random patchwork, sanctified only by appeal to the accidents of past history. Some of the newly burgeoning industrial towns achieved parliamentary representation for the first time; some "rotten boroughs"—places with insignificant populations or an unusual susceptibility to corruption—disappeared from the parliamentary map. In the years that followed there were various further reforms, some of them favorable to the working classes (for example, the Factory Act of 1833, which limited the working hours of women and children in the textile mills and provided government inspectors to enforce the limitation). Others were, in contemporary eyes at least, unfavorable, the leading example being the

New Poor Law of 1834. This attempted to tighten the boundaries of poor relief by limiting it to the inmates of workhouses, by prohibiting relief payments supplemental to wages, and by creating a central authority (the Poor Law Commission) which could enforce the rules nationally and prevent local generosity from making the relief rolls too attractive.

The protest against the Poor Law was formidable, especially in the industrial north. Led by an odd mixture of political radicals and paternalistic Tories, this protest movement was the most direct prelude to Chartism. But there were others. One was disillusionment with the 1832 Reform Act. Working-class leaders had joined energetically in the agitation for the bill, but the expansion of the electorate had stopped well short of their followers, and the Whigs now announced that this very limited reform was in their eyes final and unalterable. Another factor in the Chartist background was the failure of industrial organization, and of the vaguely socialist or syndicalist aspirations that had motivated Robert Owen's Grand National Consolidated Trades Union in 1833–34. Not for the last time British working men were to argue that political power was a necessary prelude to trade union success.

In short, there were both general and specific causes for unrest in the late 1830's. The vehicle for expression of discontent was supplied by "the People's Charter," a program drawn up in 1837. There was nothing original about the six points of the Charter: manhood suffrage, the secret ballot, no property qualifications for Members of Parliament, payment of salaries to M.P.'s, equal election districts, and annual parliamentary elections. In one form or another, these had been the stuff of radical politics for two generations. The Charter is, however, the single thread connecting the many changes and chances of working-class politics over the next dozen years.

Whether Chartism was one movement or several may be debated. "Perhaps, indeed, we are wrong to speak of a Chartist movement," says R. K. Webb. "Perhaps Chartism was more an attitude than a movement, an attitude which found certain concrete outlets in particular times. . . ." [1] The political program had little direct relevance to social miseries, but it was a basis upon which men who disagreed on much else could cooperate. Whether the democratic electorate, once it was created, would use its power to promote socialism, agrarian reform, temperance (always a major force in nineteenth-century British reform movements), mass education, or trade unionism— this was never decided, but the Chartist ranks included staunch advocates of each, and many more besides.

Chartism as a general movement had its peaks and troughs, which corresponded quite clearly with economic trends. It grew prominent whenever times were hardest: in 1839, again in 1842, finally in 1848. Of these, the first was the most severe threat to the stability of England, although it may be debated how close to revolution a nation can be said to have come when its propertied and governing elements were solidly opposed to the

[1] Webb, *The British Working-Class Reader, 1790–1848* (London, 1955), p. 102.

Chartist thrust, and when the principal potential leaders of "revolution" showed little stomach for a fight. There was much talk of resort to physical force, should moral force fail, and much argument over "ulterior measures." But the Chartists talked the summer away, and when a local rising finally came at Newport, near the Welsh border, it was suppressed with almost ridiculous ease by a handful of Her Majesty's soldiers.

In 1842 there were the Plug Riots, so called because gangs of men went from one factory to another in the textile districts calling their fellows out on strike and pulling the plugs of the steam boilers to make sure that production stopped. Initially a fight against wage reductions, this movement was adopted by the Chartist leaders as a vehicle for their political purposes. But strikes seldom succeed in a depression, and hunger did most of the work of the authorities in 1842.

The final major show of Chartist activity, in 1848, produced one more mammoth petition to Parliament and a remarkable burst of defensive activity on the part of the government, especially in the London area. The Cabinet were doubtless more nervous in that year of European revolutions than they had any cause to be. The Chartists met, petitioned, and disbursed; thenceforth their movement went into a decline as inexorable as it was protracted. The Victorian prosperity removed enough of the sting from the grievances of the poor to make further mass agitation impossible. When next the British working classes stirred, it would be to promote another highly respectable Reform Bill (in 1867). By that time, Chartism was already becoming a legend, a myth, fit to inspire latter-day radicals with the heroes and sufferings of a bygone era, but no longer part of the living fabric of political life.

DOCUMENTS

1] Background: The Troubles of a Nascent Industrial Society

A] MISERY ON THE PERIPHERY: THE HAND-LOOM WEAVERS

Chartism drew much of its strength from large groups of industrially displaced persons such as the hand-loom weavers, who were being pushed, with
agonizing slowness, out of a field that was overcrowded even before the
power-driven loom appeared on the scene. The following excerpts from the
1834 "Report from Select Committee on Hand-Loom Weavers' Petitions"
illustrate the conclusions reached by a parliamentary investigation and include
a sample of the evidence on which these were based.*

THE SELECT COMMITTEE . . . Have examined the matters referred to them,
and agreed to the following REPORT:

Your Committee have, as far as the late period of the Session at which
they were appointed would admit, made inquiry into the facts and allegations
contained in the Petitions of the Hand-Loom Weavers, referred to their
consideration; and they feel deep regret at finding the sufferings of that large
and valuable body of men, not only not exaggerated, but that they have for
years continued to an extent and intensity scarcely to be credited or conceived, and have been borne with a degree of patience unexampled.

This distress is attributed by the Witnesses to various causes, and among
others to the extensive use of Machinery,—to heavy and oppressive Taxation,—to the present system of Corn Laws; but more especially to the great
competition amongst Manufacturers, which, it is stated, has had the effect
of producing the present deplorable condition of the Hand-loom Weavers,
comprising, as it appears from the Evidence, a body of not less than eight
hundred thousand Individuals dependent on this occupation for subsistence.

·   ·   ·

HUGH MACKENZIE CALLED IN; AND EXAMINED

663. Are you a hand-loom weaver or a manufacturer?—I am a hand-loom
weaver.

* From "Report from Select Committee on Hand-Loom Weavers' Petitions," 1834,
Parliamentary Papers (556).

664. Of what description of manufacture?—In the plain muslin line. . . .

665. Is there sufficient employment in that line?—In the city of Glasgow there lately was an apparent shade of dulness, but there is not a hand going idle that I know of.

666. What is the condition of the operatives as to wages and their circumstances?—Their Condition is extremely poor in that respect, both with regard to food and clothing.

667. Have they worse food and clothing than they used to have formerly? —Yes, considerably so. When they had possibly three or four times the wages that they have at present for the same fabric, of course they must necessarily [have] be[en] able to purchase more of the necessaries of life, food and clothing included.

668. Have they worse furniture?—Their furniture is in a great measure run out, and they are certainly not able to purchase new furniture at the present time. And their houses, taking them in general, are extremely poorly furnished.

669. Do they attend public worship as much as they did formerly?—Ever since their condition has deteriorated, they have in a great measure lost heart; and because they have not the same outward look as other tradesmen, they generally stay at home or take skulking walks in the country to get out of sight.

670. Do they educate and watch over the conduct of their children as they did formerly?—It is a very natural thing for a parent to educate and superintend his children. The first they neglect for want of means; and with respect to the last, especially when their children grow up, they have lost influence over them, more so than they did at a former period.

671. When did this change commence in the condition of the operatives, and in the influence they have over their families?—To answer that question properly, it may be necessary to state, that a weaver's family, in former times, was under his own roof till they were pretty well grown up, and he himself provided for them, and he had a parental authority over them. It has so happened among many weavers' families at the present time, that the children have gone to steam-loom factories and other public works; and in consequence of this, the children are able to make double the earnings of the father, and they conceive, in their own minds, before they have come properly to the years of discretion, that they may throw off the parental authority, and in that case they threaten to leave the house and take up other lodgings; they consider that they are able to maintain themselves.

672. Can you explain what led to the low prices and the reduced condition of the weavers, in your description of manufacture?—We have paid particular attention to that for many years, and we certainly do attribute the sufferings principally to the unprincipled competition amongst the manufacturers at home.

B] SLUMS AND SQUALOR

The extracts below are taken from one of the most famous of all the parliamentary "bluebooks." Written by Edwin Chadwick, a disciple of the Utilitarian philosopher Jeremy Bentham, the report prepared the way for sanitary legislation which eventually solved some of the worst problems of the slums. But such solutions were distant in the time of the Chartists.*

The following is a brief notice of the condition of the residences of the population amidst which the cholera first made its appearance in this country.

MR. ROBERT ATKINSON, Gateshead, states, that—

'It is impossible to give a proper representation of the wretched state of many of the inhabitants of the indigent class, situated in the confined streets called Pipewellgate and Killgate, which are kept in a most filthy state, and to a stranger would appear inimical to the existence of human beings, where each small, ill ventilated apartment of the house contained a family with lodgers in number from seven to nine, and seldom more than two beds for the whole. The want of convenient offices in the neighborhood is attended with many very unpleasant circumstances, as it induces the lazy inmates to make use of chamber utensils, which are suffered to remain in the most offensive state for several days, and are then emptied out of the windows. The writer had occasion a short time ago to visit a person ill of the cholera; his lodgings were in a room of a miserable house situated in the very filthiest part of Pipewellgate, divided into six apartments, and occupied by different families to the number of 26 persons in all. The room contained three wretched beds with two persons sleeping in each; it measured about 12 feet in length and 7 in breadth, and its greatest height would not admit of a person's standing erect; it received light from a small window, the sash of which was fixed. Two of the number lay ill of the cholera, and the rest appeared afraid of the admission of pure air, having carefully closed up the broken panes with plugs of old linen.'

.   .   .

[The following tables give mortality rates for 1839. Leeds was a textile town; Liverpool was a seaport. The final table compares Rutland, a rural county, with Manchester, a textile manufacturing city.]

* From "Report . . . from the Poor Law Commissioners on . . . the Sanitary Condition of the Labouring Population of Great Britain," 1842, pp. 21–22, 157–59.

Leeds Borough

Number of Deaths		Average Age
79	Gentlemen and persons engaged in professions, and their families	44
824	Tradesmen, farmers, and their families	27
3,395	Operatives, labourers, and their families	19

Liverpool, 1840

137	Gentry and professional persons, etc.	35
1,738	Tradesmen and their families	22
5,597	Labourers, mechanics and servants, etc.	15

Manchester and Rutlandshire

	Average Age at Death	
	In Manchester	In Rutlandshire
Professional persons and gentry, and their families	38	52
Tradesmen and their families (in Rutlandshire, farmers and graziers are included with shopkeepers)	20	41
Mechanics, labourers, and their families	17	38

c] UNCERTAINTIES OF THE NEW INDUSTRIAL ECONOMY

Friedrich Engels, the closest collaborator of Karl Marx, was hardly an unbiased witness to conditions of industrial England. But his vivid description of the instability of the economic system in the 1840's, taken from The Condition of the Working Class in England, *is scarcely exaggerated.**

In the modern world both industrial production and the division of the means of subsistence are wholly unplanned; no attempt is made to satisfy undoubted needs. On the contrary profits alone determine what shall be produced and who shall consume it. Everyone works on his own with an eye to his own profits. It is hardly surprising that such a system should be continually breaking down. England, for example, supplies a number of countries with a very wide variety of manufactured goods. The individual manufacturer may well know how many articles of a particular kind are consumed annually in particular countries, but he does not know how many goods are being stored abroad. Still less does he know how many goods his competi-

* From Friedrich Engels, *The Condition of the Working Class in England*, trans. and ed. by W. O. Henderson and W. H. Chaloner (New York: Macmillan, 1958), pp. 95–97. Reprinted by permission of Basil Blackwell, Publisher.

tors are exporting. All he can do is to make estimates of a dubious character about such matters from the evidence of continually fluctuating prices. He exports his goods in the hope that they will be absorbed by the market. He sends everything blindly overseas and leaves the rest to chance. On the slightest indication that some particular market is a favourable one, everyone exports as much as possible and consequently such a market is soon overstocked. There follows a fall both in sales and cash returns and before long English industry has no more employment to offer the workers. In the early phase of the Industrial Revolution these crises were confined to particular branches of trade and particular markets. In time, however, the small individual crises coalesced and they have now developed into a recurrent cycle of major depressions. This development has been due to the unifying force of competition. The unemployed workers of one branch of industry are thrown on to such other branches of manufacture as are easiest for them to learn. Similarly goods which are superfluous in one overseas market are thrown on to other markets. A crisis now comes once every five years, after a short period of boom for the manufacturers and prosperity for the workers. In times of depression, home and foreign markets are glutted with English manufactured goods and their disposal inevitably takes time. Practically all branches of industry are adversely affected. There are failures among the smaller factory owners and those merchants who cannot carry on without the remittances due to them. At the height of the crisis the larger manufacturers transact no business. They either close their factories or put their workers on 'short time', i.e., about half a day. Wages fall owing to competition between the unemployed as well as the reduction of working hours and the lack of profitable orders. The workers suffer great distress. The small savings of the individual worker are soon spent and charitable organizations are overwhelmed with appeals for help. The poor rates are doubled or even trebled and, even so, are inadequate to alleviate the distress. The number of those who are starving increases and general panic is created by the sudden realisation of the existence of a great mass of 'superfluous population.' . . . Eventually, however, rising prices, combined with more favourable reports of trade prospects, encourage manufacturers to increase production. . . . And so it goes on. English industry passes through a continuous series of cycles of boom and slump.

2] The Reforming Impulse: Its Limits and Frustrations

A] WORKING-CLASS DISAPPOINTMENT WITH THE 1832 REFORM BILL

The London Working Men's Association was a small group of skilled artisans led by William Lovett and founded in 1836. The next year, in consultation with several middle-class Radical Members of Parliament, the L.W.M.A. produced the "People's Charter." This selection is taken from a general manifesto issued by the L.W.M.A. for the parliamentary election of 1837.*

FELLOW COUNTRYMEN,

—It is now nearly six years since the Reform Bill became a part of the laws of our country. To carry that measure despite the daring advocates of corruption, the co-operation of the millions was sought for and cheerfully and honestly given. They threw their hearts into the contest, and would have risked their lives to obtain that which they were led to believe would give *to all* the blessings of LIBERTY. Alas, their hopes were excited by promises which have not been kept, and their expectations of freedom have been bitterly disappointed in seeing the men, whom they had assisted to power, spurning their petition with contempt, and binding them down by still more slavish enactments. . . . But the people have learnt a profitable lesson from experience, and will not again be stimulated to contend for any measure which excludes them from its advantages. They now perceive that most of our oppressive laws and institutions, and the consequent ignorance and wretchedness to which they are exposed, *can be traced to one common source*—EXCLUSIVE LEGISLATION; *and they therefore have their minds intently fixed on the destruction of this great and pernicious monopoly;* being satisfied that while the power of law making is confined *to the few,* the exclusive interests *of the few* will be secured at the expense of the many.

B] THE NEW POOR LAW OF 1834

The selections below represent three points of view on the New Poor Law of 1834. The first is from the *Edinburgh Review,* the most famous Whig periodical of the time; the second is a poster issued by Richard Oastler (1789–1861), a Tory leader of working-class agitations in Yorkshire (the county in which the textile towns of Wakefield and Huddersfield are located); the third is a report by R. G. Gammage (in *History of the Chartist Movement*) of a speech given in 1838 by the Reverend Joseph Rayner Stephens (1805–79), a Methodist minister and one of the most popular leaders of the Anti-Poor Law Campaign. †

* From "An Address to the Reformers on the Forthcoming Elections," issued by the L.W.M.A. in 1837, from William Lovett, *Life and Struggles,* ed. R. H. Tawney, 2 vols. (London: G. Bell & Sons, Ltd., 1920), Vol. I, pp. 118–20. Reprinted in G. D. H. Cole and A. W. Filson, eds., *British Working Class Movements* (London: Macmillan, 1951), p. 348. Reprinted by permission of St Martin's Press, Inc., New York; The Macmillan Company of Canada, Limited; and Macmillan & Co., Ltd., London.

  † From the *Edinburgh Review* (July 1836) 502–04, 506–07.

  From Cecil Driver, *Tory Radical: The Life of Richard Oastler* (New York: Oxford University Press, 1946), p. 361.

  From a speech at Newcastle, January 1, 1838, quoted in R. G. Gammage, *History of the Chartist Movement, 1837–1854* (London, 1894), pp. 56–57.

A FRIENDLY VIEW, 1836

The [Poor Law] Commissioners laid it down as a principle, that it was ruinous and demoralizing to offer to persons of the best characters more than a simple subsistence [by way of relief], and that the person of bad character, if he were allowed anything, could not be allowed less. By this means a self-acting test was established, and a line drawn betweeen those who do and those who do not need relief. For if the claimant does not comply with the terms on which relief is given to the destitute, he gets nothing; and if he does comply, the compliance proves the truth of his claim, namely, his destitution. It is impossible to state briefly how much the practical working of this subject is facilitated by the clear perceptions and steady undeviating application of this principle. . . .

The Commissioners declared that . . . if the vital evil of the system, relief to the able-bodied on terms more eligible than regular industry, were allowed to continue, pauperism, with its train of evils, the demoralization of the labouring classes, the deterioration of their labour, the reduction of the demand for their employment, the decrease or efflux of capital, and the destruction of property, and all the elements of prosperity must steadily advance. . . .

The effects of the measure, so far as it has hitherto been carried, have fully answered the most sanguine anticipations of its proposers.

. . .

The effect of the progressive discontinuance of the allowance system, and the entire cessation of out-door relief to the able-bodied, has been to cause the absorption of almost the whole of the surplus of able-bodied labourers. For example, in the four following unions in the county of Kent, the effects of the measure have been as under-mentioned:—

Name of Union	Total number of able-bodied Paupers at the formation of Union	Number of able-bodied Paupers in June instant	Population
Milton	291	1	10,689
Bridge	272	1	9,244
Blean	241	1	10,639
River	150	2	10,837
Totals:	954	5	41,409

Close enquiries have been made as to what has become of these labourers, and it is found that nearly the whole of them are accounted for as at work within their parishes. Only about half-a-dozen men in each union have quitted it in search of work elsewhere. These were fellows whom no one would intrust [sic] in their farms. It is presumed, that they have most of them gone to places where they may renew their characters. One or two of them have gone to seek glory and pay in the service of the Queen of Spain.

AN ANTI–POOR LAW POSTER, 1837

ARE YOU FOR HAVING YOUR TOWNS AND VILLAGES FILLED WITH METROPOLITAN POLICE, ARMED WITH TRUNCHEONS AND PISTOLS? AND GIRT WITH MURDEROUS SWORDS? . . . WILL YOU OR WILL YOU NOT DECLARE TO THE IRISH SECRETARY, LORD MORPETH [i.e., to the government], AT WAKEFIELD NEXT MONDAY, THAT THIS HORRIBLE BASTILLE LAW SHALL NOT BE ESTABLISHED HERE AND THAT YOU WILL NOT BE CONTENT TILL IT HAS BEEN UPROOTED EVERYWHERE? . . .
THE HUDDERSFIELD MEN WILL BE THERE, AND SO I TRUST WILL YOU. THEY HAVE ASSISTED ME LIKE MEN TO GAIN THE VICTORY OVER THE POOR LAW COMMISSIONERS, DESPITE THEIR BLUE JACKETS AND CUTLASS-ARMED POLICE. . . .
MEN OF HUDDERSFIELD—ONE MORE TUG AND WE WILL GIVE THAT EXECRABLE LAW ITS DEATH BLOW. . . .

TO WAKEFIELD! TO WAKEFIELD!

STEPHENS THREATENS VIOLENCE, 1838

The people were not going to stand this, and he [Stephens] would say, that sooner than wife and husband, and father and son, should be sundered and dungeoned, and fed on 'skillee,'—sooner than wife or daughter should wear the prison dress—sooner than that—Newcastle ought to be, and should be—one blaze of fire, with only one way to put it out, and that with the blood of all who supported this abominable measure.

He (Mr. Stephens) was a revolutionist by fire; he was a revolutionist by blood, to the knife, to the death. If an unjust, unconstitutional, and illegal parchment was carried in the pockets of the Poor Law Commissioners, and handed over to be slung on a musket, or a bayonet, and carried through their bodies by an armed force, or by any force whatever . . . then it would be law for every man to have his firelock, his cutlass, his sword, his pair of pistols, or his pike, and for every woman to have her pair of scissors, and for every child to have its paper of pins and its box of needles, (here the orator's voice was drowned in the cheers of the meeting) and let the men with a torch in one hand and a dagger in the other, put to death any and all who attempted to sever man and wife.

3] The First Phase of Chartism, 1837–39

a] THE NATIONAL PETITION, MAY 1838

Drawn up under the auspices of the Birmingham Political Union, the National
Petition served as the rallying point for Chartist groups throughout the country
in this phase of the movement. It began with a discourse on the theme of
poverty-amidst-plenty, and then attacked the 1832 Reform Act for having
"effected a transfer of power from one domineering faction to another." Note
that five of the six Chartist points are included; equal election districts was
omitted, perhaps because it was thought to be implied by universal suffrage.*

We come before your honourable house to tell you, with all humility, that
this state of things must not be permitted to continue. That it cannot long
continue, without very seriously endangering the stability of the throne, and
the peace of the kingdom, and that if, by God's help, and all lawful and
constitutional appliances, an end can be put to it, we are fully resolved that
it shall speedily come to an end. We tell your honourable house, that the
capital of the master must no longer be deprived of its due profit; that the
labour of the workman must no longer be deprived of its due reward. That
the laws which make food dear, and the laws which make money scarce,
must be abolished. That taxation must be made to fall on property, not on
industry. That the good of the many, as it is the only legitimate end, so
must it be the sole study of the government. As a preliminary essential to
these and other requisite changes—as the means by which alone the interests of the people can be effectually vindicated and secured, we demand that
those interests be confided to the keeping of the people. When the State
calls for defenders, when it calls for money, no consideration of poverty or
ignorance can be pleaded in refusal or delay of the call. Required, as we are
universally, to support and obey the laws, nature and reason entitle us to
demand that in the making of the laws the universal voice shall be implic-
itly listened to. We perform the duties of freemen; we must have the privileges of freemen. Therefore, we demand universal suffrage. The suffrage, to
be exempt from the corruption of the wealthy and the violence of the powerful, must be secret. The assertion of our right necessarily involves the power
of our uncontrolled exercise. We ask for the reality of a good, not for its
semblance, therefore we demand the ballot. The connection between the
representatives and the people, to be beneficial, must be intimate. The legislative and constituent powers, for correction and for instruction, ought to
be brought into frequent contact. Errors which are comparatively light, when
susceptible of a speedy popular remedy, may produce the most disastrous

* From R. G. Gammage, *History of the Chartist Movement, 1837–1854* (London, 1894),
pp. 87–90.

effects when permitted to grow inveterate through years of compulsory endurance. To public safety, as well as public confidence, frequent elections are essential. Therefore, we demand annual parliaments. With power to choose, and freedom in choosing, the range of our choice must be unrestricted. We are compelled, by the existing laws, to take for our representatives men who are incapable of appreciating our difficulties, or have little sympathy with them; merchants who have retired from trade and no longer feel its harassings; proprietors of land who are alike ignorant of its evils and its cure; lawyers by whom the notoriety of the senate is courted only as a means of obtaining notice in the courts. The labours of a representative who is sedulous in the discharge of his duty are numerous and burdensome. It is neither just, nor reasonable, nor safe, that they should continue to be gratuitously rendered. We demand that in the future election of members of your honourable house, the approbation of the constituency shall be the sole qualification, and that to every representative so chosen, shall be assigned out of the public taxes, a fair and adequate remuneration for the time which he is called upon to devote to the public service. The management of this mighty kingdom has hitherto been a subject for contending factions to try their selfish experiments upon. We have felt the consequences in our sorrowful experience. Short glimmerings of uncertain enjoyment, swallowed up by long and dark seasons of suffering. If the self-government of the people should not remove our distresses, it will, and it alone can, bring true and lasting peace to the nation; we firmly believe that it will also bring prosperity. May it therefore please your honourable house, to take this our petition into your most serious consideration, and to use your utmost endeavours, by all constitutional means, to have a law passed, granting to every male of lawful age, sane mind, and unconvicted of crime, the right of voting for members of parliament, and directing all future elections of members of parliament to be in the way of secret ballot, and ordaining that the duration of parliament, so chosen, shall in no case exceed one year, and abolishing all property qualifications in the members, and providing for their due remuneration while in attendance on their parliamentary duties.

And your petitioners shall ever pray.

B] THE CHARTIST NATIONAL CONVENTION MEETS

Its very name designed to stir memories of the French Revolution, the Convention of Chartist delegates met in London on February 4, 1839. The mixture of fear and contempt with which outsiders viewed this gathering is apparent in the contemporary reporting of the Convention and of related events elsewhere. (*The Times* [London] reports of February 5, 1839, are given in their entirety.) The extravagant hopes of the Chartists also emerge clearly from the tone of the *Northern Star* of February 9, 1839, a weekly paper published by the most colorful (if not very reliable) Chartist leader Feargus O'Connor.*

* From *The Times* (London), February 5, 1839.
From the *Northern Star* (Leeds), February 9, 1839.

The Times (LONDON)

Meeting of the Chartist Delegates

A meeting of the Chartist delegates was held yesterday at the British Coffee-house, Cockspur-street. Mr. Feargus O'Connor, Dr. Wade, Mr. Hetherington, Mr. Lovett, Mr. O'Brien, and others were also present. Dr. Wade implored the divine blessing on the objects of the Chartists. Mr. Baillie, of Ayrshire, was called to the chair. Among the petitions brought to town by the delegates those from the following places bore the greatest number of signatures:—Birmingham, 94,600 odd; Fifeshire, 45,060; Glasgow, 80,000; Newcastle, 35,000; portions of the West Riding of York, 52,000; different portions of Lancashire, 20,000; Oldham, 13,000; Ayrshire, 13,000; and Ashton-under-Line, 13,000.—Evening paper.

The Chartists

Another 'grand demonstration,' as it was ludicrously termed, of the Chartists, took place on Brandon-hill on Thursday night. About 9 o'clock a procession was formed at the head-quarters of the demagogue [Henry] Vincent, in Thomas-street, preceded by all the ragged boys in the city that could be raked together, consisting of some 700 persons, in the midst of whom rode the would-be modern Masaniello [leader of an abortive seventeenth-century Neapolitan revolt]. Parading the streets in this guise, gathering adherents as they went from every sink of iniquity, and disturbing the peaceful citizens with their frightful yells, they reached Brandon-hill, where Vincent addressed the mob in his usual incendiary style. It would be vain to attempt to give anything like a report of his speech, which was a very counterpart of those delivered by his co-agitators at similar meetings. Repeal of the corn laws, universal suffrage &c., were of course advocated, with assertions that four monarchs were maintained by the sweat of the labouring man, indiscriminate abuse of the Conservatives and the Government, denunciations of the aristocracy, as blood-sucking, money-mongering tyrants, and of the country magistrates generally as lick-spittle creatures, with turnips for heads, &c. The oration being finished, the mob returned through the city in the same order.—Bristol Journal.

THE *Northern Star*

The Glorious Convention

The Convention has met; and never did the eye of freeborn man light upon a more heavenly spectacle. A number of men thrown together without other concert than that which general fame had attached to the character of each, and yet, as a body, presenting an appearance, a power, and a disposition which does not belong to either or any of those bodies, who declare that the people are incompetent to judge for themselves in the selection of representatives. The respectable appearance of the delegates, however, is trifling compared to the harmony, union, and good feeling which pervaded the whole body. O yes! thanks be to God, over and over again, all our misgivings have been but whimsical anticipations; the elements which, when apart, seemed somewhat discordant, have, on their meeting, subsided into a calm. Men of the Empire! learn then that your servants seem true and faithful; that in your councils there is neither jealousy nor intrigue; but an honourable vying to emulate in the boldest deeds of patriotism and philanthropy.

c] THE NORTHERN AGITATION: GENERAL NAPIER KEEPS THE PEACE

Throughout the spring and summer the threat of violence in support of the Chartist demands hung over England. Major General Sir Charles James Napier, a veteran of the Napoleonic wars, was put in command of troops in the northern district, comprising much of the industrial area of the country and therefore most major centers of Chartism. The first two excerpts are from Napier's letters to Samuel Phillipps, Permanent Under-Secretary, Home Department, April 25 and May 25, 1839; the rest are from Napier's diary.*

LETTER OF APRIL 25, 1839

We have now the same men to encounter [as those who organized agitations for Parliamentary reform in 1830–31], but their object is to overthrow the throne. Their number, though not ascertained, is probably greater than before; the arms possessed then they still possess, with the addition of a great number of pikes, so we may fairly suppose every man has a weapon. We have also those indications of commotion described by Colonel Kennedy as the precursors of an outbreak, namely, the beer-house meetings, the small assemblies, rumours, threats, agitators, and exciting pamphlets. So far the analogy is complete: but we have more, for we know that printed extracts from Maceroni's book on pike exercise are also in circulation; and we have information, though vague, that drilling without arms goes on nightly. We are also informed, and of this our information is tolerably certain, that the purchase of fire-arms and the manufacture of pikes goes on in some places with more vigour, in some with less, but still goes on.

We have also the fragment of a letter shewing that barricades are contemplated and understood, the example of Paris being held out. Finally, the conversation among the poorest classes who meet in public houses is, that one hundred Chartists may destroy fifty soldiers in billets and small detachments; and that the first thing is to cut the railroad and all communications between towns: these are all sound military operations, and taken as a whole afford some ground for apprehending that an outbreak will take

* From William Napier, *Life and Opinions of General Sir Charles James Napier* (London, 1857), Vol. II, pp. 18–19, 39, 69, 72–74.

place sooner or later. Of its being speedily put down there can be no doubt, because funds, leaders, and that discipline which is required to move large bodies, are all wanting; there are leaders for a midnight massacre but not for a mid-day battle; moreover, the avowed objects of the Chartists is [*sic*] said to be plunder and assassination. Such we hear is their language in the public houses, and that alone would destroy them even if a resolute and loyal army were not at hand to crush insurrection. The state of the unhappy hand-loom weavers is distressing in the greatest degree; an industrious man in full work and on the highest rate of wages starves: this is very dreadful, and in such parts the Chartists are most numerous and most resolute. If this state of distress can be ameliorated one great source of Chartism will soon be tarried.

With the foregoing general view of the subject I have constantly asked myself, what is to be done by me as a military man? The answer is—Secure your detachments from surprise as far as practicable, seek for information and abide events.

LETTER OF MAY 25, 1839

I am just about to mount for Kersall Moor to have a look at the meeting and see their temper. One wing of the 10th came by a morning train yesterday; the other by an evening train, which made everybody suppose two regiments had arrived. We made also a great show on the 23rd, and it is generally thought we had then 3,000 men under arms; we had not 1,000! The civil force here is quite inadequate. What are five hundred constables and specials [i.e., special constables] in a town which would turn out fifty thousand people to see a dog-fight? Manchester should have a well-organized police of at least a thousand men.

DIARY ENTRIES

August 5th. Meetings every night in the market-place, and good sense talked by the speakers: some a little outrageous, but nothing to demand notice. My advice to the magistrates is not to interfere unless the peace be broken: why should they? If the mob break the peace I will break their heads; we will have no burnings, no disgraceful proceedings, which the honest part of the Chartists deprecate: but when men assemble to express their political opinions it is unjust as well as foolish to disperse them.

August 6th. The plot thickens. Meetings increase and are so violent, and arms so abound, I know not what to think. The Duke of Portland tells me there is no doubt of an intended general rising. Poor people! They will suffer. They have set all England against them and their physical force:—fools! We have the physical force, not they. They talk of their hundred thousands of men. Who is to move them when I am dancing round them with cavalry, and pelting them with cannon-shot? What would their 100,000 men do with my 100 rockets wriggling their fiery tails among them, roaring, scorching, tearing, smashing all they came near? And when in desperation and despair they broke to fly, how would they bear five regiments of cavalry careering through them? Poor men! Poor men! How little they know of physical force!

.   .   .

August 13th. Magistrates again read the riot act on the race-course. We scolded, laughed . . . but three or four times was I obliged to mount, and indeed remained on horseback until long after dark. The mob was abusive but very timid, the approach of a dragoon made them fly like sheep.

.   .   .

August 19th. Everywhere a sudden calm has succeeded the storm; it is unnatural, for the causes of discontent still exist. The fact is that the Chartist leaders' calculations are quite at fault; they have found the difficulty of uniting their people in simultaneous efforts. Many of the chief men have been seized, there has been no resistance, and in this Lord John Russell has deserved well of the country. His failure has been in not making concessions, and not diminishing taxation: he cannot take a great view of affairs.

4] The End of the First Phase

A] PARLIAMENT REJECTS THE CHARTIST NATIONAL PETITION

The Chartist National Petition was not debated in Parliament until July 12, 1839. Thomas Attwood, Birmingham banker, currency reformer, and political Radical, then moved "that the House do resolve itself into a Committee of the Whole House, for the purpose of taking into consideration the petition called the National Petition." Excerpts below are from *Hansard's Parliamentary Debates*: a speech by the Home Secretary, Lord John Russell, a leading Whig politician and the government spokesman in this debate; a report of a speech by the young Benjamin Disraeli, a Tory backbench Member who was to become Prime Minister almost thirty years later; and a report of a speech by Attwood, offering his final arguments before the vote was taken.*

LORD JOHN RUSSELL

Those persons, I say, who have promoted this petition, have been found going through the country, from town to town, and from place to place, exhorting the people in the most violent and revolutionary language—language

* From *Hansard's Parliamentary Debates*, Third Series, Vol. XLIX, cols. 236–38, 245–46, 250, 274.

not exceeded in violence and atrocity in the worst times of the French Revolution—to subvert the laws by force of arms. We owe it to the good sense of the people in general, that they have not listened to such exhortations. Unfortunately, a certain number of them have been misled—not into entertaining particular opinions, for with their political opinions I am not now quarrelling, but into the assumption of a menacing attitude towards those who administer the laws, and towards the rest of their fellow-subjects who wish to live peaceably, and to conduct themselves according to the laws of the realm. . . . But I do conceive, that at the bottom of all those opinions . . . there is a most grievous error. The hon. Gentleman [Mr. Attwood] supposes . . . that if you have a certain representation, framed in a certain manner,—if you have a law enacted with certain provisions, then you can by your mere will establish enduring and lasting prosperity in a country. . . . Sir, I cannot conceive of any form of political government or mode of legislation by which you can insure to the whole community of a country a perpetual and lasting state of prosperity, or by which, in a country depending very much upon commerce and manufactures, you can prevent that state of low wages and consequent distress which at all times affect those who are at the bottom of the scale,—or prevent those alternate fluctuations from prosperity to distress which occur in every community of the kind. . . . My own opinion is, that these are the exhortations of persons, several of them, no doubt, conscientious persons, but others very designing and insidious persons, wishing not the prosperity of the people, but exhorting the people, by those means most injurious to themselves, to produce a degree of discord—to produce a degree of confusion—to produce a degree of misery, the consequence of which would be to create a great alarm, that would be fatal, not only to the constitution as it now exists, not only to those rights which are now said to be monopolised by a particular class, but fatal to any established government.

BENJAMIN DISRAELI

Mr. D'Israeli entirely agreed with the noble Lord as to the fallacy he had pointed out, as pervading this petition—that political rights necessarily ensured social happiness. But although they did not approve the remedy suggested by the Chartists, it did not follow they should not attempt to cure the disease complained of. He did not think they had, up to the present moment, clearly seen what the disease really was. He could not believe, that a movement which, if not national, was yet most popular, could have been produced by those common means of sedition to which the noble Lord had referred. . . . But if the noble Lord supposed, that in this country he could establish a permanent Government on what was styled now-a-days, a monarchy of the middle classes, he would be indulging a great delusion, which, if persisted in, must shake our institutions and endanger the Throne. He believed, such a system was actually foreign to the character of the people of England. He believed, that in this country, the exercise of political power

must be associated with great public duties. The English nation would con-
cede any degree of political power to a class making simultaneous advances
in the exercise of the great social duties. . . . [The Chartists] complained
only of the government by the middle classes. They made no attack on the
aristocracy . . . but upon the newly enfranchised constituency, not on the
old—upon that peculiar constituency which was the basis of the noble Lord's
Government.

THOMAS ATTWOOD

He [Mr. Attwood] trusted the House would see the propriety of going into
a Committee to investigate, if not to agree, upon the points mentioned in
this petition of 1,200,000 honest, hard-working men. Hon. Members would
then prove that they were actuated by honest and conscientious motives, and
that some faith at least might be had in them. And besides all this, if the
House would consent to go into Committee, that evidence of a disposition
to entertain the wishes of their fellow subjects would go a long way towards
soothing the disappointments that the petitioners had hitherto suffered.

The House divided: Ayes 46; Noes 235; Majority 189.

B] THE CONVENTION DWINDLES

Between February and July 1839, the Chartist Convention awaited the results
of the petition, meeting first in London, then in Birmingham, then back in
London. While waiting, the delegates argued about strategy and tactics. What
should be done if the petition were to be rejected by Parliament? The leading
suggestion, a partial compromise between militants and moderates, "physical
force" men and "moral force" men, was the "sacred month," or general
strike. But as dissensions continued and the number of delegates dwindled,
the plan's impracticability became plain. The Convention approved the following resolution on July 24 by 12 votes to 6, with 7 abstentions: *

Resolved:—

That while the Convention continues to be unanimously of opinion, that
nothing short of a general strike, or suspension of labour throughout the
country, will ever suffice to re-establish the rights and liberties of the industrial classes, we nevertheless cannot take upon ourselves the responsibility of
dictating the time or circumstances of such strike, believing that we are incompetent to do so for the following reasons:—

1st—Because our numbers have been greatly reduced by the desertion, absence, and arbitrary arrests of a large portion of our members.

2nd—Because great diversity of opinion prevails amongst the remaining

* From R. G. Gammage, *History of the Chartist Movement, 1837–1854* (London,
1894), p. 146.

members as to the practicability of a general strike, in the present state of trade in the manufacturing districts.

3rd—Because a similar diversity of opinion seems to prevail out of doors amongst our constituents and the working class generally.

4th—Because, under these circumstances, it is more than doubtful whether an order from the Convention for a general holiday would be generally obeyed, or whether the strike would not be a failure.

5th—Because, while we firmly believe that an [sic] universal strike would prove the salvation of the country, we are at the same time equally convinced that a partial strike would only entail the bitterest privations and sufferings on all parties who take part in it, and, in the present exasperated state of public feeling, not improbably lead to confusion and anarchy.

6th—Because, although it is the duty of the Convention to participate in all the people's dangers, it is no part of our duty to create danger unnecessarily, either for ourselves or others. To create it for ourselves would be folly —to create it for others would be a crime.

7th—Because we believe that the people themselves are the only fit judges of their right and readiness to strike work, as also of their own resources and capabilities of meeting the emergencies which such an event would entail. Under these circumstances, we decide that a committee of three be appointed to reconsider the vote of the 16th instant, and to substitute for it an address, which shall leave to the people themselves to decide whether they will or will not commence the sacred month on the 12th of August, at the same time explaining the reasons for adopting such a course, and pledging the Convention to co-operate with the people in whatever measures they may deem necessary to their safety and emancipation.

c] The Newport Rising

The Convention disbanded in September 1839. The long summer had passed without the violent uprising feared by General Napier (and many others). Then suddenly, in November, came a brief outburst in the coal and iron country on the borders of Wales, centering on the town of Newport, Monmouthshire. To what extent this was intended as the signal for a more general resort to arms we shall probably never discover, for direct evidence is lacking. Some notion of the kind of planning that went into the rising may be derived from this contemporary account from the 1839 *Annual Register*, a reference book covering the year's events that has appeared since 1759. With the failure at Newport, Chartism's first phase may be said to have ended.*

Nov. 4. CHARTIST INSURRECTION.—Disturbances of a very serious character occurred among the working population of South Wales, chiefly in the neighborhood of Newport, Monmouth, Brecon, Merthyr Tydvil, and in the mountainous districts. On Sunday, the 3rd of November, the magistrates of New-

* From "Chronicle," in the *Annual Register* (1839), pp. 221–22.

port received information, that large bodies of men collected from the districts above-mentioned were marching upon Newport, headed by John Frost, formerly a draper in Newport, but better known as a chartist delegate, and as the magistrate dismissed by Lord John Russell from the commission of the peace, to which he had been appointed under the municipal act. It was the intention of the rioters to have attacked Newport, about one o'clock on Monday morning; but the extreme wetness of the weather prevented many from attending at the appointed places of meeting, and it was not till ten o'clock, on Monday, that they entered the town, in two divisions, one headed by Frost, the other by his son, a lad of fourteen or fifteen. They were armed with guns, pistols, pikes, swords, and heavy clubs. When they entered the town, their first enquiry was for the military, and where they were stationed; and being informed that a small detachment of them was stationed at the Westgate Hotel, the mob formed in front of it, and immediately commenced an attack by firing through the windows into the house. The military (about thirty soldiers of the forty-fifth regiment,) under the direction of the mayor, Mr. Thomas Phillips, junior, promptly returned the fire; and in a very short time several of the rioters were deprived of life, and lay weltering in blood to the dismay of the survivors, who very soon retreated in great disorder and in every direction. The mayor was wounded by a gun-shot in the left arm, and by a severe cut in the right side, which for some time quite disabled him. A sergeant and a private, and two shopkeepers of Newport, Mr. Henry Williams and Mr. Morgan, were seriously wounded, and several other special constables slightly.

The mayor, who behaved with much coolness and intrepidity, read the riot act, amongst showers of bullets, before he ordered the military to fire. The number of the rioters was variously estimated at from 7,000 to 10,000; but a much larger number were collected on the hills.

At night, Mr. Frost's house was searched and his papers secured, by Mr. Jones Phillips, a solicitor. Mr. Phillips then proceeded to the residence of Partridge, Frost's printer; and there apprehended Mr. Frost himself, who was quietly supping on bread and cheese, and apparently unconscious of danger, though a reward of £100 had been offered for his apprehension. Partridge was also secured. Both the prisoners had pistols, percussion caps, powder, and bullets, on their persons. Many of the rioters were made prisoners. The bodies of many rioters were found in the streets and in the fields. Their dress and appearance indicated them to be working men in full employ; as are, indeed, the Welsh miners generally. The number killed was upwards of twenty; the wounded, much more numerous.

5] Ideas and Issues of the Chartist Movement

A] CHARTISM AND MIDDLE-CLASS RADICALISM

"Radical" had a special meaning in nineteenth-century British politics: "one who holds the most advanced views of political reform on democratic lines." [2] There is no connotation of revolution here, and middle-class Victorian Radicals were generally staunch supporters of private enterprise, the rights of property, and economy in government. The main attempt to form a Radical-Chartist alliance was the Complete Suffrage Union, founded in 1841 by Joseph Sturge (1793–1859), a Birmingham Quaker. The union was attacked by many Chartist leaders, including James Bronterre O'Brien (1805–64), a journalist and one of the ablest intellects in the movement. At the climactic meeting of December 1842 Sturge's appeal for moderation failed; a majority voted to proceed on the basis of the Charter itself, rather than the Union's program. At this the Sturge group walked out, thus ending the most serious attempt to link Chartism with middle-class Radicalism. The selections below are from a letter that O'Brien wrote to a friend in Edinburgh on March 31, 1841, and a speech by Sturge to the Conference of Complete Suffrage and Chartist Delegates given in December 1842.*

JAMES BRONTERRE O'BRIEN

The middle classes can remove all our political and social evils whenever they like, without either convulsing society, or forming any pretended 'Unions' with us for the purpose. You must also admit that we have a perfect right to hold them responsible for those evils—seeing they will neither remove them themselves, nor suffer us to do so—and that no sane person would think of uniting for any purpose with known enemies; our proper business, as Chartists, is to combine together as one man, not *with* the middle classes, but *against* them, in order to put an end to their usurpations.

But, it is said, 'Some of them are friendly to us; would you exclude them?' &c. Certainly not; if they be really friendly, they will unite with us to get the *Charter*—if they be not, they will exclude themselves. We cannot reject any man, of any class, who, *bona fide*, admits our principles; nor have we ever spurned the cooperation of middle-class Chartists. . . . But we can form no alliance—we can enter into no compact with men who require from us, as the conditions [sic] of their joining us, that we renounce the Charter. To renounce the Charter, would be either to renounce our rights—which would be madness—or to barter away the rights of others, which would be wickedness.

---

[2] *Shorter Oxford English Dictionary* (1933). *Editor.*

* From James Bronterre O'Brien, "A letter to a friend in Edinburgh," dated March 31, 1841, from the *Northern Star*, April 24, 1841.

From Henry Richard, *Memoirs of Joseph Sturge* (London, 1864), pp. 316–17.

JOSEPH STURGE

The success we have already met with gives us good ground to hope that, by forbearance and argument, we shall do much to remove the alienation [between middle and working classes] which has been so lamentably fostered and increased by the events of the last few years. Having at a former conference adopted all six points which involve any question of principle in what is called 'the people's charter,' I had hoped it would at least have removed suspicion towards us from the minds of all upright friends of the people; and while we invite the most vigilant watchfulness of our every movement on the part of our fellow-countrymen, we consider we are entitled to claim credit for honesty of intention until the contrary is proved against us; but we are resolved not to be parties to any steps whatever which involve the slightest violation of our peaceable principles, or go further in offending the prejudices of those at whose hands we seek redress, than is called for by a firm adherence to the claim of full justice for our unenfranchised brethren. . . . I wish therefore emphatically to assure this assembly, and I am persuaded I speak the sentiments of every member of the Complete Suffrage Council, that we cannot knowingly act in unison with any who recommend or countenance violence for the attainment of their object; or who, instead of cordially uniting with all honest men to obtain the rights of the people, waste their time in abusing those who do not exactly tread in their steps. At the same time I trust that when any who have thus acted prove by future deeds as well as words that they have seen their error, the past will be for ever buried in oblivion.

B] THE CHARTIST LAND SCHEME

Some Chartists (such as William Lovett) accepted industrialism; others appealed to the yearning of many a transplanted peasant for a return to the land. Among the latter was Feargus O'Connor (1794–1855), "the Lion of Freedom," as a popular Chartist song called him, or (in Lovett's words) "the chief marplot of our movement . . . this great 'I am' of Chartism." The giant, bull-voiced Irishman was the chief promoter of a scheme for mobilizing the resources of the poor and using them to purchase land on which some of the shareholders (chosen by lot) would then be settled. Associated with this scheme was to be a "National Land Bank," which would hopefully produce further funds for the purchase of estates.

The selections below, taken from the "First Report from the Select Committee on the National Land Company" (1847–48), include a printed circular issued by the company on April 1, 1847; an excerpt from the testimony of the Financial Secretary of the company, Philip McGrath, to the House of Commons; and part of the final report on the company given the House by the committee.

Twenty shillings make one pound; the average worker in a cotton textile factory in 1840 earned ten shillings a week, and the total expenditure of Her Majesty's government, excluding charges on the national debt, was just under £20 million in 1840.*

PRINTED CIRCULAR

National Land Company, provisionally registered. Shares £1 6s. each. The object of this company is to enable working men, for a trifling sum, to obtain possession of land and dwellings upon such terms, that by honourable and independent labour they may maintain themselves and families in comfort and respectability. Benefits assured. The following are the benefits which the Company guarantees to its members: holders of two shares, a comfortable house, two acres of good land, and £15. Holders of three shares, a house, three acres, and £22 10s. Holders of four shares, a house, four acres, and £30. Leases forever will be granted to the occupants, thus ensuring to them the value of every improvement they may make upon their allotments. The company affords great facilities to those members who have the means of purchasing their allotments. The rent will be moderate, as it will be regulated by a charge of five per cent. upon the capital extended. The company having been called into existence for the benefit of the working classes, the rules enable the poorest to avail themselves of its advantages; as to the shares they may be paid by instalments as low as 3d. per week. The rules of the company, price 4d., can be obtained of Mr. Wheeler, the secretary, at the office, 83, Dean-street, Soho, London, where members may be enrolled, and every information obtained, or of John Gathard.

TESTIMONY OF PHILIP MCGRATH

1502. It appears, by the rules of the company, that the capital is to be £130,000, and the number of shares 100,000, and the calculation which is made in page 7 of the rules of the company allows to each shareholder three shares?—Yes.

1503. You will therefore have 33,333 for the number of shareholders? —Yes.

1504. And the cost of locating each individual, on the plan laid down in page 7, is £242 10s., is it not?—Yes, that is the case supposed here.

1505. If you divide the capital of £130,000 by that sum, you will get 536 for the number of shareholders which the capital will suffice to locate?—You will.

1506. Therefore out of the whole number of shareholders of 33,333, only 536 will get an allotment?—Just so, with the original capital.

1507. What will become of the remaining 32,797 shareholders; what benefit

* From "First Report from the Select Committee on the National Land Company" (398), p. 6; the examination of Philip McGrath, Financial Secretary to the Company, "Second Report" (420), pp. 27–28; and "Sixth Report" (577), p. iii; in *Parliamentary Papers*, 1847–48.

are they to derive from the company?—They enter the company for the purpose of getting upon the land, just the same as those who are put upon the land by the original capital; their hope is in the reproductive machinery of the company. Their hope is that the banking department of the company will so work as to reproduce the original sum, and thus enable the directors to locate as many more, and so on until all are located.

1508. How much will the bank have to reproduce to locate the whole of the 33,333 shareholders at £242 10s. each; will not the bank have to provide the sum of £8,083,252?—It will.

THE COMMITTEE'S FINAL REPORT

The Select Committee appointed to inquire into the National Land Company, who were empowered to Report the Evidence taken before them, from time to time, and their Opinion, to The House;—

Have further considered the Matters to them referred, and have agreed to the following RESOLUTIONS and REPORT:—

. . .

3. THAT the National Land Company, as at present constituted, is an illegal scheme, and will not fulfil the expectations held out by the Directors to the Shareholders.

4. THAT it appearing to this Committee by the evidence of several witnesses that the books of proceedings of the National Land Company, as well as the accounts of the Company, have been most imperfectly kept, and that the original balance-sheets signed by the auditors of the Company have been destroyed, and only three of those balance-sheets, for the quarters ending the 29th of September and the 25th of December 1847, and the 25th of March 1848 respectively, have been produced; but Mr. Feargus O'Connor having expressed an opinion that an impression had gone abroad that the monies subscribed by the National Land Company had been applied to his own benefit, this Committee are clearly of opinion, that although the accounts have not been kept with strict regularity, yet that irregularity has been against Mr. Feargus O'Connor's interest, instead of in his favour; and that it appears by Mr. Grey's account there is due to Mr. Feargus O'Connor the sum of £3,298 5s. 3½ d., and by Mr. Finlaison's account the sum of £3,400.

5. THAT, considering the great number of persons interested in the scheme, and the bona fides with which it appears to have been carried on, it is the opinion of this Committee that powers might be granted to the parties concerned, if they shall so desire, to wind up the undertaking and to relieve them from the penalties to which they may have incautiously subjected themselves.

c] Democracy for What? The Conflict over Objectives

Taunted by their opponents with the criticism that the Charter's six points would do nothing to remedy the economic situation of the poor, Chartists often proposed a broadening of the movement to include social and economic legislation. For example, in the first selection below, from the *London Democrat* of June 1, 1839, George Julian Harney (1817–95) argues that political democracy is not enough. Harney was leader of the London Democratic Association, founded in 1837 in protest against the moderation of the L.W.M.A. There were also counterarguments, exemplified by P. H. Muntz's address to the "Grand Midland Demonstration" at Birmingham on August 6, 1838, the second selection given below. The last selection is the legislative program from the "Address to the Electors and Nonelectors of Halifax" (published in the *Northern Star* July 3, 1847) by Ernest Jones (1816–69), a lawyer with some literary talent who became the chief leader of Chartism in its long decline after 1848. The six points of the Charter preceded the legislative program in the address; note the program's concern with attacking aristocratic (rather than middle-class) privilege in numbers six and seven.*

GEORGE JULIAN HARNEY

Now I have no objection to the 'People's Charter', as a fundamental law of this country, but I have a great objection to its being considered as a panacea for all the evils under which you labour. No, my friends, the disease which is now preying on your vitals, is much too deeply seated to be affected by remedies of that kind. Your whole social system requires 'revolution', your commercial system requires 'revolution', your political system requires 'revolution', and nothing short of actual convulsion will enable you to effect a cure.

As I said in my last, you must inscribe on your banners, 'the land national property', 'no usury laws', and 'no exclusive monopolies or charters'. Now these are fundamental principles, and well understood, and would immediately effect a change in the system; but establish the 'People's Charter' tomorrow, and the working man would not have one difficulty the less to contend with. I know very well that the 'mountebanks', who are now travelling the country [delegates on mission from the Convention], will

* From the *London Democrat*, June 1, 1839. Reprinted in G. D. H. Cole and A. W. Filson, eds., *British Working Class Movements* (London: Macmillan, 1951), p. 357. Reprinted by permission of St Martin's Press, Inc., New York; The Macmillan Company of Canada, Limited; and Macmillan & Co., Ltd., London.

From a contemporary pamphlet. Reprinted in G. D. H. Cole and A. W. Filson, eds., *British Working Class Movements* (London: Macmillan, 1951), p. 355. Reprinted by permission of St Martin's Press, Inc., New York; The Macmillan Company of Canada, Limited; and Macmillan & Co., Ltd., London.

From the *Northern Star*, July 3, 1847. Reprinted in John Saville, ed., *Ernest Jones: Chartist* (London: Lawrence & Wishart, Ltd., 1952), pp. 95–97. Reprinted by permission of the publishers.

endeavour to persuade you that all these things would follow the establishment of the 'People's Charter' . . . [but] this is a monstrous delusion.

P. H. MUNTZ

But they must get rid of both Tories and Whigs. They must get up a general system of agitation. They must not agitate for every paltry question. And above all they must beware of the old motto, 'Divide and Conquer.' They must make their stand upon the national petition, throwing aside all minor points that caused dissension (cheers). The question of the corn laws must for the time, be laid aside, as well as every other question that set the manufacturer against the farmer, the man against the master, or the landlord against the tenant. These must all be laid aside, and they must join hand and heart in one great and general effort. (Loud cheers). Let them once get a fair and just representation of the people, and they would ultimately secure the peace, the happiness, and the permanent welfare of the people (cheers). Let not the attention for a moment be withdrawn from the main point of universal suffrage. All other evils, the corn laws, the poor laws—forget all these for an instant—let nothing be thought of but the principle which will give you the power of returning such men as, when returned, will repeal, if necessary, a dozen such laws a day.

ERNEST JONES

1. THE SEPARATION OF CHURCH AND STATE, and the abolition of all religious endowment at the hands of the Government—since those who worship Mammon cannot worthily serve God; since religion is far too sacred to be made the tool of party politics, being an emanation from the Deity, and not of the Houses of Parliament.

2. THE RESTORATION of that portion of the CHURCH PROPERTY, taken from the poor, to its rightful owners, leaving the support of Ministers of religion to those who follow their guidance.

3. A VOLUNTARY SYSTEM OF EDUCATION, enabling every section of the community to give their children religious and secular instruction in accordance with their own convictions, without any Government interference or control.

4. THE ABOLITION OF CAPITAL PUNISHMENTS, since the respite between condemnation and execution does not afford the opportunity for true repentance, and since a sanguinary law exercises an injurious effect, by familiarising the popular mind with acts of cruelty.

5. THE ABOLITION OF THE NEW POOR LAW, and the establishment of a system of relief and remuneration in accordance with the spirit of Christianity and justice.

6. THE REPEAL OF THE LAWS OF PRIMOGENITURE AND ENTAIL, since these

laws tend to lock up the land in the hands of a few, and keep a body of political tools at the beck of Government in the pauper-sons of titled houses.

7. THE REPEAL OF THE GAME LAWS, since, as game is kept at the expense of all, it ought not to be exclusively enjoyed by the few.

8. A SYSTEM OF DIRECT TAXATION, and no secret service money, since where money is honestly spent, no one need be ashamed to own how it has been applied.

9. AN EXTENSION OF THE SMALL PROPRIETORY SYSTEM, by means of the Government support, for reclaiming waste land, and the purchase of land for the people.

10. A consistent development of the principle of FREE TRADE, by a repeal of the NAVIGATION LAWS and other monopolies pressing on the mechanical and agricultural industry of the country.

Gentlemen—I have but to add in conclusion that, if returned, I shall lend my support to these measures, facilitating, by railroads and cheap postage, the means of easy and rapid transmission and intercourse; that I shall oppose all foreign wars, not rendered necessary for self defence, or the purposes of humanity; and that I shall feel it my duty annually to present myself before the inhabitants of your borough, in public meeting assembled, and there to resign my trust into their hands, should such be the will of the majority.

CONCLUSION

I T W A S not only prosperity that smothered the Chartist movement after 1848. There were also alternative outlets for working-class energy and self-help—consumers' cooperatives, born in the 'forties and advancing in the 'fifties; trade unions for the skilled elite of labor, carefully managed and practical, eschewing dreams of the millennium in favor of benefits in the here and now. Yet while Chartism was dying, the Charter was becoming a reality: its six points were beginning to edge their way into the British constitution. The property qualification for Members of Parliament was abolished in 1858. Although the second Reform Act, in 1867, did not bring about a democratic electorate, it did extend the franchise to large numbers of the more prosperous manual workers. The Ballot Act followed in 1872, while the general principle of equal election districts achieved recognition in the third Reform Act of 1884–85. Further extensions of the right to vote made Britain a democracy in the twentieth century, and Members of Parliament began to receive salaries in 1911. Of the six points, only annual elections failed to materialize.

Doubtless these things would have happened had the Chartists never lived. Chartism is interesting today not so much because its program was destined to be enacted by later generations, with different motivations and in different circumstances from those of Feargus O'Connor's day, but because it offers a vast field for the study of a society under the stress of rapid economic change. Seen in this light, the failures and frustrations of the Chartists become as interesting and instructive to us as the eventual triumph which they could not live to see.

STUDY QUESTIONS

1] How much danger of revolution was there in Britain as a result of Chartism, as far as you can judge from the documents presented?

2] Was Disraeli's view of Chartist attitudes toward the upper (aristocratic) class and middle classes correct?

3] Poor leadership is often cited as one of the main causes of Chartism's failure; do you find evidence of this?

4] Compare the attitudes toward Chartism of Lord John Russell, General Sir Charles Napier, and George Julian Harney.

5] What tactical alternatives had the Chartist leaders in late July 1839? What do you think they should have done (assuming, for the purposes of analysis, that it was desirable for the Chartist program to succeed)?

RECOMMENDED READINGS

PRIMARY

CARLYLE, THOMAS. *Chartism* (London, 1839).

COLE, G. D. H. AND A. W. FILSON, eds. *British Working Class Movements: Select Documents, 1789–1875* (London, 1951).

DISRAELI, BENJAMIN. *Sybil, or The Two Nations* (a novel) (London, 1845).

GAMMAGE, R. G. *History of the Chartist Movement, 1837–1854* (London, 1854).

LOVETT, WILLIAM. *Life and Struggles* (London, 1876).

NAPIER, WILLIAM. *Life and Opinions of General Sir Charles James Napier*, Vol. II (London, 1857).

SAVILLE, JOHN. *Ernest Jones: Chartist—Selections from the Writings and Speeches of Ernest Jones* (London, 1952).

YOUNG, G. M. AND W. D. HANDCOCK, eds. *English Historical Documents, 1833–1874*, Vol. XII(I) (London, 1956).

SECONDARY

BRIGGS, ASA, ed. *Chartist Studies* (London, 1959).

COLE, G. D. H. *British Working Class Politics, 1832–1914* (London, 1941).

———. *Chartist Portraits* (London, 1941).

———. *Short History of the British Working Class Movement, 1789–1947* (London, 1949).

FAULKNER, H. V. *Chartism and the Churches* (New York, 1910).

HAMMOND, J. L. AND BARBARA HAMMOND. *The Age of the Chartists* (London, 1930).

HOVELL, MARK. *The Chartist Movement* (Manchester, 1918).

MACCOBY, S. *English Radicalism, 1832–1852* (London, 1935).

MATHER, F. C. *Public Order in the Age of the Chartists* (Manchester, 1959).

O'HIGGINS, RACHEL. "The Irish Influence in the Chartist Movement," *Past and Present*, XX (November, 1961), 83–96.

ROSENBLATT, F. F. *The Chartist Movement in Its Social and Economic Aspects* (New York, 1916).

SCHOYEN, A. R. *The Chartist Challenge: A Portrait of George Julian Harney* (London, 1958).

SLOSSON, PRESTON. *Decline of the Chartist Movement* (New York, 1916).

THOMPSON, E. P. *The Making of the English Working Class* (London, 1963). A massive study of the background of Chartism.

WILLIAMS, DAVID. *John Frost: A Study in Chartism* (Cardiff, 1939).

British Imperialism:
The Scramble for Africa,
1870–1914

ROBIN W. WINKS

YALE UNIVERSITY

CONTENTS

B] Schumpeter, Sociology, and Psychology, 1919
(Schumpeter, *Imperialism and Social Classes*)

CHRONOLOGY

1868   Gladstone forms his first cabinet.
1869   The opening of the Suez Canal.
1871   Henry M. Stanley finds David Livingstone; the end of the Maori wars in New Zealand.
1872   Disraeli's Crystal Palace speech.
1874   Britain annexes the Fiji Islands; Disraeli forms his second Cabinet.
1875   British intervention in Malaya.
1876   The Brussels Conference on African affairs.
1878   The Congress of Berlin; Britain occupies Cyprus.
1880   Gladstone forms his second Cabinet.
1881   The British North Borneo Company is chartered; the French occupy Tunis and begin expansion.
1882   The British occupy Cairo; the Triple Alliance is formed.
1884   The Berlin Conference and the partition of Africa; the French war in Tonkin.
1885   Gordon is massacred at Khartoum; the British acquire Bechuanaland at the urging of Cecil Rhodes; Lord Salisbury forms his first Cabinet.
1886   The Roger Niger Company is chartered.
1887   The Reinsurance Treaty.
1888   Britain acquires Zanzibar; the Imperial East African Company is formed.
1890   The British and French agree on spheres of influence in West Africa; Cecil Rhodes becomes Prime Minster of Cape Colony; Bismarck is dismissed in Germany.
1893   Uganda Protectorate.
1894   Russo-French Alliance.
1895   Jameson's Raid; Lord Salisbury forms his third Cabinet.
1898   The Fashoda Incident; the British acquisition of Hong Kong; the Spanish-American War.
1899   The beginning of the Boer War (ends in 1902).
1900   The Boxer Rebellion; the Nigeria Protectorate.
1902   The British-Japanese Alliance.
1903   The Berlin-to-Bagdad Railroad.
1904   The Entente Cordiale.
1905   The First Moroccan crisis.
1907   The Triple Entente.
1911   The Second Moroccan crisis.

1914 The United States completes the Panama Canal; World War I begins following the assassination of Archduke Francis Ferdinand.

1919 The League of Nations and the mandate system.

1926 The Balfour Declaration on the independence of Dominions.

INTRODUCTION

IMPERIALISM is one of those strange words whose meaning depends on the time and place in which it is used. In recent years both American capitalists and Russian Communists have attacked imperialism and empire, even though both the United States and the Soviet Union have been imperial nations in their own ways, and very few people indeed would defend the practices normally thought to be associated with imperialism. Marx and Lenin denounced imperialism as capitalism's means of oppressing the weak, and today Communist rhetoric labels the United States an "imperialist capitalist" nation. But in the twentieth century the United States has consistently opposed imperialism, at least as it defines it, and when Winston Churchill declared that he would not preside over the dissolution of the British Empire, he was thinking of American attacks on that empire as fully as attacks from the extreme left. In short, imperialism in the mid-twentieth century is everyone's whipping boy.

Such was not the case in the nineteenth century. The word itself was little used until comparatively late in the century, and in 1878 Lord Carnarvon, who had just resigned as Colonial Secretary in Disraeli's second Cabinet, confessed that the "newly coined word" puzzled him. He did not shrink from it, however, for at the time it seemed to embody much that Victorian England found virtuous. Evelyn Baring, the first Earl Cromer, who virtually ruled Egypt from 1883 to 1907, argued that "a sound but reasonable Imperialist" was one who understood the uses of power both to strengthen the imperial nation and to benefit the colonies through imperialism's "civilising and moralising mission." Writing shortly before World War I Philip Jourdan, private secretary to Cecil Rhodes, the empire-builder of southern Africa, declared that, largely because of Rhodes, "At the present day we are all proud to call ourselves Imperialists." The men who fell at Rorke's Drift before Cetawayo's Zulus, or who stood with "Chinese" Gordon at Khartoum, or who read London's halfpenny press, the *Daily Mail*, were imperialists who took seriously Kipling's call to "take up the white man's burden." To attack imperialism today is proper, for new occasions teach new duties, but to fail to understand the myriad motives that led men sincerely to espouse aggressive annexation, or empire by treaty, or moral overlordship and the protectorate system, is to fail as historian.

What was imperialism? Amid the welter of conflicting meanings and interpretations by different countries one can at least discern agreement that, on the whole, imperialism was manifested through the annexation, or extension of a protectorate over, territories already populated by an indigenous people thought to be incapable, by various and varying standards, of governing themselves. Occupation of a totally unpopulated land, such as parts of

Canada, or the implantation of settlers of British stock in an area basically uninhabited, such as Australia, is generally thought to fall under the rubrics of "expansionism" or "colonialism" but not "imperialism." Since "imperialism" is most closely associated with the period 1870 to 1914, and since the areas acquired at that time already were populated by Africans and Asians, imperial thought is generally considered to contain a racist strain as well. Finally, imperialism often arose because of a sense of competition with another power.

Historians have explained imperialism in several different ways. However, all will agree that imperialism was a powerful force that unleashed in its train other forces as dynamic, as sweeping, and as genuinely revolutionary as those released by the Protestant Reformation or the French Revolution. Imperialism contributed to the late nineteenth and early twentieth centuries' major wars, and from these flowed the great depression, World War II, and many of the difficulties of the modern world. Imperialism, racism, and romantic nationalism were inextricably linked, each feeding the other; the disintegration of empires, under the force of twentieth-century nationalism, created yet other forces with which we have only begun to reckon. And the basic problem of the 1960's and 1970's, race relations, was shaped by the age of imperialism. Indeed, the changes flowing from Europe's expansion into Asia, Africa, Latin America, and the Pacific have been so great that it is surprising more historians do not speak of the Imperial Revolution.

The motivations for imperialism fall into three rough categories, and schools of history offering variant interpretations have grown up around these categories. The first interpretation remains the most accepted by the "man in the street": that the chief motive for empire was commercial gain. An Englishman, John A. Hobson, published his *Imperialism: A Study* in 1902, in which he answered his own rhetorical question, *Cui bono?* Who profits from imperialism? with a single answer, "the investor." The munitions and arms manufacturers, industrialists in search of consumers to replace glutted domestic markets, and capitalists with idle funds—these all promoted empire, he argued. So, too, did the civil and military establishment which fed off the expanding empire. In 1933 the British historian Charles R. Fay added the phrase "informal empire" to our lexicon when he pointed out that British influence often was greatest where Britain did not annex: in the Near East and in parts of Latin America. The informal empire was one built entirely by alliances, trade concessions, market rights, and guaranteed sources of raw materials to feed the British industrial machine; annexation as such was unnecessary. These two points of view, while in basic disagreement over why Britain chose politically to acquire possessions in a certain area, were in agreement on the fundamental point: Britain committed itself overseas, whether formally or informally, largely for reasons of the marketplace. In *Wealth of Nations* (1776) Adam Smith had referred to the British as a "nation of shopkeepers," and their first empire, based on mercantilism, also had been stimulated by commercial concerns. The nature of commerce had changed, and so too, therefore, had the nature of empire, but the fundamental motivation was still discernible: money.

More recent historians, although not yet the "man in the street," have come to question Hobson's economic interpretation of imperialism. Modern economists are far less certain than their classical counterparts that they can filter out from a complex series of historical events the purely economic components. Today economists admit that many noneconomic, indeed nonrational, influences shape the decisions men make. Hobson saw a small clique of financiers working behind the scenes to mold the empire; modern economists and historians doubt that such a clique existed in precisely the way Hobson thought, or that it could make itself felt through an imperial crusade without the cooperation of many other conditions. A second broad school of historical thought has therefore come to attribute the basic motivation for imperialism to the strategic and diplomatic conditions of the time.

Until the end of the nineteenth century, Britain in particular had based its foreign policy on a balance of power. Britain wished to prevent any alliance system from developing in Europe by which two or more of its strongest rivals might stand together. To hold the balance of power Britain either had to be more powerful than any potential competitor or combination of competitors, or Britain had to be able to strike up alliances of its own to counterbalance those mounted against it. Power did not necessarily rest upon military or naval might, however, and not until near the end of the century did the European nations engage in arms races. To the British, power lay in strategic control of geopolitically important resources and areas. Direct annexation of an area was expensive, since annexation required both a military and a civil establishment. It was also dangerous, since it might provoke counterannexation moves by another power. Britain preferred to annex only those points which strategically dominated large areas, as Singapore dominated the East Indies.

At the Congress of Berlin in 1878, after the Russo-Turkish War, Germany's Bismarck played "honest broker" in parceling out strategic and ethnically important areas. Previously, by a secret Anglo-Turkish agreement, Britain had been given permission to occupy Cyprus, then nominally Turkish territory, in exchange for a promise to defend Turkey against further attack. The Congress of Berlin now gave multilateral support to this occupation; at the same time, France was promised that it might occupy Tunis. The Ottoman Empire was left fragmented and weak. The acquisition of Cyprus by Britain, following closely upon Disraeli's purchase of the Egyptian Khedive's shares in the Suez Canal, made Britain the dominant power in the Near East and provided a guaranteed access route to the "jewel in the crown of England," India. Four years later, after bombarding Alexandria, Britain occupied Cairo in order to protect the canal against an Egyptian nationalist leader, Ahmed Arabi. Thereafter the dual control of Cairo initiated by the French and British ended, and Egypt was virtually ruled by the British, first under Sir Evelyn

Baring (1883–1907) and later under General Lord Kitchener (1911–14). These proconsuls, as they have come to be called, worked to develop the economic stability of Egypt, abolished many practices objectionable to Europeans, and brought order to the administration of the Nile Valley. They also strengthened Britain's position in the area at the cost of other European powers and of the Egyptian nationalists. Between 1896 and 1898 Kitchener reconquered the Sudan, partly to suppress the dervishes but largely to ensure the Egyptian water supply. In September 1898 Kitchener moved well up the Nile and encountered Captain J. B. Marchand, who had placed a French force on the river at Fashoda in order to establish France's claim to the region. Kitchener was claiming the territory for Egypt by right of conquest, and ultimately, after the sharpest crisis in Anglo-French relations of the decade, Marchand was instructed by his government to withdraw. Thereafter British competition around and above the headwaters of the Nile was with the Germans.

Although these facts are not under dispute, their significance has been debated at length. Many historians hold that Britain expanded, as in the Sudan, solely in order to assure firm control over the strategically important regions to which the new conquests were tributary. Most recently three British scholars, Ronald Robinson, John Gallagher, and Alice Denny, in *Africa and the Victorians* (1961), have argued cogently that Britain acquired all of East Africa in an attempt to make safe the Suez Canal and, later, the Cape-to-Cairo communications route. Certainly there is no question that strategic considerations or purely diplomatic problems arising in European chanceries contributed to British intervention in many areas, and that the acquisition of colonies was sometimes an outgrowth of the chief power disputes in Europe. But one must also remember, in support of the commercial argument for imperial expansion, that the Suez Canal acquired its strategic importance largely because of the canal's relationship to Britain's economic interests in India and the Far East.

Recently historians also have stated in modified form the nineteenth-century view that a nation was like an organism: It could either grow or shrink, but it could not stand still. In the nineteenth century the Englishman Walter Bagehot saw a close relationship between certain physical laws and political behavior, and in the twentieth century Arnold Toynbee, another Englishman, spoke of the "dysgenic effects" at work in society, likened certain unprogressive peoples to vestigial organs, and argued that nations grew (or faltered) naturally in the face of recurrent cycles of challenge and response. One recent theory which is related to these views, and to the singularly influential conceptions of the British father of geopolitics, Halford John Mackinder, who was most active around the turn of the century, is the "vacant lands" thesis. This thesis holds that nations expanded into unpacified, unorganized, and unoccupied areas because vacant lands not only presented a potential power vacuum, but because one could not hope for orderly progress at the center unless the center dominated the periphery and because an occupied and controlled area inevitably was influenced by what happened in the unoccupied areas adjacent to it. Hence, the Americans had to occupy their western lands, pacify the Indians, and give way to the attractions of ever moving westward if the eastern seaboard of the nation was to mature. The same argument has been presented with respect to South Africa, Malaya, Canada, and to a lesser extent Australia.

The third major school of historians emphasizes neither commerce nor strategy but speaks rather of man's mind. Joseph Schumpeter, an economist, suggested as early as 1919 that the basic imperial thrust was a social atavism, coming from the simple, even primitive, psychological desire for power, for conquest, for dominance. In 1960 Elias Canetti refined this thesis to argue that men in a group of any sort—a missionary band, an army, or a nation— naturally seek to enforce the standards of their group upon others. Many rationalizations for the desire to persuade others to one's way of thought or way of life present themselves: because one's God will save others, because one's economy will make others prosperous, because one's political system will give others dignity. This is the most subtle source of imperial power, for it joins duty, morality, and the desire for power. Surely the British were, in the main, sincere about wishing to bring "good government," health, and a sound economy to natives whom they saw as children in need of guidance. In the twentieth century, in the midst of a wave of philosophical relativism, we reject (at least theoretically) such attempts to enforce the standards of one people upon another. But in 1957 a British administrator defended his nation's colonial policy by arguing that it had attempted to do for dependent territories only what the Marshall Plan and Point Four (and now the Peace Corps) attempt to do for underdeveloped lands. The desire to help others and the desire to demonstrate that one's own ideas are superior, to be benevolent and also paternal, lead readily to the desire to chastise, to dominate, to make anew a people in one's own image.

Finally, related to this psychological school are the historians who point out that no over-all generalization will cover the many reasons for European imperialism. Rather, they say, we must emphasize the individual explorer, the individual administrator, the individual Colonial Secretary, the "man-on-the-spot" and his psychology. They may argue that responsibility for British intervention in Malaya, for example, ultimately rests not with some vague cluster of ideas which may or may not have influenced men who themselves may or may not have been influential; responsibility in this case rests with one man, W. F. D. Jervois, then governor of the Straits Settlements, who through personal ambition, ignorance, and pride carried Britain into an area where Britain did not wish to go. This body of historians maintains that we must examine anew each instance of British, French, or German imperialism, to learn that some men are indeed motivated primarily by greed and others primarily by God. History, they remind us, is the essence of innumerable biographies. With Reinhold Niebuhr, they know that "goodness, armed with power, is corrupted; and pure love without power is destroyed."

Imperialism presents a problem which ultimately resides in that nebulous but all-important area known as "intellectual history" as much as within the more traditional bounds of political or diplomatic history. No collection of documents, however large, can present the ideas that stood behind what we so casually call "imperialism," and the following selection attempts only to provide evidence for various points of view. Those nations which have now emerged from colonial to independent status will long serve to remind us, as they remind themselves repeatedly, that because of imperialism Europe is no longer only a place—it is also an idea.

DOCUMENTS

1] Spokesmen for Empire

A] DISRAELI AT THE CRYSTAL PALACE, 1872

For Great Britain the "New Imperialism" traditionally is said to have begun with a speech by Benjamin Disraeli, then leader of the Conservative opposition, before a banquet audience at the Crystal Palace in London on June 24, 1872. British involvement already was clear in Africa, but when Disraeli came to power for the second time, early in 1874, he made imperialism his special preserve. His particular focus was India, and his Colonial Secretary, the fourth Earl Carnarvon, moved in his first year in office to acquire the Malay Peninsula and the Fiji Islands. In the Crystal Palace speech Disraeli made imperialism the keystone in the Tory arch. His primary concern, however, was to solidify the loyalty of the old empire—Canada, Australia, New Zealand, and South Africa—rather than to acquire new territories.*

If you look to the history of this country since the advent of Liberalism— forty years ago—you will find that there has been no effort so continuous, so subtle, supported by so much energy, and carried on with so much ability and acumen, as the attempts of Liberalism to effect the disintegration of the Empire of England. And, gentlemen, of all its efforts, this is the one which has been the nearest to success. Statesmen of the highest character, writers of the most distinguished ability, the most organised and efficient means, have been employed in this endeavour. It has been proved to all of us that we have lost money by our Colonies. It has been shown with precise, with mathematical demonstration, that there never was a jewel in the Crown of England that was so truly costly as the possession of India. How often has it been suggested that we should at once emancipate ourselves from this incubus! Well, that result was nearly accomplished. When those subtle views were adopted by the country under the plausible plea of granting self-government to the Colonies, I confess that I myself thought that the tie was broken. Not that I for one object to self-government; I cannot conceive how our distant Colonies can have their affairs administered except by self-government.

But self-government, in my opinion, when it was conceded, ought to have been conceded as part of a great policy of Imperial consolidation. It ought to have been accompanied by an Imperial tariff, by securities for the people of England for the enjoyment of the unappropriated lands which belonged

---

* From W. F. Monypenny and G. E. Buckle, *The Life of Benjamin Disraeli, Earl of Beaconsfield*, 1868–1876 (London: John Murray, 1920), Vol. V, pp. 194–96. Reprinted by permission of the publishers.

to the Sovereign as their trustee, and by a military code which should have precisely defined the means and the responsibilities by which the Colonies should be defended, and by which, if necessary, this country should call for aid from the Colonies themselves. It ought, further, to have been accompanied by the institution of some representative council in the metropolis, which would have brought the Colonies into constant and continuous relations with the Home Government. All this, however, was omitted because those who advised that policy—and I believe their convictions were sincere—looked upon the Colonies of England, looked even upon our connection with India, as a burden upon this country; viewing everything in a financial aspect, and totally passing by those moral and political considerations which make nations great, and by the influence of which alone men are distinguished from animals.

Well, what has been the result of this attempt during the reign of Liberalism for the disintegration of the Empire? It has entirely failed. But how has it failed? Through the sympathy of the Colonies for the Mother Country. They have decided that the Empire shall not be destroyed; and in my opinion no Minister in this country will do his duty who neglects any opportunity of reconstructing as much as possible our Colonial Empire, and of responding to those distant sympathies which may become the source of incalculable strength and happiness to this land.

. . .

The issue is not a mean one. It is whether you will be content to be a comfortable England, modelled and moulded upon Continental principles and meeting in due course an inevitable fate, or whether you will be a great country, an Imperial country, a country where your sons, when they rise, rise to paramount positions, and obtain not merely the esteem of their countrymen, but command the respect of the world.

B] CHAMBERLAIN ON BRITAIN'S DUTY IN EGYPT, 1890

The single most important new commitment by the British between 1878 and 1884 was to an imperial stance in Egypt. In 1882 the British occupied Cairo and set about reorganizing the chaotic Egyptian administration. Britain's desire to control Egypt and the Suez Canal, the lifeline of empire to India, the Far East, and the Pacific Islands, carried her deeper and deeper into East Africa. On March 24, 1890, Joseph Chamberlain, a Liberal, justified Britain's presence in Egypt in an address to the West Birmingham Liberal Unionist Association.*

I want to say a word or two to you about the future. I am going to make a confession. I admit I was one of those—I think my views were shared by

* From Joseph Chamberlain, *Foreign and Colonial Speeches* (London: George Routledge and Sons, 1897), pp. 41–44.

the whole Cabinet of Mr. Gladstone—who regretted the necessity for the occupation of Egypt. I thought that England had so much to do, such enormous obligations and responsibilities, that we might well escape, if we could, this addition to them; and, when the occupation was forced upon us, I looked forward with anxiety to an early, it might be even, to an immediate evacuation. The confession I have to make is that having seen what are the results of this occupation, having seen what is the nature of the task we have undertaken, and what progress we have already made towards its accomplishment, I have changed my mind. (Cheers.) I say it would be unworthy of this great nation if we did not rise to the full height of our duty, and complete our work before we left the country. (Cheers.) We have no right to abandon the duty which has been cast upon us, and the work which already shows so much promise for the advantage of the people with whose destinies we have become involved.

This great alteration is due to the influence of a mere handful of your fellow-countrymen, a few scores of Englishmen acting under Sir Evelyn Baring, our Minister at Cairo. They, by their persevering devotion, and their single-minded honesty, have wrought out this great work, and have brought Egypt from a condition which may fairly be described as one of ruin, to the promise of once more being restored to its ancient prosperity. I hear sometimes of pessimists who think the work of England is accomplished, who will tell you that we have lost the force and the capacity to govern. No; that is not true; and as long as we can spare from our abundance men like these, who, after all, are only ordinary Englishmen—men like these, who are able and willing to carry their zeal and their intelligence wherever it may conduce to the service of humanity, and to the honour of their native land—so long as we can do that we need not despair of the future of the United Kingdom. (Cheers.) But we owe it to them, we owe it to ourselves, that their work shall not be in vain. You cannot revolutionise a country like Egypt—you cannot reform all that is wrong in her system, all that is poor and weak in the character of the people—in a few minutes, or a few years. Egypt has been submitted for centuries to arbitrary despotism. I believe there is hardly any time in her history, even if you go back to almost prehistoric ages, when she has not been in the grasp of some foreign ruler; and, under these circumstances, you cannot expect to find ready to your hands a self-governing people. They are not able—they cannot be able—to stand alone; and they do not wish to stand alone. They ask for your support and assistance, and, without it, it is absolutely impossible that their welfare can be secured. If you were to abandon your responsibility, your retirement would be followed by an attempt once more to restore the old arbitrary methods and the old abuses, which in turn would no doubt be followed by anarchy and disorder; and then in time there would be again a foreign intervention, this time the intervention of some other European country. I have too much confidence in the public spirit of the country to believe that it will ever neglect a national duty. (Hear, hear.) A nation is like an individual; it has duties which it must fulfil, or else it cannot live honoured and respected as a nation. (Loud cheers.)

c] Bismarck Advocates Imperial Growth, 1884

Portugal, Spain, and France had preceded Britain into imperial power in the seventeenth century. By the end of the eighteenth, Britain had displaced these powers and now dominated the world overseas. The American Revolution divested Britain of its early empire at approximately the same time another empire—based on India, Singapore, and Australasia—was rising. The Dutch, too, had acquired extensive colonial possessions, especially in Southeast Asia. After 1870 both Asia and Africa became the imperial goals of a resurgent France, and Africa in particular (and belatedly) drew the attention of Germany and Italy. The molder of modern Germany, Prince Otto von Bismarck, was at first an anticolonialist, concentrating on German unification. By 1884, however, as the following précis of his address to the Reichstag on June 23 shows, he was prepared to enter the colonial race.*

[I]t would not be right for Germany to occupy land where we have no interests. . . . It is another matter to place under the protection of the German Reich the free settlements of German citizens in areas which are not under the acknowledged sovereignty of other nations. The Reich Chancellor holds it to be an imperial duty to give her protection to overseas settlements by German citizens, not only to their factories but also to the territory they have acquired.

2] Motives for Imperialism

a] Racism

Justifications for empire and for imperialism were many and varied. Under the impact of vulgarized and popularized forms of Charles Darwin's *Origin of Species*, first published in 1859, the prevailing climate of opinion focused increasingly on catch phrases such as "survival of the fittest" and "lesser breeds." Some argued that an empire was akin to an organism in that it must grow or die. Others spoke of proven Anglo-Saxon superiority. Certainly racism was one thrust to imperial expansion. Sir Harry Johnston, British explorer and administrator in Central and East Africa, represents racism in its less virulent form.†

[L]et us proceed to define who and what these backward or unprogressive peoples are and to what extent they may be considered to be retrograde and

* Translated by Robin W. Winks from the *Norddeutschen Allgemeinen Zeitung*. Reprinted in Hans Delbrück, ed., *Das Staatsarchiv: Sammlung der officiellen Actenstücke zur Geschichte der Gegenwart* (Leipzig: Duncker & Humblot, 1884), pp. 361–64.

† From Sir Harry Johnston, *The Backward Peoples and Our Relations with Them* (London: Humphrey Milford, Oxford University Press, 1920), pp. 7–9. Reprinted by permission of the publishers.

ineffective as compared with the dominating white race. The chief and obvious distinction between the backward and the forward peoples is that the former, with the exception of about 20,000,000 in the Mediterranean basin and the Near East, are of coloured skin; while the latter are white-skinned or, as in the case of the Japanese and the inhabitants of Northern China, nearly white.

I think if we took all the factors into consideration—religion, education (especially knowledge concerning the relations between this planet and the universe of which it is a minute speck, the history and geography of the planet, the sciences that are a part of earth-study), standard of living, respect for sanitation, infant death rate, bodily strength, manner of government, regard for law and order, position in agriculture and manufactures,—we might appraise mathematically, according to the following ratio, the principal nations and peoples into which humanity is divided:—

100 per cent.

1. Great Britain and Ireland, Canada and Newfoundland, White Australia, New Zealand, White South Africa (south of the Zambezi), Malta and Mauritius, United States, France, Corsica, much of Algeria and Tunis, Belgium and Luxembourg, Holland, Germany, Austria, Chekho-Slovakia, Italy, Switzerland, Hungary, Norway, Sweden, Denmark and Iceland, Finland, Esthonia, Spain, Chile, Argentina, Japan

98 per cent.

2. Poland and Lithuania, Serbia and Croatia, Bulgaria, Rumania, Portugal, Greece, Cyprus, Brazil, Peru, Colombia, British Guiana, French and Dutch Guiana, British and French West Indies, Cuba and Porto Rico, Hawaii, Uruguay

97 per cent.

3. Russia, Russian Siberia, Russian Central Asia, the Caucasus, Egypt, British India, French Indo-China, Siam, British Malaysia, Mexico, Central America, Bolivia, Venezuela, Ecuador, Paraguay, Java, . . . Armenia

95 per cent.

4. Albania, Asia Minor, Morocco, Southern Algeria, Tripoli, Palestine, Syria, Persia, China, Tibet, Afghanistan, Zanzibar

90 per cent.

5. Madagascar, Black South Africa, French West Africa, British West Africa, Uganda, British Central and East Africa, Sumatra, Borneo, the Philippines, the Anglo-Egyptian Sudan, Angōla, Santo Domingo

80 per cent.

6. Abyssina, Arabia, Portuguese East Africa, the Belgian Congo, Portuguese Congo, Liberia, Haiti, Celebes, Timor, New Caledonia, British Papua

75 per cent.

7. Dutch New Guinea and New Hebrides, Portuguese Guinea, French Central Africa

This rough estimate of civilization and culture does not imply that the nations or peoples which are classed together resemble one another in all their stages of culture. Some will excel in one direction, some in another. In certain directions a people may be very forward, coupled with retrograde features which reduce their average value.

Obviously, the foremost nations in the world at the present day are Britain and the regions of the British Empire in which the white race predominates; the United States; France; and Germany,—not only by the numbers of their peoples and the degree of their national wealth, but by their industry, commerce and the proportion of educated to uneducated people in their population. In all elements of greatness, but not in potency of numbers, Denmark, Sweden, Norway, Finland, Holland, Luxembourg and Belgium, are on an equal footing. From their magnificent parts in history, one would like to class Spain, Portugal and Italy with these powers of the first rank. . . .

It is the peoples of 95 per cent. to 90 per cent. that may be put in the unprogressive or retrograde class, unable at present to govern themselves in a manner conducive to progress; while those that are graded 80 and 75 per cent. still contain in their midst elements of sheer savagery. Such regions, if left alone by the controlling white man, might easily relapse into the unprofitable barbarism out of which they have been lifted with the white man's efforts during the past fifty years.

B] DUTY

Victorians thrilled to the call of duty in a way at once admirable and dangerous. Indeed, of all the rationalizations for imperial expansion, surely the one most widely accepted was the doctrine of stewardship. Stemming from St. Thomas Aquinas, this doctrine held that godly men were but stewards who held in trust the good that was to come until such time as human beings were sufficiently advanced morally to receive God's universal word. The British would act as trustees for the "backward peoples" until they were ready, through colonial tutelage, for some form of self government. Sir Frederick Lugard, British explorer and administrator, justified the mandate system in this way.*

It has been well said that a nation, like an individual, must have some task higher than the pursuit of material gain, if it is to escape the benumbing influence of parochialism and to fulfil its higher destiny. If high standards

* From Sir Frederick Dealtry Lugard, *The Dual Mandate in British Tropical Africa* (Edinburgh and London: William Blackwood & Sons, 1922), pp. 58–61. Reprinted by permission of the publishers.

are maintained, the control of subject races must have an effect on national character which is not measurable in terms of material profit and loss. And what is true for the nation is equally true for the individual officers employed. If lower standards are adopted—the arrogant display of power, or the selfish pursuit of profit—the result is equally fatal to the nation and to the individual. . . .

But if the standard which the white man must set before him when dealing with uncivilised races must be a high one for the sake of his own moral and spiritual balance, it is not less imperative for the sake of the influence which he exercises upon those over whom he is set in authority. The white man's prestige must stand high when a few score are responsible for the control and guidance of millions. His courage must be undoubted, his word and pledge absolutely inviolate, his sincerity transparent. There is no room for "mean whites" in tropical Africa. Nor is there room for those who, however high their motives, are content to place themselves on the same level as the uncivilised races. They lower the prestige by which alone the white races can hope to govern and to guide.

Turning now to questions of economic policy, we find that the two chief Powers have adopted radically different principles in Africa. The French . . . adopt "a sort of economic nationalism," which aims at preserving the products and markets of her colonies for the exclusive use of France by every means in her power. It was . . . only in certain specified colonies, for a limited period, and as the price of territorial adjustments in her favour, that she agreed to break down the tariff wall.

This principle is regarded as essential to the theory that her colonies form an integral part of France, mutually interdependent and sufficing. After the war of 1870, and again [in 1917], the doctrine was proclaimed that "France can only remain a great Power by knowing how to draw from her colonies all she requires."

.   .   .

When Great Britain undertook the control of great regions in tropical Africa, she not only gave to her commercial rivals the same opportunities as were enjoyed by her own nationals, but she assisted in the development of these territories from Imperial revenues—not as loans to be repaid when they grew rich, but as free gifts—and later by the use of Imperial credit to float loans for development, while her Navy, and on occasion her troops, ensured their protection. She secured to their inhabitants an unrestricted market for their produce, and to all engaged in their development, of whatever nationality, equality of commercial opportunity and uniform laws.

She recognised that the custodians of the tropics are, in the words of Mr Chamberlain, "trustees of civilisation for the commerce of the world"; that their raw materials and foodstuffs—without which civilisation cannot exist—must be developed alike in the interests of the natives and of the world at large, without any artificial restrictions. . . . [T]he tropics are the heritage of mankind, and neither, on the one hand, has the suzerain Power a right to their exclusive exploitation, nor, on the other hand, have the races which inhabit them a right to deny their bounties to those who need them. The responsibility for adequate development rests on the custodian on behalf of civilisation—and not on behalf of civilisation alone, for much of these products is returned to the tropics converted into articles for the use and comfort of its peoples.

The democracies of to-day claim the right to work, and the satisfaction of that claim is impossible without the raw materials of the tropics on the one hand and their markets on the other. Increased production is more than ever necessary now, to enable England to pay the debts she incurred in preserving the liberties of the world. The merchant, the miner, and the manufacturer do not enter the tropics on sufferance, or employ their technical skill, their energy, and their capital as "interlopers," or as "greedy capitalists," but in fulfilment of the mandate of civilisation. . . .

. . . The tropics can only be successfully developed if the interests of the controlling Power are identical with those of the natives of the country, and it seeks no individual advantage, and imposes no restriction for its own benefit.

c] God

Many men went to the tropics God-impelled. To save souls was imperative. The problem was: By which dogma might they be saved? Lugard was friendly to the missionary impulse, but secular, or Colonial Office, conceptions of stewardship ultimately were to be given priority.*

The beneficial effect of Mission work in Africa is marred—no less than religious work in Christian countries—by sectarian rivalries and differences in teaching. The antagonism between the Protestants and Roman Catholics . . . was no doubt accentuated by national rivalry, and resulted . . . in actual war [in Uganda]. Elsewhere it is often disguised under a thin veneer.

The special dogmas of the "Memnonite [sic] Brothers in Christ," the "Pentecostal Missions," and many others, confuse the African, and have no doubt encouraged that secessional movement which in West Africa has led to the establishment of various African Churches in which polygamy is recognised, or some other departure from orthodoxy is introduced.

.   .   .

Some few Missions carry the ideal of the equality of man to a point which the intelligence of the primitive savage does not appreciate in its true sig-

* From Sir Frederick Dealtry Lugard, *The Dual Mandate in British Tropical Africa* (Edinburgh and London: William Blackwood & Sons, 1922), pp. 588–89. Reprinted by permission of the publishers.

nificance. That a white man should come to Africa to do menial work in the furtherance of an altruistic ideal is not comprehensible to him, and the result is merely to destroy the missionary's own influence for good, and to lessen the prestige of Europeans, upon which the avoidance of bloodshed and the maintenance of law and order so largely depend in Africa.

The Colonial Office issued a regulation towards the close of the war that missionaries must obtain sanction before proceeding to West Africa. Its object, no doubt, was not primarily concerned with the financial position or the physical fitness of the applicant and his family for life in the tropics, but these things merit attention too. We read of the arrival of a ship with "several small children, being taken by their parents to stations many miles from medical aid, there to stay for two or three years"; of a missionary and his wife whose joint salary, in these times of excessive prices, was £160 per annum—too poor to buy meat. I recollect a case of a missionary too poor to take his dying wife out of the country. These things do not promote the cause of the gospel. They do harm.

d] ROMANCE

Romance and adventure, the lure of the exotic, the desire to escape the commonplace drew many into the distant realm of the nineteenth-century world. Novelists contributed to imperial sentiment, especially for the armchair imperialist and pub-room diplomatist, and H. Rider Haggard in particular carried his readers vicariously to the world's four corners. His most popular novel, *King Solomon's Mines* (1885), contained a scene he was to repeat in other novels: the ignorant savage put to rout by the cool and courageous adventurer.*

"Have they not told thee how we strike with death from afar?" I [said].

"They have told me, but I believe them not. Let me see you kill. Kill me a man among those who stand yonder"—and he pointed to the opposite side of the kraal—"and I will believe."

"Nay," I answered; "we shed no blood of man except in just punishment; but if thou wilt see, bid thy servants drive in an ox through the kraal gates, and before he has run twenty paces I will strike him dead."

"Nay," laughed the king, "kill me a man, and I will believe."

"Good, O king, so be it," I answered, coolly; "do thou walk across the open space, and before thy feet reach the gate thou shalt be dead; or, if thou wilt not, send thy son Scragga." . . .

On hearing this suggestion Scragga gave a sort of howl, and bolted into the hut.

Twala frowned majestically; the suggestion did not please him.

"Let a young ox be driven in," he said.

* The extract from *King Solomon's Mines* by H. Rider Haggard [London, Cassell & Co., 1885] by permission of his Executors and Cassell & Co., Ltd. [Pp. 144–50.]

Two men at once departed, running swiftly.

"Now, Sir Henry," said I, "do you shoot. I want to show this ruffian that I am not the only magician of the party."

. . .

Then came a pause, till presently we caught sight of an ox running straight for the kraal gate. It came on through the gate, and then, catching sight of the vast concourse of people, stopped stupidly, turned round, and bellowed.

"Now's your time," I whispered.

Up went the rifle.

Bang! thud! and the ox was kicking on his back, shot in the ribs. The semi-hollow bullet had done its work well, and a sigh of astonishment went up from the assembled thousands.

I turned coolly round—

"Have I lied, O king?"

"Nay, white man, it is a truth," was the somewhat awed answer.

"Listen, Twala," I went on. "Thou hast seen. Now know we come in peace, not in war. See here" (and I held up the Winchester repeater); "here is a hollow staff that shall enable you to kill even as we kill, only this charm I lay upon it, thou shalt kill no man with it. If thou liftest it against a man, it shall kill thee. Stay, I will show thee. Bid a man step forty paces and place the shaft of a spear in the ground so that the flat blade looks toward us."

In a few seconds it was done.

"Now, see, I will break the spear."

Taking a careful sight, I fired. The bullet struck the flat of the spear and broke the blade into fragments.

Again the sigh of astonishment went up.

"Now, Twala" (handing him the rifle), "this magic tube we give to thee, and by and by I will show thee how to use it; but beware how thou usest the magic of the stars against a man of earth," and I handed him the rifle. He took it very gingerly, and laid it down at his feet. As he did so I observed [a] wizened, monkey-like figure creeping up from the shadow of the hut. It crept on all fours, but when it reached the place where the king sat it rose upon its feet, and, throwing the furry covering off its face, revealed a most extraordinary and weird countenance. It was (apparently) that of a woman of great age, so shrunken that in size it was no larger than that of a year-old child, and was made up of a collection of deep, yellow wrinkles. . . . [T]he whole countenance might have been taken for that of a sun-dried corpse had it not been for a pair of large black eyes, still full of fire and intelligence, which gleamed and played under the snow-white eyebrows and the projecting parchment-colored skull, like jewels in a charnel-house. As for the skull itself, it was perfectly bare, and yellow in hue, while its wrinkled scalp moved and contracted like the hood of a cobra.

The figure to whom this fearful countenance, which caused a shiver of fear to pass through us as we gazed on it, belonged stood still for a moment, and then suddenly projected a skinny claw armed with nails nearly an inch long, and laid it on the shoulder of Twala, the king, and began to speak in a thin, piercing voice:

"Listen, O king! Listen, O people! Listen, O mountains and plains and rivers, home of the Kukuana race! Listen, O skies and sun, O rain and storm and mist! Listen, all things that live and must die! Listen, all dead things that must live again—again to die! Listen, the spirit of life is in me, and I prophesy. I prophesy! I prophesy!"

The words died away in a faint wail, and terror seemed to seize upon the hearts of all who heard them, including ourselves. The old woman was very terrible.

"*Blood! blood! blood!* rivers of blood; blood everywhere. I see it, I smell it, I taste it—it is salt; it runs red upon the ground, it rains down from the skies.

"*Footsteps! footsteps! footsteps!* the tread of the white man coming from afar. It shakes the earth; the earth trembles before her master."

.   .   .

Here the features of this extraordinary creature became convulsed, and she fell to the ground foaming in an epileptic fit and was carried off into the hut.

The king rose up trembling, and waved his hand. Instantly the regiments began to file off, and in ten minutes, save for ourselves, the king, and a few attendants, the great space was left clear.

"White people," he said, "it passes in my mind to kill ye. . . . What say ye?"

I laughed. "Be careful, O king, we are not easy to slay. Thou hast seen the fate of the ox; wouldst thou be as the ox?"

The king frowned. "It is not well to threaten a king."

"We threaten not, we speak what is true. Try to kill us, O king, and learn."

The great man put his hand to his forehead.

"Go in peace," he said, at length. "To-night is the great dance. Ye shall see it. Fear not that I shall set a snare for ye. To-morrow I shall think."

"It is well, O king," I answered, unconcernedly, and then, accompanied by Infadoos, we rose and went back to our kraal.

E] PRIDE

A sense of pride arose from the empire and spurred men to new efforts. Empire fed upon empire. Rudyard Kipling, the unofficial poet laureate of imperial growth, dedicated "If," his rousing challenge to be up and be doing, to Dr. L. S. Jameson, an unscrupulous empire-builder, and it was W. E. Henley, author of the century's stirring declaration, "I am the master of my

fate; / I am the captain of my soul," who found Haggard his publisher for
King Solomon's Mines. None of Kipling's poems spoke of imperial pride more
clearly than "The Song of the Cities" (1893).*

THE SONG OF THE CITIES

Bombay

Royal and Dower-royal, I the Queen
    Fronting thy richest sea with richer hands—
A thousand mills roar through me where I glean
    All races from all lands.

Calcutta

Me the Sea-captain loved, the River built,
    Wealth sought and Kings adventured life to hold.
Hail, England! I am Asia—Power on silt,
    Death in my hands, but Gold!

.   .   .

Rangoon

Hail, Mother! Do they call me rich in trade?
    Little care I, but hear the shorn priest drone,
And watch my silk-clad lovers, man by maid,
    Laugh 'neath my Shwe Dagon.

Singapore

Hail, Mother! East and West must seek my aid
    Ere the spent gear may dare the ports afar.
The second doorway of the wide world's trade
    Is mine to loose or bar.

Hong-Kong

Hail, Mother! Hold me fast; my Praya sleeps
    Under innumerable keels to-day.
Yet guard (and landward), or to-morrow sweeps
    Thy war-ships down the bay!

Halifax

Into the mist my guardian prows put forth,
    Behind the mist my virgin ramparts lie,
The Warden of the Honour of the North,
    Sleepless and veiled am I!

* From *Rudyard Kipling's Verse: Inclusive Edition*. Reprinted by permission of Mrs.
George Bambridge and Doubleday & Company, Inc. "The Song of the Cities" by Rudyard
Kipling from *The Seven Seas* by permission of Mrs. George Bambridge, the Macmillan
Company of Canada, Ltd., and Methuen & Co. Ltd.

Quebec and Montreal

Peace is our portion. Yet a whisper rose,
  Foolish and causeless, half in jest, half hate.
Now wake we and remember mighty blows,
  And, fearing no man, wait!

Victoria

From East to West the circling word has passed,
  Till West is East beside our land-locked blue;
From East to West the tested chain holds fast,
  The well-forged link rings true!

Cape Town

Hail! Snatched and bartered oft from hand to hand,
  I dream my dream, by rock and heath and pine,
Of Empire to the northward. Ay, one land
  From Lion's Head to Line!

Melbourne

Greeting! Nor fear nor favour won us place,
  Got between greed of gold and dread of drouth,
Loud-voiced and reckless as the wild tide-race
  That whips our harbour-mouth!

Sydney

Greeting! My birth-stain have I turned to good;
  Forcing strong wills perverse to steadfastness:
The first flush of the tropics in my blood,
  And at my feet Success!

Brisbane

The northern strip beneath the southern skies—
  I build a Nation for an Empire's need,
Suffer a little, and my land shall rise,
  Queen over lands indeed!

.   .   .

Auckland

Last, loneliest, loveliest, exquisite, apart—
  On us, on us the unswerving season smiles,
Who wonder 'mid our fern why men depart
  To seek the Happy Isles!

F] COMMERCE

But there were men who would admit that race, romance, and religion, or
even pride and duty, were not the chief sources of the imperial processional.
Lugard himself recognized that commerce stood behind much of the imperial
movement.*

The Chambers of Commerce of the United Kingdom have unanimously
urged the retention of East Africa on the grounds of commercial advantage.
The Presidents of the London and Liverpool chambers attended a deputation [October 20, 1892] to her Majesty's Minister for Foreign Affairs to urge
"the absolute necessity, for the prosperity of this country, that new avenues
for commerce such as that in East Equatorial Africa should be opened up,
in view of the hostile tariffs with which British manufactures are being everywhere confronted." Manchester followed with a similar declaration; Glasgow,
Birmingham, Edinburgh, and other commercial centres gave it as their opinion that "there is practically no middle course for this country, between a
reversal of the free-trade policy to which it is pledged, on the one hand, and
a prudent but continuous territorial extension for the creation of new markets, on the other hand." Such is the view of the Chambers of Commerce,
and I might quote endless paragraphs from their resolutions and reports in
the same sense.

. . . The "Scramble for Africa" by the nations of Europe—an incident
without parallel in the history of the world—was due to the growing commercial rivalry, which brought home to civilised nations the vital necessity
of securing the only remaining fields for industrial enterprise and expansion.
It is well, then, to realise that it is for our *advantage*—and not alone at the
dictates of duty—that we have undertaken responsibilities in East Africa. It
is in order to foster the growth of the trade of this country, and to find an
outlet for our manufactures and our surplus energy, that our far-seeing statesmen and our commercial men advocate colonial expansion.

Money spent in such extension is circulated for the ultimate advantage
of the masses. It is, then, beside the mark to argue that while there is want
and misery at home money should not be spent in Africa. It has yet to be
proved that the most effective way of relieving poverty permanently, and in
accordance with sound political economy, is by distributing half-pence in the
street. If our advent in Africa introduces civilisation, peace, and good government, abolishes the slave-trade, and effects other advantages for Africa,
it must not be therefore supposed that this was our sole and only aim in
going there. However greatly such objects may weigh with a large and powerful section of the nation, I do not believe that in these days our national

* From Sir Frederick Dealtry Lugard, *The Rise of Our East African Empire: Early
Efforts in Nyasaland and Uganda* (Edinburgh and London: William Blackwood & Sons,
1893), Vol. I, pp. 379–82. Reprinted by permission of the publishers.

policy is based on motives of philanthropy only. Though these may be our *duties*, it is quite possible that here (as frequently if not generally is the case) advantage may run parallel with duty. There are some who say we have no *right* in Africa at all, that "it belongs to the natives." I hold that our right is the necessity that is upon us to provide for our ever-growing population—either by opening new fields for emigration, or by providing work and employment which the development of over-sea extension entails —and to stimulate trade by finding new markets, since we know what misery trade depression brings at home.

While thus serving our own interests as a nation, we may, by selecting men of the right stamp for the control of new territories, bring at the same time many advantages to Africa. Nor do we deprive the natives of their birth-right of freedom, to place them under a foreign yoke. It has ever been the key-note of British colonial method to rule through and by the natives, and it is this method, in contrast to the arbitrary and uncompromising rule of Germany, France, Portugal, and Spain, which has been the secret of our success as a colonising nation, and has made us welcomed by tribes and peoples in Africa, who ever rose in revolt against the other nations named. In Africa, moreover, there is among the people a natural inclination to submit to a higher authority. That intense detestation of control which animates our Teutonic races does not exist among the tribes of Africa . . . and if there is any authority that we replace, it is the authority of the Slavers and Arabs, or the intolerable tyranny of the "dominant tribe."

G] POWER

A lust for power, neither pure nor simple, also moved many men. Wilfrid Scawen Blunt, a poet who once had been in the British diplomatic service, but who had turned to advocating Irish and Indian Home Rule, recorded one such reaction in his diary. George Wyndham, whom Blunt quotes, was a brilliant young Tory who eventually became Chief Secretary for Ireland.*

"*17th Oct.* [1898]—. . . I have had it out with George [Wyndham] about Fashoda. He states the English case with brutal frankness. 'The day of talking,' he says, 'about legality in Africa is over, all the international law there is there consists of interests and understandings. It is generally agreed by all the Powers that the end of African operations is to "civilize" it in the interests of Europe, and that to gain that end all means are good. The only difference between England and France is which of them is to do it in which particular districts. England intends to do it on the Nile, and it makes no difference what the precise legal position is. We may put forward the Khedive's rights if it is convenient or we may put forward a right of conquest,

* From Wilfrid Scawen Blunt, *My Diaries: Being a Personal Narrative of Events, 1888–1914* (London: Martin Secker, 1919), Part I, pp. 368–69, 464. Printed by permission of the Syndics of the Fitzwilliam Museum, Cambridge, England, and Alfred A. Knopf, Inc.

or a right of simply declaring our intentions. One is as good as another to get our end, which is the railway from Cairo to the Cape. We don't care whether the Nile is called English or Egyptian or what it is called, but we mean to have it and we don't mean the French to have it. The Khedive may be kept on for some years as a sort of Indian Maharajah, but it will end in a partition of the Ottoman Empire between England, Germany, and Russia, France will be allowed North-western Africa. It is not worth while drawing distinctions of right and wrong in the matter, it is a matter entirely of interest.'

"This of course is the true thought of our Government, and has been for at least ten years, but for the first time to-day it is beginning to be avowed. George represents all that is most extreme, most outrageous, in modern English politics, and it marks the decline of the higher traditions to find one like him proclaiming and defending it. . . . The dispute between France and England is a dispute between rival card sharpers, and the very best thing that can happen is that they should beat in each other's heads.

. . .

"*22nd Dec.* [1900]—The old century is very nearly out, and leaves the world in a pretty pass, and the British Empire is playing the devil in it as never an empire before on so large a scale. We may live to see its fall. All the nations of Europe are making the same hell upon earth in China, massacring and pillaging and raping in the captured cities as outrageously as in the Middle Ages. The Emperor of Germany gives the word for slaughter and the Pope looks on and approves. In South Africa our troops are burning farms under [Horatio Herbert Lord] Kitchener's command, and the Queen and the two Houses of Parliament, and the bench of bishops thank God publicly and vote money for the work. The Americans are spending fifty millions a year on slaughtering the Filipinos; the King of the Belgians has invested his whole fortune on the Congo, where he is brutalizing the negroes to fill his pockets. The French and Italians for the moment are playing a less prominent part in the slaughter, but their inactivity grieves them. The whole white race is revelling openly in violence, as though it had never pretended to be Christian. God's equal curse be on them all! So ends the famous nineteenth century into which we were so proud to have been born."

3] The Scramble for Empire: Why?

A] GERMANY, WAKE UP! 1890

The British often insisted that they annexed areas only in order to keep them from falling to a European rival, which would upset the balance of power in Europe. Certainly this was true in many, though not in all, instances. In particular, Britain was concerned with the growth of German industrial strength after 1880; by the final decade of the nineteenth century Germany clearly was the chief power on the Continent. In 1890 the British gave Germany Heligoland in exchange for recognition of a British protectorate over Zanzibar and Pemba. The Kaiser had dropped his pilot, Bismarck, by then, and the German imperialists, led by Dr. Karl Peters, attacked the earlier German policy of attempting to retain British friendship by assuming second-rate imperial status in Africa. The following advertisement appeared in the Cologne *Zeitung* in June 1890.*

The diplomacy of the English works swiftly and secretly. What they created burst in the face of the astonished world on June 18 like a bomb—the German-English African Treaty. With one stroke of the pen—the hope of a great German colonial empire was ruined. . . . Shall this treaty really be? No, no, and again no. The German people must arise as one and declare that this treaty is unacceptable! . . . Men of all parties who, in this situation, think of themselves only as Germans wish to take the matter into their hands. The Reichstag will, we hope, go to the government with an overpowering majority and say: The treaty with England harms our interests and wounds our honor; this time it *dares* not become a reality! We are ready at the call of our Kaiser to step into the ranks and allow ourselves dumbly and obediently to be led against the enemy's shots, but we may also demand in exchange that the reward come to us which is worth the sacrifice, and this reward is: that we shall be a conquering people which takes its portion of the world itself, and does not seek to receive it by the grace and benevolence of another people.

Deutschland wach auf!

b] Jules Ferry Defends the French Empire, 1890

The French also were interested in Africa and Asia, and Jules Ferry, who had served twice as premier of the Third Republic, and who had annexed Tunisia, defended French expansion when writing of Tonkin (Indochina) in 1890.†

Colonial policy is the child of the Industrial Revolution. For rich states, where capital is abundant and accumulates rapidly . . . exports are an essential factor in public prosperity, and the scope for employing capital, as well as the demand for labor, depend upon the foreign market. If it had

* From O. Bonhard, *Geschichte des Alldeutschen Verbandes* (Berlin, 1920), p. 2. Translated by Mildred S. Wertheimer in M. S. Wertheimer, *The Pan-German League, 1890–1914* (*Studies in History, Economics and Public Law*, Vol. CXII) (New York: Columbia University Press, 1924), pp. 31–32. Reprinted by permission of the publishers.

† Translated by Robin W. Winks from Jules Ferry, *Le Tonkin et la mère-patrie: Témoignages et documents*, 15th ed. (Paris: Victor-Havard, 1890), pp. 40–44.

been possible to establish among the chief industrial nations some method-ical and rational division of production, according to national aptitudes, eco-nomic conditions, and natural and social differences . . . Europe might not have had to seek markets for its products elsewhere. But today everyone wants to do his own spinning and weaving, forging and distilling. All of Europe makes sugar, for example, and must then attempt to export it. Upon the arrival on the scene of the last industrial giants—the United States on the one hand, Germany on the other, as well as the advent of the smaller states, once sleepy or exhausted, such as regenerated Italy, Spain enriched by French capital, the enterprising and shrewd Swiss—all of the West, with Russia now preparing to expand, is engaged in the industrial life in all its forms and cannot turn back.

On the other side of the Vosges and across the Atlantic the rise of pro-tectionism has multiplied the number of manufactured goods, suppressed traditional markets, and thrown all the markets of Europe into formidable competition. Each country defends itself by raising its own tariff barrier, but that is not sufficient. . . .

The protective system is a steam engine without a safety valve, unless cor-rected and accompanied by a serious and sane colonial policy. An excess of capital engaged in industry not only diminishes the profits from capital but also arrests the rise of wages. . . . Social peace in this industrial age de-pends upon markets. The economic crisis which has hung heavily over Euro-pean labor since 1876 or 1877, with its frequent, long, harmful strikes, al-ready formidable today, is only the sad symptom, coinciding in France, in Germany, and in England, of the same notable and persistent drop in ex-ports. . . . The European consumer market is saturated, and unless we de-clare modern society a failure and prepare in the dawn of the twentieth cen-tury for the liquidation of our society by revolution, new consumer markets will have to be created in all parts of the world. . . .

Colonial policy is an international manifestation of the eternal laws of competition.

c] GEORGE GOLDIE MOVES TO ELIMINATE THE FRENCH, 1894

Competition with the French definitely promoted British expansion in Africa, as the following instructions, written on July 24, 1894, by Sir George Goldie, Deputy Governor of the Royal Niger Company, to then Captain Frederick D. Lugard, show. Goldie wished to consolidate British claims to the Niger River and West Africa in general.*

* From the Lugard Papers, Bodleian Library, Oxford University, as quoted in Margery Perham and Mary Bull, eds., *The Diaries of Lord Lugard*, Vol. IV: *Nigeria, 1894–5 and 1898* (London: Faber and Faber, 1963), pp. 58–59. Reprinted by permission of the publishers.

[W]e want treaties *south* and *west* of Say, even with people who are really tributary to Gandu. In your itinerary westwards it may be necessary for you to zig-zag a good deal, so as to run networks of treaties across and between the few treaties obtained by [Colonel Parfait-Louis] Monteil, Crozat and (in a portion of your region) [Lieutenant Louis-Gustave] Binger, for France.

The last sentence conveys the objects of your journey. France has obtained a few treaties with powerful chiefs on the strength of which she claims immense regions in the great bend of the Niger, known in France as 'le boucle du Niger'. Yet although her own rights in these vast regions are so slight and unfounded, she sends her adventurers into a recognized British Sphere to make treaties with persons who are undoubtedly subjects or tributaries of kings having treaties with England, and she defends this policy in the only possible manner by asserting the independence of these subject or tributary princes. I do not think that in your journey westward you will need to follow her example; as it is probable that great numbers of tribes and States are really quite independent of the chiefs with whom the French explorers have made treaties. I do not for a moment anticipate that you will be able to found a continuous British Protectorate from the Niger to Long. 4° W. It will be sufficient to secure great numbers of small regions, which can be reached by strips (however narrow and however circuitous) either from Gandu or Borgu or Illorin or the Gold Coast Colony—including the Neutral Zone, over which free transit exists. Your objects will therefore be as follows:—

a. In places where the French pretend that they have made treaties, to obtain a written declaration from the rulers that such statements are false, and then to make treaties for us.

b. In places where no such pretence has been made, to secure treaties accompanied by a short declaration that no previous treaties have been made with any European. Wherever you cannot obtain a written declaration in Hausa, or some other language which your interpreter can read, you had better have the verbal declaration written in English and after carefully explaining each point to the chief, ask him to set his X to it and have that mark duly attested by your companions.

c. To collect the fullest information as to the extent (mileage in every direction) of the jurisdiction of *all* the above places, so as to enable the fullest claims to be made for British rights and proper limits to be set to the pretensions of France.

d. To collect general information of every kind about the regions you visit, which you will remember is one of the most important objects of your expedition, but especially to make inquiries as to the existence of gold, either alluvial or in reefs, and to bring home for investigation any specimens of rock or sand which the natives assure you contain gold. The gradual lightening of your loads as you proceed will enable you to do this on a considerable scale.

e. To check Mr. [Guy N.] Mottram's astronomical observations by your own calculations of your marches, and to insist on his taking as many independent observations as possible in each place so that mistakes can be rejected.

f. To urge on all chiefs and men of influence the importance to them of Europeans bringing goods to their country, which can only be done if they sign the treaties.

g. To obtain from natives and especially from caravan men (Hausas and others) the greatest possible number of lists of itineraries, with the number of days march, from every town of importance to every other. These lists cannot be obtained from too many independent persons, so as to enable us to reject those which differ too widely from the average.

h. To note specially prevalence of Gum trees, Shea Butter trees and rubber vines.

i. To remember, above all, that diplomacy and not conquest is *the* object of your expedition westwards. The French Press for the last six years have incessantly boasted that French officers and travellers, with (or even without) a single French companion and with very few native carriers and armed men, are able to cross new regions peacefully, and acquire valuable treaty rights where Englishmen can only make their way by force, leaving behind them a hatred and fear of Europeans. I do not for a moment admit the truth of this; but it is possible that, in regions where Europe has absolutely no military power, the gaiety, cajolery and sympathetic manner of the French have more effect in obtaining treaties than the sterner and colder manners of our countrymen. I suggest this only to emphasize the fact that in your expedition west, the exercise of force cannot further your objects, but must on the contrary prevent them being attained. On the other hand, it is vital that by constant vigilance, entrenching yourself and other precautions, you should secure yourself against treachery and violence.

4] The First Efforts to Understand

A] LENIN, *Imperialism: The Highest Stage of Capitalism,* 1916

Imperialists insisted upon justifying their acts by theoretical constructions, forgetting, as Voltaire said, that "virtue debases itself in justifying itself." Those who opposed imperialism replied in kind. Far removed from the specific question of why Britain chose to annex a particular area, or the problem of the effect of that annexation on indigenous peoples, is the more abstract question: What forces drove the imperialists, especially into Africa? While imperial growth still was in progress, V. I. Lenin launched his now classic, much debated, attack on imperialism "as a special stage of capitalism" (1916).*

* From V. I. Lenin, *Imperialism: The Highest Stage of Capitalism,* rev., trans., 2nd ed. (London: Martin Lawrence, 1934), pp. 80–81, 111–13. Reprinted by permission of International Publishers Co., Inc.

Imperialism emerged as a development and direct continuation of the fundamental properties of capitalism in general. But capitalism became capitalist imperialism only at a definite, very high stage of its development, when certain of its fundamental properties had begun to change into their opposites, when the features of a period of transition from capitalism to a higher socio-economic system had begun to take shape and reveal themselves all along the line. Economically fundamental in this process is the replacement of capitalist free competition by capitalist monopolies. . . .

If it were necessary to give the briefest possible definition of imperialism, we should have to say that imperialism is the monopoly stage of capitalism. Such a definition would include the essential point, for, on the one hand, finance capital is bank capital of the few biggest monopolist banks, merged with the capital of the monopolist combines of industrialists; on the other hand, the division of the world is the transition from a colonial policy which has extended without hindrance to territories unoccupied by any capitalist power, to a colonial policy of monopolistic possession of the territories of the world, which has been completely divided up.

But too brief definitions, although convenient, since they sum up the main points, are nevertheless inadequate, because very fundamental features of the phenomenon to be defined must still be deduced. And so . . . we must give a definition of imperialism that will include the following five essential features:

1. The concentration of production and capital, developed to such a high stage that it has created monopolies which play a decisive rôle in economic life.

2. The merging of bank capital with industrial capital and the creation, on the basis of this "finance capital," of a financial oligarchy.

3. The export of capital, as distinguished from the export of commodities, becomes of particularly great importance.

4. International monopoly combines of capitalists are formed which divide up the world.

5. The territorial division of the world by the greatest capitalist powers is completed.

Imperialism is capitalism in that stage of development in which the domination of monopolies and finance capital has taken shape; in which the export of capital has acquired pronounced importance; in which the division of the world by the international trusts has begun, and in which the partition of all the territory of the earth by the greatest capitalist countries has been completed.

.   .   .

We have seen that by its economic essence imperialism is monopolist capitalism. This fact alone determines the place of imperialism in history. . . . We must take special note of four main aspects of monopolies. . . .

First, monopoly arose out of the concentration of production at a very high stage of development. This refers to the monopolist capitalist combines: cartels, syndicates and trusts. . . . Towards the beginning of the twentieth century, they acquired complete supremacy in the advanced countries, and although the initial steps towards the formation of combines were first taken by countries with high protective tariffs (Germany, America), Great Britain, with her system of free trade, was not far behind. . . .

Second, monopolies have accelerated seizure of the most important sources of raw materials, especially for the coal and iron industry, which is the basic and most highly trustified industry in capitalist society. . . .

Third, monopoly arose out of the banks. The banks changed from modest intermediary enterprises into the monopolists of finance capital. Some three or five of the biggest banks in any of the most advanced capitalist countries have achieved a "personal union" of industrial and banking capital, and have concentrated in their hands the control of billions upon billions, which form the greatest part of the capital and revenue of an entire country. . . .

Fourth, monopoly arose out of colonial policy. To the numerous "old" motives of colonial policy finance capital has added the struggle for sources of raw materials, for the export of capital, for "spheres of influence," *i.e.*, spheres of good business, concessions, monopolist profits, and so on; in fine, for economic territory in general. When the colonies of the European powers in Africa comprised only one-tenth of that territory, as was still the case in 1876, colonial policy was able to develop in a non-monopolist manner, like "freebooters" taking land, so to speak. But when nine-tenths of Africa had been seized (by 1900); when the whole world had been divided up, there was inevitably ushered in a period of monopolist possession of colonies, and, consequently, of particularly intense struggle for the partition and for the re-partition of the world.

. . .

Monopolies, oligarchy, striving for domination instead of striving for liberty, exploitation of an increasing number of small or weak nations by an extremely small group of the richest or most powerful nations—all these have given birth to those distinctive characteristics of imperialism which compel us to define it as parasitic or decaying capitalism. More and more prominently there appears, as one of the tendencies of imperialism, the creation of the "rentier-state," the usurer state, whose bourgeoisie lives more and more on capital exports and by "clipping coupons." . . . [I]n the epoch of imperialism, now one, now another of these tendencies is displayed, to greater or less degree by certain branches of industry, by certain strata of the bourgeoisie, and by individual countries. As a whole, capitalism is growing far more rapidly than before, but not only is this growth becoming more and more uneven, but also this unevenness is showing itself in particular in the decay of the countries which are richest in capital (such as England).

B] Schumpeter, Sociology, and Psychology, 1919

Joseph Schumpeter, an Austrian-born economist who moved to the United States, provided quite a different explanation for the peculiar contours of imperial development. Writing in 1919, at the close of the war which Lenin saw as a product of capitalist imperialism, Schumpeter spoke of the darker nature of man's soul in his *Zur Soziologie der Imperialismus*. Imperialism, he said, was atavistic, and man would outgrow it. It was in the same year that the ideas of Sigmund Freud, who also stressed man's nature rather than man's acts, were first made widely known in the United States, a nation which had joined in the imperial fervor in 1898.*

Our analysis of the historical evidence has shown, first, the unquestionable fact that "objectless" tendencies toward forcible expansion, without definite, utilitarian limits—that is, non-rational and irrational, purely instinctual inclinations toward war and conquest—play a very large role in the history of mankind. It may sound paradoxical, but numberless wars—perhaps the majority of all wars—have been waged without adequate "reason"—not so much from the moral viewpoint as from that of reasoned and reasonable interest. . . . Our analysis, in the second place, provides an explanation for this drive to action, this will to war—a theory by no means exhausted by mere references to an "urge" or an "instinct." The explanation lies, instead, in the vital needs of situations that molded peoples and classes into warriors—if they wanted to avoid extinction—and in the fact that psychological dispositions and social structures acquired in the dim past in such situations, once firmly established, tend to maintain themselves and to continue in effect long after they have lost their meaning and their life-preserving function. Our analysis, in the third place, has shown the existence of subsidiary factors that facilitate the survival of such dispositions and structures—factors that may be divided into two groups. The orientation toward war is mainly fostered by the domestic interests of ruling classes, but also by the influence of all those who stand to gain individually from a war policy, whether economically or socially. Both groups of factors are generally overgrown by elements of an altogether different character, not only in terms of political phraseology, but also of psychological motivation. Imperialisms differ greatly in detail, but they all have at least these traits in common, turning them into a single phenomenon in the field of sociology. . . .

Imperialism thus is atavistic in character. It falls into that large group of surviving features from earlier ages that play such an important part in every concrete social situation. In other words, it is an element that stems from the living conditions, not of the present, but of the past—or, put in terms of the economic interpretation of history, from past rather than present re-

---

* Reprinted by permission of The President and Fellows of Harvard College from *Imperialism and Social Classes* by Joseph Schumpeter, copyright 1951 by the Trustees of Elizabeth B. Schumpeter. First published in English in 1951 by Augustus M. Kelley, Inc.; now available only through Meridian Books, New York. [Pp. 64–65, 69–73.]

lations of production. . . . Since the vital needs that created it have passed away for good, it too must gradually disappear, even though every warlike involvement, no matter how non-imperialist in character, tends to revive it. It tends to disappear as a structural element because the structure that brought it to the fore goes into a decline, giving way, in the course of social development, to other structures that have no room for it and eliminate the power factors that supported it. It tends to disappear as an element of habitual emotional reaction, because of the progressive rationalization of life and mind, a process in which old functional needs are absorbed by new tasks, in which heretofore military energies are functionally modified.

.   .   .

[I]nstinctual tendencies can survive only when the conditions that gave rise to them continue to apply, or when the "instinct" in question derives a new purpose from new conditions. . . . [W]e must expect to see this impulse, which rests on the primitive contingencies of physical combat, gradually disappear, washed away by new exigencies of daily life. There is another factor too. The competitive system absorbs the full energies of most of the people at all economic levels. Constant application, attention, and concentration of energy are the conditions of survival within it, primarily in the specifically economic professions, but also in other activities organized on their model. There is much less excess energy to be vented in war and conquest than in any precapitalist society. What excess energy there is flows largely into industry itself, accounts for its shining figures—the type of the captain of industry—and for the rest is applied to art, science, and the social struggle. In a purely capitalist world, what was once energy for war becomes simply energy for labor of every kind. Wars of conquest and adventurism in foreign policy in general are bound to be regarded as troublesome distractions, destructive of life's meaning, a diversion from the accustomed and therefore "true" task.

A purely capitalist world therefore can offer no fertile soil to imperialist impulses. That does not mean that it cannot still maintain an interest in imperialist expansion. . . . The point is that its people are likely to be essentially of an unwarlike disposition. Hence we must expect that anti-imperialist tendencies will show themselves wherever capitalism penetrates the economy and, through the economy, the mind of modern nations—most strongly, of course, where capitalism itself is strongest. . . . The facts that follow are cited to show that this expectation, which flows from our theory, is in fact justified.

1. Throughout the world of capitalism, and specifically among the elements formed by capitalism in modern social life, there has arisen a fundamental opposition to war, expansion, cabinet diplomacy, armaments, and socially entrenched professional armies. This opposition had its origin in the country that first turned capitalist—England—and arose coincidentally with

that country's capitalist development. "Philosophical radicalism" was the first politically influential intellectual movement to represent this trend successfully, linking it up, as was to be expected, with economic freedom in general and free trade in particular. . . . True, pacifism as a matter of principle had existed before, though only among a few small religious sects. But modern pacifism, in its political foundations if not its derivation, is unquestionably a phenomenon of the capitalist world.

2. Wherever capitalism penetrated, peace parties of such strength arose that virtually every war meant a political struggle on the domestic scene. The exceptions are rare—Germany in the Franco-Prussian war of 1870–1871, both belligerents in the Russo-Turkish war of 1877–1878. That is why every war is carefully justified as a defensive war by the governments involved, and by all the political parties, in their official utterances—indicating a realization that a war of a different nature would scarcely be tenable in a political sense. . . . In the distant past, imperialism had needed no disguise whatever, and in the absolute autocracies only a very transparent one; but today imperialism is carefully hidden from public view. . . . Every expansionist urge must be carefully related to a concrete goal. All this is primarily a matter of political phraseology, to be sure. But the necessity for this phraseology is a symptom of the popular attitude. . . .

3. The type of industrial worker created by capitalism is always vigorously anti-imperialist. In the individual case, skillful agitation may persuade the working masses to approve or remain neutral—a concrete goal or interest in self-defense always playing the main part—but no initiative for a forcible policy of expansion ever emanates from this quarter. . . .

4. Despite manifest resistance on the part of powerful elements, the capitalist age has seen the development of methods for preventing war, for the peaceful settlement of disputes among states. The very fact of resistance means that the trend can be explained only from the mentality of capitalism as a mode of life. It definitely limits the opportunities imperialism needs if it is to be a powerful force. . . .

5. Among all capitalist economies, that of the United States is least burdened with precapitalist elements, survivals, reminiscences, and power factors. Certainly we cannot expect to find imperialist tendencies altogether lacking even in the United States, for the immigrants came from Europe with their convictions fully formed, and the environment certainly favored the revival of instincts of pugnacity. But we can conjecture that among all countries the United States is likely to exhibit the weakest imperialist trend. This turns out to be the truth. . . . [T]he United States was the first advocate of disarmament and arbitration. It was the first to conclude treaties concerning arms limitations (1817) and arbitral courts (first attempt in 1797). . . . Since 1908 such treaties have been concluded with twenty-two states. In the course of the nineteenth century, the United States had numerous occasions for war, including instances that were well calculated to test its patience. It made almost no use of such occasions. . . .

These facts are scarcely in dispute. And since they fit into the picture of the mode of life which we have recognized to be the necessary product of capitalism . . . it follows that capitalism is by nature anti-imperialist. Hence we cannot readily derive from it such imperialist tendencies as actually exist, but must evidently see them only as alien elements, carried into the world of capitalism from the outside, supported by non-capitalist factors in modern life.

CONCLUSION

G E R M A N Y did not come to the aid of the Boers when, in 1899, the South African War broke out. Baron von Holstein, who shaped German policy in the 1890's, was unable to forge the Triple and Dual Alliances into a cooperative instrument against Britain, for he was unwilling to fight to give France what it wanted most: Egypt. And while Britain subdued the Boers, the United States acquired its first overseas empire, to add to its own earlier continental empire west of the Mississippi. In a few short years the Republic was caught up first in the general global war and later in reaping the fruits of earlier imperial gain: the Philippine Islands, acquired from Spain in the Spanish-American War, were to be the Achilles heel of American policy in the Far East, making it difficult for the United States to take a hard line with Japan in the 1930's.

Ultimately war came to the imperial powers, but imperialism was not the chief cause. Each European nation shaped its colonial policy according to the Continental balance of power; only as long as the colonies contributed to maintaining the balance were they closely associated with European diplomacy. Yet often the colonies were unimportant to the balance of power. After 1900 there were no major colonial disputes between Britain and Germany, for the powers were more concerned with the development of informal empire in the Far East. The Boxer Rebellion in that year was the signal for European cooperation against the Chinese and for a period of grand diplomatic doodling during which spheres of influence rather than outright annexations were the chief goals. When war at last came, it was sparked by the alliance system which had grown out of basically Continental needs, and the match was applied to the tinder in the Balkans, not in Africa. Britain continued to expand imperially up to and even after the war, and under the League of Nations' mandate system additional territories—those captured in Africa, the Far East, and the Pacific—fell to Britain or to the Dominions.

At the turn of the century all this lay ahead. Strength, the British thought, lay on the sea and within the empire. An imperial race was being bred both at home and abroad, a race that would regenerate the world, providing order where there was chaos—sanitation, paved roads, and daily prayers. While many in Britain also foresaw the day when some, if not all, of the colonies would be independent nations in their own right, such fruitage was thought to be a century or more away. Yet by the Statute of Westminster in 1931 the Commonwealth of Nations was to come into being, consisting then of only five independent states but, by 1965, of twenty-two free nations. Before the century was half over the imperial gem in Victoria's crown, India, placed there symbolically by Disraeli, would be independent. Britain and France between them would, by the mid-1960's, have spawned a quarter of the world's nations.

To assess this imperial heritage is the future task of historians; to judge it, the role of present moralists. As Voltaire remarked, "There are truths which are not for all men, nor for all times." Imperialism was one such "operable truth"; intensely if briefly effective, now condemned, its meaning and its influence stretch forward into the heavily thickening future.

STUDY QUESTIONS

1] Which of the many motives for imperial expansion seems to have been most consistently present for Britain in the period 1870–1919?
2] Britain was active in many other parts of the world in addition to Africa during this period of time. Why have historians placed such emphasis on the African phase of imperial expansion?
3] To what extent do the other selections tend to support Schumpeter's view of capitalism and its relation to imperialism?
4] To what extent were contemporaries under illusions about their own motives in the scramble for empire?
5] To what extent do individual personalities override the larger, more impersonal forces at work during a period of imperial expansion, and to what extent are individuals merely the product of those forces?
6] In the long run imperialism fathered many nations, for it helped give rise to nationalist movements around the world. In what ways can the history of the imperial period be distorted by modern nationalist hindsight?

RECOMMENDED READINGS

PRIMARY

BENNETT, GEORGE, ed. *The Concept of Empire: Burke to Attlee, 1774–1947*, 2nd ed., pp. 243–386 (London, 1962).
HERTSLET, SIR EDWARD, ed. *The Map of Africa by Treaty*, 3 vols., 2nd rev. ed. (London, 1896).
KEITH, ARTHUR BERRIEDALE, ed. *Selected Speeches and Documents on British Colonial Policy, 1763–1917*, repr. ed., Part 2, pp. 3–403 (London, 1961).
PERHAM, MARGERY AND MARY BULL, eds. *The Diaries of Lord Lugard*, 4 vols. (London, 1959–63).
WALLBANK, T. WALTER, ed. *Contemporary Africa: Continent in Transition*, pp. 104–21 (Princeton, 1956).
WINKS, ROBIN W., ed. *British Imperialism: Gold, God, Glory* (New York, 1963).

WRIGHT, HARRISON M., ed. *The "New Imperialism": Analysis of Late Nineteenth-Century Expansion,* pp. 4–38, 47–67 (Boston, 1961).

SECONDARY

BODELSEN, C. A. *Studies in Mid-Victorian Imperialism,* repr. ed. (London, 1960).
COHEN, MORTON. *Rider Haggard: His Life and Works* (London, 1960).
COWAN, C. D. *Nineteenth Century Malaya: The Origins of British Political Control* (London, 1961).
CREIGHTON, DONALD G. "The Victorians and the Empire," *The Canadian Historical Review,* XIX (March, 1938), 138–53.
EYCK, ERICH. *Bismarck and the German Empire* (London, 1950).
HALÉVY, ELIE. *Imperialism and the Rise of Labour* (A History of the English People in the Nineteenth Century, Vol. V), 2nd rev. ed. (New York, 1961).
KOEBNER, RICHARD AND HELMUT DAN SCHMIDT. *Imperialism: The Story and Significance of a Political Word, 1840–1960* (Cambridge, 1964).
LANGER, WILLIAM L. *European Alliances and Alignments, 1871–1890* (New York, 1931).
MANSERGH, NICHOLAS. *The Coming of the First World War: A Study in the European Balance, 1878–1914* (London, 1949).
MOON, PARKER T. *Imperialism and World Politics* (New York, 1927).
OLIVER, ROLAND. *Sir Harry Johnston and the Scramble for Africa* (London, 1957).
OLIVER, ROLAND AND J. D. FAGE. *A Short History of Africa* (Baltimore, 1962).
PERHAM, MARGERY. *The Colonial Reckoning: The End of Imperial Rule in Africa in the Light of British Experience* (New York, 1962).
———. *Lugard: The Years of Adventure, 1858–1898* (London, 1956).
ROBINSON, RONALD, JOHN GALLAGHER, AND ALICE DENNY. *Africa and the Victorians: The Climax of Imperialism in the Dark Continent* (New York, 1961).
SEMMEL, BERNARD. *Imperialism and Social Reform: English Social-Imperial Thought, 1895–1914* (Cambridge, Mass., 1960).
STRACHEY, JOHN. *The End of Empire* (New York, 1960).
TAYLOR, A. J. P. *Bismarck: The Man and the Statesman* (New York, 1955).
THORNTON, A. P. *The Imperial Idea and Its Enemies: A Study in British Power* (London, 1959).
TROTTER, REGINALD G. *The British Empire–Commonwealth: A Study in Political Evolution* (New York, 1932).

Crisis in Man's Self-knowledge: The Psychology of Sigmund Freud

MARGOT DREKMEIER

STANFORD UNIVERSITY

CONTENTS

CHRONOLOGY

1882

On the advice of his teacher Ernst Brücke, Freud abandons his research career in physiology and enters the General Hospital in Vienna, where he begins the study of nervous diseases.

Freud is introduced to the case of Anna O, an hysterical patient of his colleague Josef Breuer, who refers to her manner of detailing her symptoms as "the talking cure."

1885

Freud goes to Paris to study problems of hysteria and the technique of hypnosis with the neuropathologist Jean Martin Charcot.

1895

Studies on Hysteria, written in collaboration with Breuer, is published; the chapter on psychotherapy indicates the evolution of the psychoanalytic method of free association from the cathartic method of Breuer.

1895–99

Freud works on *The Interpretation of Dreams* (published in 1900) and makes some of his most basic and crucial discoveries.

1897

Freud begins his famous self-analysis, his exploration of his own unconscious.

1904

Publication of *The Psychopathology of Everyday Life,* which analyzes the way unconscious motives function in slips of the tongue, accidents, and commonplace mistakes.

1905

Publication of *Three Essays on the Theory of Sexuality,* a presentation of his conception of sexual deviations and perversions, the sexual factor in neurosis, infantile sexuality, and the phases of psychosexual development; *Fragment of an Analysis of a Case of Hysteria,* the Dora analysis; and *Wit and Its Relation to the Unconscious.*

1908

The First International Psychoanalytical Congress is held at Salzburg.

1909
President G. Stanley Hall of Clark University in Worcester, Massachusetts, invites Freud to give a lecture series on psychoanalysis; these lectures provide the first account of the development and content of psychoanalysis.

1910
The International Psychoanalytic Association is founded.

1911–13
Alfred Adler and C. G. Jung, two prominent psychoanalytic theorists, break with Freud.

1912–13
Publication of *Totem and Taboo,* a collection of essays dealing with similarities between primitive customs, values, and beliefs and neurotic symptoms and fantasies.

1914
Publication of *The History of the Psychoanalytic Movement,* which Freud wrote primarily to distinguish the main line of psychoanalysis from deviations of Jung and Adler that could not be reconciled with it.

1915–17
Freud lectures at the University of Vienna; the lectures delivered in his three courses will later be published as *A General Introduction to Psychoanalysis.*

1920
Publication of one of Freud's most controversial works, *Beyond the Pleasure Principle,* in which he reformulates his instinct theory: the instinct of aggression is pitted against the libidinal instincts.

1921
Publication of *Group Psychology and the Analysis of the Ego.*

1923
Publication of *The Ego and the Id,* an analysis of "the regions of the mind" and their functioning.

1925
Publication of Freud's *Autobiographical Study,* which gives a detailed account of Freud's professional history and the growth of psychoanalysis.

1926
Publication of *Inhibitions, Symptoms, and Anxiety* (later titled *The Problem of Anxiety*).

1927

Publication of *The Future of an Illusion,* which focuses on the character of religion, the needs that give rise to it, and the prospects for facing life without it.

1930

Publication of *Civilization and Its Discontents,* which argues that civilization is dependent on the suppression or sublimation of basic gratifications.

The German Government awards Freud the Goethe Prize for literature.

1933

Publication of *New Introductory Lectures on Psychoanalysis,* which contains seven essays, including one on philosophies of life.

1939

Publication of *Moses and Monotheism,* which argues that Moses was an Egyptian who converted the Jews to a monotheism of Egyptian origin.

1940

Posthumous publication of *An Outline of Psychoanalysis,* a succinct guide to fundamental principles of psychoanalysis.

INTRODUCTION

THE MAIN current of European philosophy, from the classical age until our own, has centered on an image of man as the one creature with a command over his mental life. While the passions as well as the rational faculties were fundamental to his nature, it was in exercising control over these passions that man asserted his humanity. To the layman as well as to the trained philosopher mental activity meant conscious activity, and it was believed that the will, the soul, or the conscience governed thought and action. The achievement of Sigmund Freud, as the founder of psychoanalysis, the science of unconscious processes, was to challenge this view of mental functioning and recast the bases of our understanding not only of the self but of human culture and social organization.

According to Freud, the consciousness is only the surface of mental life, and what takes place in the unconscious depths is of critical importance in determining human behavior. Motivation for conduct arises from unconscious drives and instincts, from responses fixated in childhood, from traditions and habits absorbed without the test of reason. In short, ideas, feelings, memories, and goals may be unconscious yet at the same time play a more telling part in motivation than do those conscious purposes to which men attribute their behavior. Mental life, characterized by interplay among various elementary instincts, is more authentically approached through dreams, fantasies, and the ways of children than through philosophical treatises on human nature. While remaining within the tradition of "know-thyself" philosophers and stressing the importance of objective self-knowledge, Freud exposed what usually passed for self-knowledge as being incomplete and even superficial. Men expend enormous energy in hiding from themselves, in protecting their feelings from the realities of existence.

Freud's *Interpretation of Dreams*, though it failed to arouse much stir until some time after its first appearance in 1900, in effect laid the cornerstone of psychoanalysis. Freud himself saw the theory of dreams as fundamental to the development of psychoanalysis—the point at which it stopped being simply a therapeutic method and became a depth psychology. In this famous study he demonstrated the similarities between the structure of dreams and that of neurosis, and what he had to say about infantile activity, the relationships between children and parents, and the powerful role of mental conflict, resistance, and repression applied to neurotic and healthy men alike.

Trained as a physician, Freud had pursued research in neurology and brain physiology before going into medical practice in Vienna, where he concentrated on the treatment of nervous disorders. His interest in research persisted, and throughout his career he carried on therapy and scientific research together. Psychoanalysis had originally been a therapy for dealing with neurotic disorders: phobias, obsessional states, and particularly conversion hysteria. Patients suffering from hysteria, for example, evidenced somatic symptoms (paralyses, nervous tics or coughs, migraine headaches, etc.) for which there seemed to be no apparent physical explanation. The distinctive method that Freud had evolved for getting at the source of their troublesome symptoms stressed the analysis and interpretation of their "free associations." Once in a relaxed and almost dreamlike state, the patients were encouraged to report everything that came into their minds, no matter how painful or seemingly irrelevant. Freud soon found that symptoms were physical expressions of psychological conflict; they served to shield the patient from conscious awareness of repressed impulses of a sexual nature. Sexual impulses too painful or too disturbing to gain conscious acceptance, in other words, had found outlet in the substitute form of a symptom.

It was in his experimentation with various techniques for treating mental disorders, then, that Freud developed his hypotheses regarding the normal as well as the malfunctioning personality. It had become apparent to him that the so-called normal and healthy person participates in the same difficulties and variety of responses as the ill, and that health is a matter of degree—of the ability to cope with anxiety so that it does not interfere with performance. "The borderline between the nervous, normal, and abnormal states is indistinct," he wrote. "We are all slightly nervous." In arguing that no sharp line could be drawn between the normal and the abnormal, that the study of neurotics could yield an understanding of the normal functioning of mental life, Freud put himself in opposition to most of the physicians of his day. To them the symptoms of the hysterical neurosis were a form of malingering and the neurotic was commonly looked upon as the least desirable type of patient.

In his *Interpretation of Dreams,* as in *Psychopathology of Everyday Life* and subsequent works, Freud stressed that he was dealing with conditions of normal mental life and not merely with the symptoms of neurotic individuals. Dreams, like neurotic symptoms, serve a purpose; as fulfillments of hidden wishes, dreams reflect the perennial pleasure-seeking of the unconscious forces within man. The instinctual life of the unconscious regions of the mind to which dreams provide access is dominated by desire—that is, by the pleasure principle, which seeks the reduction of tension. The essence of mental life is conflict between the pleasure principle and the reality principle —between the urge for immediate gratification of impulse and the demands for delay and control imposed by reality, or the external environment. In the healthy as well as in the neurotic person, dreams represent "inroads of the repressed." The screening and protective mechanisms of conscious life have been relaxed, but on the other hand the repressed material does not appear in naked form; rather, a process of symbolization and unconscious elaboration has taken place. As Freud put it, the dream is meaningful, but like a chapter in a foreign language it needs translating. Similarly, every other expression of the individual is to be treated as part of a related whole. All behavior is motivated; there is no such thing as accidental, or "chance," behavior. Usually it is experiences and fixations of childhood that provide the unconscious motivation for seemingly accidental behavior. While free association and dream analysis provide the most notable paths to the unconscious, there are others as well: humor and wit, slips of the tongue, forgetting names or resolutions or appointments, faulty recollections, mistakes in reading or transcribing. Like dreams, though to a less significant extent, all these make possible the expression of thoughts which could not be tolerated in consciousness. Thus everyday happenings ignored or dismissed as irrelevancies by earlier scientific investigators become meaningful with Freud's argument that they follow "lawful and rational paths."

The analysis of dreams and the study of symptom formation, which continually led Freud back to early childhood, resulted in his discovery of infantile sexuality. Of all his contributions, Freud's work on infantile sexuality probably aroused the greatest stir and, along with the libido theory as a whole, accounted for the major dissent on the part of certain of his followers. Early in his treatment of hysterics, Freud had found that the crucial point in analysis seemed to be regaining the memory of a traumatic experience of childhood—often a seduction scene—which appeared to provide the foundation for later symptom formation. It was not long, however, before he made the further discovery that most of the seductions his patients supposedly "remembered" were fantasies rather than actual incidents, which meant that the problem could not be reduced to traumas but must ultimately be rooted in an instinctual life that had not hitherto been associated with childhood. In place of the innocence of childhood so long romanticized by society, Freud posited the existence of pregenital sexuality. He called the parts of the body which give sexual pleasure—the mouth, genitals, certain skin surfaces, etc.—erogenous zones. Sexual energy, which he termed *libido,* he considered a kind of life force basic to the biological organism.

Even in an infantile state, then, libidinous impulses are crucial in the shaping of behavior; the so-called sexual instinct comprises a whole series of separate instincts associated with the different erogenous zones of the body, instincts which are not subordinated to the genital sexuality of adulthood until a later date. Sexual life in this sense begins in the earliest years of infancy, and on the basis of his investigations Freud held that all men go through a universal course of development from an oral stage of erotism through an anal stage, a phallic stage, and a latency phase to the genital stage characteristic of adult life. Holdovers from infantile stages influence adult character traits, both normal and abnormal; repressed orality, for example, takes such forms as self-accusation and melancholy, whereas repressed anality takes the form of stubbornness, compulsive neatness, and parsimony. The unconscious knows no abrupt division between childhood and the sexually mature adult; rather, all the early stages of development persist along with later stages that have emerged from them. Instinctual demands are persistent and inflexible: they cannot be eliminated through education and training, but only redirected or rechanneled; that is, pregenital libido may be *sublimated*, or diverted to aims other than the immediate sexual ones. Sublimation involves a change in both the object and the aim of the instinct; what was initially a sexual instinct finds outlet in social or cultural activities, for example. Much culture and civilization, Freud contends, is in fact bought at the price of restricting sexuality.

Freud argues that "an instinct differs from a stimulus in that it arises from sources of stimulation within the body, operates as a constant force, and is such that the subject cannot escape from it by flight as he can from an external stimulus." The theory thus provides little basis for optimism, especially in its later formulation of instinctual life as a battleground between Eros and aggression. According to this dualistic theory, individual life and civilization as a whole reflect the continual intermingling and conflict of two basic instincts: Eros (the urge to love and unite in ever-increasing unities), which is at the basis of all social organization and group life, and the death instinct (sometimes used by Freud interchangeably with aggression), which aims at destruction and the conversion of things to an inorganic state. Eros and aggression never act in isolation from one another, but are in fact entangled—sometimes working together, as in the sexual act itself, but more often working against each other. The phenomena of life are variegated according to the way these two instincts act and interact. Antisocial and aggressive inclinations are deep-rooted, and civilization is no sure defense against the primitive and savage inheritance of man. Freud refers to belief in the "goodness" of man's nature as "one of those unfortunate illusions from which mankind expects some kind of beautifying or ameliorating of its lot, but which in reality bring only disaster." In a correspondence which he carried on with Albert Einstein in 1932 on the subject of whether war could be prevented, Freud was very pessimistic about the ability of men to cope with their aggression. Aggression turned against the self is unhealthy and can even lead to suicide; aggression released against the outside world may spare the individual while promoting political and social conflict on a grand scale. It would be delightful if men could build a world ruled by reason, in which the instinctual life were firmly controlled rather than ready to erupt at any moment, but we can only hope to promote emotional bonds as defenses against our aggressive needs. Eros builds civilization, but ironically sexuality is selfish and seeks privacy. Freud says that because civilization makes arduous demand on the organism and requires that gratifications be delayed, the barbarian has a greater likelihood of being healthy than the civilized man.

Civilization requires repression and sublimation—and civilization is itself born of postponement and renunciation. Art, religion, and the social order have their bases in instincts diverted from their original aims. Freud found, for example, a common denominator between the religious practices of the pious and the obsessive acts of the neurotic. He notes that the "neurotic ceremonial"—the methodical performance of certain activities and avoidance of others—has a function that is not so different from that of the religious rite. Both are protective measures, and in the case of both there is guilt if the prescribed behavior is not followed. The major difference becomes the private character of the neurosis as opposed to the shared, symbolic character of the religious observance. Not only do morals have their source in primal taboos and the rationalization of deep-seated inhibitions, but conscience itself—far from representing a divine spark—has roots in the aggressive instinct. Freud hoped that the unmasking of the unconscious motivations manifested in religion and morality would make it possible for men to find more valid and satisfying forms of expression which were not dependent on illusion. His occasional appeals for rational morality and the value he attached to science as the model of intellectual activity are reminiscent of eighteenth-century philosophy.

Freud's work met with reactions ranging from ridicule to shock and disgust. Freud was accused of undermining morality and inviting promiscuity, and—at the opposite extreme—of restoring, albeit on a secular basis, the doctrine of original sin from which enlightened mankind had so recently emancipated itself. While in many circles psychoanalysis met with stubborn resistance, in others it was welcomed as an emancipating force, generally on the basis of interpretations that Freud could hardly be expected to accept. Freud himself attributed much of the opposition to the novelty of his discoveries, arguing that few men in any time or place are really prepared to deal with scientific disclosures that threaten traditional beliefs. It was one thing, in physical science, to analyze the atom into a field of forces; it was quite another to dissect personality into a field of unconscious forces. Some critics of Freud accused him of mysticism and intuitionism, though he had resolutely maintained that knowledge, whether of man or of the physical world, can be obtained only through the "slow, tentative, and laborious" process of scientific observation and research. His challenge to the skeptical rationalists and optimists of his day was on scientific grounds; that is, he sought to show the importance of the unconscious and irrational forces, not to make a virtue of irrationalism as some of his romantic forbears had done. Whereas the romantic may have reveled in his explorations of the subterranean depths, for Freud such explorations were calculated to yield knowledge of the human psyche that would make greater rational control possible. In this sense, Freud remains in the tradition of the Enlightenment.

2] The Development of Theory and Method

A] THE DISCOVERY OF THE DREAM

In the following passage, from "My Contact with Josef Popper-Lynkeus," Freud credits the few men who were able to help him in the search for a method of dealing with neurotic patients: Charcot, who had developed a treatment based on hypnosis; Bernheim, who had made use of the technique of suggestion in his work with hospital patients; and Breuer, who had developed a form of therapy very similar to what was to become "free association" in psychoanalysis. Freud's account suggests the direct relationship between his therapeutic work with psychoneurotic patients and psychoanalytic theory, a relationship which he would stress throughout his career.*

It was in the winter of 1899 that my book on the *Interpretation of Dreams* (though its title-page was post-dated into the new century) at length lay before me. This work was the product of the labours of four or five years and its origin was unusual. Holding a lectureship in Nervous Diseases at the University, I had attempted to support myself and my rapidly increasing family by a medical practice among the so-called 'neurotics' of whom there were only too many in our society. But the task proved harder than I had expected. The ordinary methods of treatment clearly offered little or no help: other paths must be followed. And how was it by any means possible to give patients help when one understood nothing of their illness, nothing of the causes of their sufferings or of the meaning of their complaints? So I eagerly sought direction and instruction from the great Charcot in Paris and from Bernheim at Nancy; finally, an observation made by my teacher and friend, Josef Breuer of Vienna, seemed to open a new prospect for understanding and therapeutic success.

For these new experiments made it a certainty that the patients whom we described as neurotic were in some sense suffering from *mental* disturbances and ought therefore to be treated by psychological methods. Our interest therefore necessarily turned to psychology. The psychology which ruled at that time in the academic schools of philosophy had very little to offer and nothing at all for our purposes: we had to discover from the start both our methods and the theoretical hypotheses behind them. So I worked in this direction, first in collaboration with Breuer and afterwards independently of him. In the end I made it a part of my technique to require my patients to tell me without criticism whatever occurred to their minds, even if they were ideas which did not seem to make sense or which it was distressing to report.

* Reprinted from Sigmund Freud, "My Contact with Josef Popper-Lynkeus" (1932), *Complete Works*, Vol. XXII, pp. 219–22 (1964). Reprinted by permission of Hogarth Press, London, and Basic Books, Inc., New York.

When they fell in with my instructions they told me their dreams, amongst other things, as though they were of the same kind as their other thoughts. This was a plain hint that I should assign as much importance to these dreams as to other, intelligible, phenomena. They, however, were *not* intelligible, but strange, confused, absurd: like dreams, in fact—which for that very reason, were condemned by science as random and senseless twitchings of the organ of the mind. If my patients were right—and they seemed only to be repeating the ancient beliefs held by unscientific men for thousands of years—I was faced by the task of 'interpreting dreams' in a way that could stand up against scientific criticism.

To begin with, I naturally understood no more about my patients' dreams than the dreamers did themselves. But by applying to these dreams, and more particularly to my own dreams, the procedure which I had already used for the study of other abnormal psychological structures, I succeeded in answering most of the questions which could be raised by an interpretation of dreams. There were many such questions: What do we dream about? Why do we dream at all? What is the origin of all the strange characteristics which distinguish dreams from waking life?—and many more such questions besides. Some of the answers were easily given and turned out to confirm views that had already been put forward; but others involved completely new hypotheses with regard to the structure and functioning of the apparatus of the mind. People dream about the things that have engaged their minds during the waking day. People dream in order to allay impulses that seek to disturb sleep, and in order to be able to sleep on. But why was it possible for dreams to present such a strange appearance, so confusedly senseless, so obviously contrasted with the content of waking thought, in spite of being concerned with the same material? There could be no doubt that dreams were only a substitute for a rational process of thought and could be interpreted—that is to say, translated into a rational process. But what needed explaining was the fact of the *distortion* which the dream-work had carried out upon the rational and intelligible material.

Dream-distortion was the profoundest and most difficult problem of dream life. And light was thrown on it by the following consideration, which placed dreams in a class along with other psychopathological formations and revealed them, as it were, as the normal psychoses of human beings. For our mind, that precious instrument by whose means we maintain ourselves in life, is no peacefully self-contained unity. It is rather to be compared with a modern State in which a mob, eager for enjoyment and destruction, has to be held down forcibly by a prudent superior class. The whole flux of our mental life and everything that finds expression in our thoughts are derivations and representatives of the multifarious instincts that are innate in our physical constitution. But these instincts are not all equally susceptible to direction and education, or equally ready to fall in with the demands of the external world and of human society. A number of them have retained their primitive, ungovernable nature; if we let them have their way, they would

In the following passage from "Instincts and Their Vicissitudes," Freud presents an argument for flexible as opposed to strict definition in the early stages of scientific inquiry.*

We have often heard it maintained that sciences should be built up on clear and sharply defined basic concepts. In actual fact no science, not even the most exact, begins with such definitions. The true beginning of scientific activity consists rather in describing phenomena and then in proceeding to group, classify and correlate them. Even at the stage of description it is not possible to avoid applying certain abstract ideas to the material in hand, ideas derived from somewhere or other but certainly not from the new observations alone. Such ideas—which will later become the basic concepts of the science—are still more indispensable as the material is further worked over. They must at first necessarily possess some degree of indefiniteness; there can be no question of any clear delimitation of their content. So long as they remain in this condition, we come to an understanding about their meaning by making repeated references to the material of observation from which they appear to have been derived, but upon which, in fact, they have been imposed. Thus, strictly speaking, they are in the nature of conventions; although everything depends on their not being arbitrarily chosen but determined by their having significant relations to the empirical material, relations that we seem to sense before we can clearly recognize and demonstrate them. It is only after more thorough investigation of the field of observation that we are able to formulate its basic scientific concepts with increased precision, and progressively so to modify them that they become serviceable and consistent over a wide area. Then, indeed, the time may have come to confine them in definitions. The advance of knowledge, however, does not tolerate any rigidity even in definitions. Physics furnishes an excellent illustration of the way in which even 'basic concepts' that have been established in the form of definitions are constantly being altered in their content.

A conventional basic concept of this kind, which at the moment is still somewhat obscure but which is indispensable to us in psychology, is that of an 'instinct'.

3] The Unconscious

a] On Repression

Freud's concept of the unconscious is directly associated with his theory of repression, explained in the following extract from *The Ego and the Id*. Else-

* Reprinted from Sigmund Freud, "Instincts and Their Vicissitudes" (1915), *Complete Works,* Vol. XIV, pp. 117–18 (1957). Reprinted by permission of Hogarth Press, London, and Basic Books, Inc., New York.

where he defines repression as "a preliminary phase of condemnation, something between flight and condemnation." And when the instincts themselves are involved, it is impossible to escape in the way one can flee from an external danger. The crucial repressions take place before the individual has reached an age where he has sufficient control to reject impulses on a conscious level. Repression results when the conflict between the pleasure and reality principles ends with rejection from consciousness of that which is troublesome. The repressed material continues to influence behavior indirectly to produce neurotic symptoms. On the everyday level, the activity of the unconscious is reflected in such phenomena as slips of the tongue, forgetfulness, and bizarre dreams. In the neurotic, there are additional symptoms that are more extreme and debilitating.*

The division of the psychical into what is conscious and what is unconscious is the fundamental premiss of psycho-analysis; and it alone makes it possible for psycho-analysis to understand the pathological processes in mental life, which are as common as they are important, and to find a place for them in the framework of science. To put it once more, in a different way: psycho-analysis cannot situate the essence of the psychical in consciousness, but is obliged to regard consciousness as a quality of the psychical, which may be present in addition to other qualities or may be absent.

.   .   .

We have found—that is, we have been obliged to assume—that very powerful mental processes or ideas exist (and here a quantitative or *economic* factor comes into question for the first time) which can produce all the effects in mental life that ordinary ideas do (including effects that can in their turn become conscious as ideas), though they themselves do not become conscious. . . . It is enough to say that at this point psycho-analytic theory steps in and asserts that the reason why such ideas cannot become conscious is that a certain force opposes them, that otherwise they could become conscious, and that it would then be apparent how little they differ from other elements which are admittedly psychical. The fact that in the technique of psycho-analysis a means has been found by which the opposing force can be removed and the ideas in question made conscious renders this theory irrefutable. The state in which the ideas existed before being made conscious is called by us *repression*, and we assert that the force which instituted the repression and maintains it is perceived as *resistance* during the work of analysis.

Thus we obtain our concept of the unconscious from the theory of repression. The repressed is the prototype of the unconscious for us. We see, however, that we have two kinds of unconscious—the one which is latent but capable of becoming conscious, and the one which is repressed and which is not, in itself and without more ado, capable of becoming conscious. This

* Reprinted from Sigmund Freud, *The Ego and the Id* (1923), *Complete Works*, Vol. XIX, pp. 13–15, 17 (1961). Copyright © 1960 by James Strachey. Reprinted by permission of Hogarth Press, London, and W. W. Norton & Company, Inc., New York.

is not accomplished at all; the son remains all his life in subjection to his father, and incapable of transferring his libido to a new sexual object. In the reversed relationship the daughter's fate may be the same. In this sense the Oedipus complex is justifiably regarded as the kernel of the neuroses.

c] THE CASE OF DORA

Perhaps the most famous study in the literature of psychoanalysis is the case of Dora, a young woman suffering from hysteria. Her symptoms ranged from nervous coughing and occasional loss of voice to depression and fatigue. The psychic trauma, conflict of affections, and sexual disturbances that produced Dora's hysteria arose in the context of her family's relationship to a certain Herr and Frau K. Dora's father, unhappy in his own marriage, had been nursed through a prolonged illness by Frau K., with whom he had a love affair. Dora had herself been propositioned by Herr K. in a "scene by the lake"; while she appeared to react with disgust and horror, Freud did not accept this as an accurate assessment of her unconscious feelings. The analysis also concentrated on her desire to get her father away from Frau K., on her unconscious attempts to alarm him by her sickness. The three selections below, from "Analysis of a Case of Hysteria," illustrate Freud's style of reporting case work.*

THE SEXUAL FACTOR IN HYSTERIA

No one can undertake the treatment of a case of hysteria until he is convinced of the impossibility of avoiding the mention of sexual subjects, or unless he is prepared to allow himself to be convinced by experience. The right attitude is: '*pour faire une omelette il faut casser des oeufs.*' [1] The patients themselves are easy to convince; and there are only too many opportunities of doing so in the course of the treatment. There is no necessity for feeling any compunction at discussing the facts of normal or abnormal sexual life with them. With the exercise of a little caution all that is done is to translate into conscious ideas what was already known in the unconscious; and, after all, the whole effectiveness of the treatment is based upon our knowledge that the affect attached to an unconscious idea operates more strongly and, since it cannot be inhibited, more injuriously than the affect attached to a conscious one. There is never any danger of corrupting an inexperienced girl. For where there is no knowledge of sexual processes even in the unconscious, no hysterical symptom will arise; and where hysteria is found there can no longer be any question of 'innocence of mind' in the sense in which parents and educators use the phrase.

---

[1] To make an omelet, eggs must be broken.

* Reprinted from Sigmund Freud, "Fragment of an Analysis of a Case of Hysteria" (1905), *Complete Works*, Vol. VII, pp. 49, 57–59, 116–17 (1953). Reprinted by permission of Hogarth Press, London, and Basic Books, Inc., New York.

THE UNCONSCIOUS "YES"

When I told Dora that I could not avoid supposing that her affection for her father must at a very early moment have amounted to her being completely in love with him, she of course gave me her usual reply: 'I don't remember that'. But she immediately went on to tell me something analogous about a seven-year-old girl who was her cousin (on her mother's side) and in whom she often thought she saw a kind of reflection of her own childhood. This little girl had (not for the first time) been the witness of a heated dispute between her parents, and, when Dora happened to come in on a visit soon afterwards, whispered in her ear: 'You can't think how I hate that person!' (pointing to her mother), 'and when she's dead I shall marry Daddy.' I am in the habit of regarding associations such as this, which bring forward something that agrees with the content of an assertion of mine, as a confirmation from the unconscious of what I have said. No other kind of 'Yes' can be extracted from the unconscious; there is no such thing at all as an unconscious 'No'.

.   .   .

The 'No' uttered by a patient after a repressed thought has been presented to his conscious perception for the first time does no more than register the existence of a repression and its severity; it acts, as it were, as a gauge of the repression's strength. If this 'No', instead of being regarded as the expression of an impartial judgement (of which, indeed, the patient is incapable), is ignored, and if work is continued, the first evidence soon begins to appear that in such a case 'No' signifies the desired 'Yes'.

TRANSFERENCE

What are transferences? They are new editions or facsimiles of the impulses and phantasies which are aroused and made conscious during the progress of the analysis; but they have this peculiarity, which is characteristic for their species, that they replace some earlier person by the person of the physician. To put it another way: a whole series of psychological experiences are revived, not as belonging to the past, but as applying to the person of the physician at the present moment. Some of these transferences have a content which differs from that of their model in no respect whatever except for the substitution. These, then—to keep to the same metaphor—are merely new impressions or reprints. Others are more ingeniously constructed; their content has been subjected to a moderating influence—to *sublimation,* as I call it—and they may even become conscious, by cleverly taking advantage of some real peculiarity in the physician's person or circumstances and attaching themselves to that. These, then, will no longer be new impressions, but revised editions.

.   .   .

c] The Superego *

We have found out all kinds of things about the formation of the super-ego
—that is to say, about the origin of conscience. Following a well-known pronouncement of Kant's which couples the conscience within us with the starry
Heavens, a pious man might well be tempted to honour these two things as
the masterpieces of creation. The stars are indeed magnificent, but as regards
conscience God has done an uneven and careless piece of work, for a large
majority of men have brought along with them only a modest amount of it
or scarcely enough to be worth mentioning. We are far from overlooking the
portion of psychological truth that is contained in the assertion that conscience is of divine origin; but the thesis needs interpretation. Even if conscience is something 'within us', yet it is not so from the first. In this it is a
real contrast to sexual life, which is in fact there from the beginning of life
and not only a later addition. But, as is well known, young children are
amoral and possess no internal impulses against their impulses striving for
pleasure. The part which is later taken on by the super-ego is played to begin with by an external power, by parental authority. Parental influence gov-
erns the child by offering proofs of love and by threatening punishments
which are signs to the child of loss of love and are bound to be feared on
their own account. This realistic anxiety is the precursor of the later moral
anxiety. So long as it is dominant there is no need to talk of a super-ego
and of a conscience. It is only subsequently that the secondary situation de-
velops (which we are all too ready to regard as the normal one), where the
external restraint is internalized and the super-ego takes the place of the
parental agency and observes, directs and threatens the ego in exactly the
same way as earlier the parents did with the child.

The super-ego, which thus takes over the power, function and even the
methods of the parental agency, is however not merely its successor but actually the legitimate heir of its body. It proceeds directly out of it. . . .
However, we must dwell upon a discrepancy between the two. The super-
ego seems to have made a one-sided choice and to have picked out only
the parents' strictness and severity, their prohibitive and punitive function,
whereas their loving care seems not to have been taken over and maintained.
If the parents have really enforced their authority with severity we can easily
understand the child's in turn developing a severe super-ego. But, contrary
to our expectation, experience shows that the super-ego can acquire the same
characteristic of relentless severity even if the upbringing had been mild and
kindly and had so far as possible avoided threats and punishments.

.   .   .

* Reprinted from Sigmund Freud, "The Dissection of the Psychical Personality" (Lecture XXXI), *Complete Works*, Vol. XXII, pp. 61–64 (1964). Reprinted by permission of
Hogarth Press, London, and W. W. Norton & Company, Inc., New York.

The installation of the super-ego can be described as a successful instance of identification with the parental agency. The fact that speaks decisively for this view is that this new creation of a superior agency within the ego is most intimately linked with the destiny of the Oedipus complex, so that the super-ego appears as the heir of that emotional attachment which is of such importance for childhood. With his abandonment of the Oedipus complex a child must, as we can see, renounce the intense object cathexes which he has deposited with his parents, and it is as a compensation for this loss of objects that there is such a strong intensification of the identifications with his parents which have probably long been present in his ego. Identifications of this kind as precipitates of object-cathexes that have been given up will be repeated often enough later in the child's life; but it is entirely in accordance with the emotional importance of this first instance of such a transformation that a special place in the ego should be found for its outcome. Close investigation has shown us, too, that the super-ego is stunted in its strength and growth if the surmounting of the Oedipus complex is only incompletely successful. In the course of development the super-ego also takes on the influences of those who have stepped into the place of parents—educators, teachers, people chosen as ideal models. Normally it departs more and more from the original parental figures; it becomes, so to say, more impersonal. Nor must it be forgotten that a child has a different estimate of its parents at different periods of its life. At the time at which the Oedipus complex gives place to the super-ego they are something quite magnificent; but later they lose much of this. Identifications then come about with these later parents as well, and indeed they regularly make important contributions to the formation of character; but in that case they only affect the ego, they no longer influence the super-ego, which has been determined by the earliest parental imagos.

5] From Individual to Group Psychology

a] THE LIBIDINAL TIE

In his *Group Psychology and the Analysis of the Ego* Freud directed his attention to the nature of the ties that bind men together in groups and account for the heightening of emotional response and the numbing of critical faculties in the individual. The leader is of crucial importance in the generation of these emotional bonds. Freud's distinction between sexual and social emotions, between object-love and identification, is basic to his entire argument.*

* Reprinted from Sigmund Freud, *Group Psychology and the Analysis of the Ego* (1921), *Complete Works*, Vol. XVIII, pp. 90–91, 103–06, 94–95 (1955). Reprinted by permission of Hogarth Press, London, and Liveright, Publishers, New York.

I shall make an attempt at using the concept of *libido* for the purpose of throwing light upon group psychology, a concept which has done us such good service in the study of psychoneuroses.

Libido is an expression taken from the theory of the emotions. We call by that name the energy, regarded as a quantitative magnitude (though not at present actually measurable) of those instincts which have to do with all that may be comprised under the word 'love'. The nucleus of what we mean by love naturally consists (and this is what is commonly called love, and what the poets sing of) in sexual love with sexual union as its aim. But we do not separate from this—what in any case has a share in the name 'love'—on the one hand, self-love, and on the other, love for parents and children, friendship and love for humanity in general, and also devotion to concrete objects and to abstract ideas. Our justification lies in the fact that psycho-analytic research has taught us that all these tendencies are an expression of the same instinctual impulses; in relations between the sexes these impulses force their way towards sexual union, but in other circumstances they are diverted from this aim or are prevented from reaching it, though always preserving enough of their original nature to keep their identity recognizable (as in such features as the longing for proximity, and self-sacrifice).

We are of opinion, then, that language has carried out an entirely justifiable piece of unification in creating the word 'love' with its numerous uses, and that we cannot do better than take it as the basis of our scientific discussions and expositions as well. By coming to this decision, psycho-analysis has let loose a storm of indignation, as though it had been guilty of an act of outrageous innovation. Yet psycho-analysis has done nothing original in taking love in this 'wider' sense. In its origin, function, and relation to sexual love, the 'Eros' of the philosopher Plato coincides exactly with the love–force, the libido of psycho-analysis.

.   .   .

We should also like to know whether this kind of object-cathexis, as we know it in sexual life, represents the only manner of emotional tie with other people, or whether we must take other mechanisms of the sort into account. As a matter of fact we learn from psycho-analysis that there do exist other mechanisms for emotional ties, the so-called *identifications*. . . .

Identification is known to psycho-analysis as the earliest expression of an emotional tie with another person. It plays a part in the early history of the Oedipus complex. A little boy will exhibit a special interest in his father; he would like to grow like him and be like him, and take his place everywhere. We may say simply that he takes his father as his ideal.

.   .   .

It is easy to state in a formula the distinction between an identification with the father and the choice of the father as an object. In the first case one's father is what one would like to *be,* and in the second he is what one would like to *have.* The distinction, that is, depends upon whether the tie attaches to the subject or to the object of the ego.

. . .

The Commander-in-Chief is a father who loves all soldiers equally, and for that reason they are comrades among themselves. The army differs structurally from the Church in being built up of a series of such groups. Every captain is, as it were, the Commander-in-Chief and the father of his company, and so is every non-commissioned officer of his section. It is true that a similar hierarchy has been constructed in the Church, but it does not play the same part in it economically; for more knowledge and care about individuals may be attributed to Christ than to a human Commander-in-Chief.

. . .

It is to be noticed that in these two artificial groups each individual is bound by libidinal ties on the one hand to the leader (Christ, the Commander-in-Chief) and on the other hand to the other members of the group.

b] Religion as Mass Delusion

In *Civilization and Its Discontents* Freud describes the religions of humanity as mass delusions resulting from attempts to gain assurances of happiness and protection from suffering and pain. In the following passage, from *The Future of an Illusion,* he traces the roots of religion to infantile patterns of adjustment to life.*

I have tried to show that religious ideas have arisen from the same need as have all the other achievements of civilization: from the necessity of defending oneself against the crushingly superior force of nature. To this a second motive was added—the urge to rectify the shortcomings of civilization which made themselves painfully felt. Moreover, it is especially apposite to say that civilization gives the individual these ideas, for he finds them there already; they are presented to him ready-made, and he would not be able to discover them for himself.

. . .

Do you suppose that human thought has no practical motives, that it is simply the expression of a disinterested curiosity? That is surely very improbable. I believe rather that when man personifies the forces of nature he is

* Reprinted from Sigmund Freud, *The Future of an Illusion* (1927), **Complete Works,** Vol. XXI, pp. 23–24 (1961). Reprinted by permission of Hogarth Press, London, and Liveright, Publishers, New York.

again following an infantile model. He has learnt from the persons in his earliest environment that the way to influence them is to establish a relation with them; and so, later on, with the same end in view, he treats everything else that he comes across in the same way as he treated those persons. Thus I do not contradict your descriptive observations; it is in fact natural to man to personify everything that he wants to understand in order later to control it (psychical mastering as a preparation for physical mastering); but I provide in addition a motive and a genesis for this peculiarity of human thinking.

.   .   .

Let us transport ourselves into the mental life of a child. You remember the choice of object according to the anaclitic type [a common psychoanalytic expression for the "leaning," dependent phase of object-choice in which the mother, who has made possible the gratification of all the earliest needs, becomes the first sexual object], which psycho-analysis talks of? The libido there follows the paths of narcissistic needs and attaches itself to the objects which ensure the satisfaction of those needs. In this way the mother, who satisfies the child's hunger, becomes its first love-object and certainly also its first protection against all the undefined dangers which threaten it in the external world—its first protection against anxiety, we may say.

In this function [of protection] the mother is soon replaced by the stronger father, who retains that position for the rest of childhood. But the child's attitude to its father is coloured by a peculiar ambivalence. The father himself constitutes a danger for the child, perhaps because of its earlier relation to its mother. Thus it fears him no less than it longs for him and admires him. The indications of this ambivalence in the attitude to the father are deeply imprinted in every religion, as was shown in *Totem and Taboo*. When the growing individual finds that he is destined to remain a child for ever, that he can never do without protection against strange superior powers, he lends those powers the features belonging to the figure of his father; he creates for himself the gods whom he dreads, whom he seeks to propitiate, and whom he nevertheless entrusts with his own protection. Thus his longing for a father is a motive identical with his need for protection against the consequences of his human weakness. The defence against childish helplessness is what lends its characteristic features to the adult's reaction to the helplessness which he has to acknowledge—a reaction which is precisely the formation of religion.

6] Prospects for Man

A] THE NEW SOCIETY

The vision of the new society brought about by education and environmental change is questioned in the following discussion of Bolshevism, from "A Weltanshauung." *

Although practical Marxism has mercilessly cleared away all idealistic systems and illusions, it has itself developed illusions which are no less questionable and unprovable than the earlier ones. It hopes in the course of a few generations so to alter human nature that people will live together almost without friction in the new order of society, and that they will undertake the duties of work without any compulsion. Meanwhile it shifts elsewhere the instinctual restrictions which are essential in society; it diverts the aggressive tendencies which threaten all human communities to the outside and finds support in the hostility of the poor against the rich and of the hitherto powerless against the former rulers. But a transformation of human nature such as this is highly improbable. The enthusiasm with which the mass of the people follow the Bolshevist instigation at present, so long as the new order is incomplete and is threatened from outside, gives no certainty for a future in which it would be fully built up and in no danger. In just the same way as religion, Bolshevism too must compensate its believers for the sufferings and deprivations of their present life by promises of a better future in which there will no longer be any unsatisfied need. This Paradise, however, is to be in this life, instituted on earth and thrown open within a foreseeable time. But we must remember that the Jews as well, whose religion knows nothing of an after-life, expected the arrival of a Messiah on earth, and that the Christian Middle Ages at many times believed that the Kingdom of God was at hand.

There is no doubt of how Bolshevism will reply to the objections. It will say that so long as men's nature has not yet been transformed it is necessary to make use of the means which affect them to-day. It is impossible to do without compulsion in their education, without the prohibition of thought and without the employment of force to the point of bloodshed; and if the illusions were not awakened in them, they could not be brought to acquiesce in this compulsion. And we should be politely asked to say how things could be managed differently. This would defeat us. I could think of no advice to give. I should admit that the conditions of this experiment would have de-

* Reprinted from Sigmund Freud, "A Weltanshauung" (Lecture XXXV), *Complete Works*, Vol. XXII, p. 180 (1964). Reprinted by permission of Hogarth Press, London, and W. W. Norton & Company, Inc., New York.

terred me and those like me from undertaking it; but we are not the only people concerned. There are men of action, unshakable in their convictions, inaccessible to doubt, without feeling for the sufferings of others if they stand in the way of their intentions. We have to thank men of this kind for the fact that the tremendous experiment of producing a new order of this kind is now actually being carried out in Russia. At a time when the great nations announce that they expect salvation only from the maintenance of Christian piety, the revolution in Russia—in spite of all its disagreeable details—seems none the less like the message of a better future. Unluckily neither our scepticism nor the fanatical faith of the other side gives a hint as to how the experiment will turn out. The future will tell us; perhaps it will show that the experiment was undertaken prematurely, that a sweeping alteration of the social order has little prospect of success until new discoveries have increased our control over the forces of Nature and so made easier the satisfaction of our needs. Only then perhaps may it become possible for a new social order not only to put an end to the material need of the masses but also to give a hearing to the cultural demands of the individual. Even then, to be sure, we shall still have to struggle for an incalculable time with the difficulties which the untameable character of human nature presents to every kind of social community.

B] THE VOICE OF REASON

Freud consistently argued that while religion impeded thought and divided men, reason could conceivably become a unifying force and provide the basis for community. It was his hope that psychoanalysis could free men from the tyranny of both passion and repression and help realize the ideals associated with the Enlightenment. This famous passage from the last chapter of *The Future of an Illusion* indicates his faith in the possibility of a triumph of reason.*

We may insist as often as we like that man's intellect is powerless in comparison with his instinctual life, and we may be right in this. Nevertheless there is something peculiar about this weakness. The voice of the intellect is a soft one, but it does not rest till it has gained a hearing. Finally, after a countless succession of rebuffs, it succeeds. This is one of the few points on which one may be optimistic about the future of mankind, but it is in itself a point of no small importance. And from it one can derive yet other hopes. The primacy of the intellect lies, it is true, in a distant, distant future, but probably not in an *infinitely* distant one.

* Reprinted from Sigmund Freud, *The Future of an Illusion* (1927), **Complete Works**, Vol. XXI, p. 53 (1961). Reprinted by permission of Hogarth Press, London, and Liveright, Publishers, New York.

CONCLUSION

HAD PSYCHOANALYSIS remained simply a therapy for persons suffering from neurotic disorders, its impact would have been confined to the medical world. But in abolishing any sharp separation between neurosis and normality as far as the mechanisms of the unconscious mind were concerned, Freud challenged older conceptions of rational man and thereby necessitated new thinking and investigation in a variety of fields. At the same time, the rich and complex body of Freudian material, both clinical papers and socio-cultural commentaries, provided hypotheses and interpretations that could be extended to such fields as anthropology, art, religion, and philosophy.

In some respects the crisis initiated by Freud is a dated one. It is impossible to recapture a sense of the rabid opposition that greeted his statements about the unconscious and about the role of sexuality without having some picture of the Viennese world at the turn of the century—a society wrapped tightly in a morality of guilt in an age not yet exposed to the problems and insecurities produced by social mobility, industrialization, and mass standards. In our own day, the controversy over Freud's work has taken a somewhat different form. To be sure, there are still laymen who share at least in part the sentiments of those outraged Viennese; but so much of Freud has been absorbed (although often in a distorted form) into popular culture that the general response is hardly comparable. And, more important, in the disciplines where Freud's work initially had the greatest impact, hostile camps have formed among scholars who claim divergent and sometimes conflicting debts to Freud and psychoanalysis.

Among anthropologists as well as psychologists, for example, one finds a continuing debate as to whether the Freudian analysis of man, originally formulated with reference to patients who were apt to be hysterics of a sort that is far less common today, has the universal character Freud claimed for it—a debate in which Freud himself was actively participating until his death in 1939. In the area of psychotherapy itself, this country has seen an especially heated exchange between the more orthodox Freudians, who emphasize the instinctual bases of psychoanalytic theory, and the so-called Neo-Freudians, who stress cultural and adaptational factors and have weakened if not rejected the libido theory. There are likewise psychologists and social scientists of the behaviorist tradition and other schools of theory who consider Freudian formulations too amorphous and untestable to be taken seriously. The argument over Freud's work continues, as does the larger debate concerning the nature of man.

STUDY QUESTIONS

1] Much of what appears in Freud had been hinted at or even explicitly stated by various predecessors. How, then, do you account for the suspicion and even hostility that greeted Freud's work?

2] Why is the idea of repression so central to the psychoanalytic theory?

3] Does the deterministic base of psychoanalysis rule out any idea of freedom? If not, what would be an approach to the concept of freedom consistent with the findings of psychoanalysis?

4] What are the implications of psychoanalysis for morality? Does it provide any basis for distinguishing betweeen good and evil in an ethical sense?

5] Can it be argued in terms acceptable to Freud himself that religion may be necessary to man?

RECOMMENDED READINGS[2]

PRIMARY

BRILL, A. A., ed. and trans. *The Basic Writings of Sigmund Freud* (New York: Modern Library, 1938). This collection includes *Psychopathology of Everyday Life, The Interpretation of Dreams, Three Contributions to the Theory of Sex, Wit and Its Relation to the Unconscious, Totem and Taboo,* and *The History of the Psychoanalytic Movement.* While it is convenient to have them under one cover, the individual translations are not as good as those of James Strachey.

RICKMAN, JOHN, ed. *A General Selection from the Works of Sigmund Freud* (New York, 1957).

FREUD, SIGMUND. *An Autobiographical Study,* trans. by James Strachey (New York, 1963).

————. *Beyond the Pleasure Principle,* trans. by James Strachey (New York, 1959).

————. *Civilization and Its Discontents,* trans. by James Strachey (New York, 1962).

————. *The Ego and the Id,* trans. by James Strachey (New York, 1960).

————. *The Future of an Illusion,* trans. by W. D. Robson-Scott. Revised and newly edited by James Strachey (New York, 1961).

————. *Group Psychology and the Analysis of the Ego,* trans. by James Strachey (New York, 1940).

————. *Leonardo da Vinci: A Study in Psychosexuality,* trans. by A. A. Brill (New York, 1947).

————. *Moses and Monotheism,* trans. by Katherine Jones (New York, 1939).

---

[2] Most of these books are available in paperback and sometimes in more than one edition, as are other works of Freud not included in this brief list. His *Collected Papers,* published originally as five volumes of clinical and metapsychological writings, are now available in ten paperback volumes, edited by Philip Rieff, New York, 1963.

FREUD, SIGMUND. *New Introductory Lectures,* trans. by W. J. H. Sprott (New York, 1933).

————. *An Outline of Psychoanalysis,* trans. by James Strachey (New York, 1963).

SECONDARY

FREUD, ANNA. *The Ego and the Mechanisms of Defence,* trans. by Cecil Baines (London, 1937). A valuable sequel to the later ego psychology of Freud, written by his daughter.

FROMM, ERICH. *Escape from Freedom* (New York, 1941). One of the most famous of a number of attempts to apply psychoanalytic concepts to culture as a whole. It was written in response to the threat of Fascism. (It has appeared as an English paperback entitled *The Fear of Freedom.*)

HALL, CALVIN S. *A Primer of Freudian Psychology* (New York, 1954). Probably the most compact and lucid introduction to Freud's major theories for the beginning student.

JONES, ERNEST. *The Life and Work of Sigmund Freud,* 3 vols. (New York, 1953–57). The most comprehensive and well-written of the biographies of Freud, covering his personal life as well as the evolution of psychoanalysis. Jones was an associate of Freud for a number of years. The biography is also available in an abridged form, in paperback.

MARCUSE, HERBERT. *Eros and Civilization: A Philosophical Inquiry into Freud* (Boston, 1955). An attempt to turn Freud to the purposes of a radical critique of society by distinguishing necessary from "surplus" repression and examining the implications of the libido concept.

MAZLISH, BRUCE, ed. *Psychoanalysis and History* (Englewood Cliffs, N.J., 1963). A good introductory discussion of Freud's view of historical evolution followed by a series of essays on Freud's philosophy of history and another series suggesting ways in which psychoanalysis can assist historical interpretation.

MUNROE, RUTH L. *Schools of Psychoanalytic Thought* (New York, 1955). A careful and critical account of distinctions between Freudian and Neo-Freudian analysis with an attempt at integration.

NELSON, BENJAMIN, ed. *Freud and the Twentieth Century* (New York, 1957). A collection of essays, written from several perspectives and dealing with Freud's impact on social thought, literature, art, and philosophy, as well as on psychology.

RIEFF, PHILIP. *Freud: The Mind of the Moralist* (New York, 1959). A brilliant study of Freud in terms of the history of ideas.

RUITENBEEK, HENDRIK M., ed. *Psychoanalysis and Social Science* (New York, 1962). Eleven essays by social scientists, indicating a variety of responses to the challenge of Freud's work.

THOMPSON, CLARA (with the collaboration of Patrick Mullahy). *Psychoanalysis: Evolution and Development* (New York, 1957). A survey of theory and therapy—both Freudian and post-Freudian; it is far less detailed than the Munroe volume cited above.

TRILLING, LIONEL. *Freud and the Crisis of Our Culture* (Boston, 1955). A short essay dealing with Freud's attitude toward culture, which argues that Freud's emphasis on biology may emancipate man from the idea that culture is all-powerful.

The Bolshevik Seizure of Power, November 1917

RICHARD PIPES

HARVARD UNIVERSITY

CONTENTS

C] The Mobilization Order, November 6
(Listovki petrogradskikh bol'shevikov, 1917–1920)

4] The Seizure of Power, November 6–7

A] Lenin's Letter to the Central Committee, November 6
(Lenin, Sochineniia)

B] Protest of Menshevik and Socialist Revolutionary Deputies to the Second All-Russian Congress of Soviets, November 7
(Vtoroi vserossiiskii s'ezd sovetov rabochikh i soldatskikh deputatov)

C] Resolution of the Second Congress of Soviets Proclaiming the Overthrow of the Provisional Government, November 7–8
(Vtoroi vserossiiskii s'ezd sovetov rabochikh i soldatskikh deputatov)

5] Trotsky, "Lessons of October"
(Trotsky, Sochineniia)

CHRONOLOGY[1]

1917

MARCH 15   Nicholas II abdicates.

APRIL 16   Lenin, having crossed Germany from Switzerland, arrives in Petrograd.

MAY 17   Trotsky reaches Petrograd.

JULY 16–18   An abortive Bolshevik coup takes place in Petrograd; Lenin and other Bolshevik leaders go into hiding.

JULY 21   Kerensky becomes Prime Minister of the Provisional Government.

AUGUST 4   Trotsky is arrested.

SEPTEMBER 7–12   The so-called Kornilov uprising fails.

SEPTEMBER 14   The Provisional Government proclaims Russia a republic.

SEPTEMBER 17   Trotsky is released from prison.

OCTOBER 6   Trotsky becomes chairman of the Petrograd Soviet.

OCTOBER 20   The Provisional Government's Council of the Republic (or "Pre-Parliament") opens.

OCTOBER 22   The government orders part of the Petrograd garrison to the front; the soldiers, backed by the soviet, refuse. The same day Lenin moves from his Finnish hideaway to a place of concealment near Petrograd.

OCTOBER 23   A clandestine meeting of the Bolshevik Central Committee, with Lenin present, votes in favor of a seizure of power.

OCTOBER 24–26   The self-styled Congress of Soviets of the Northern Region is convened by the Bolshevik party in Petrograd.

OCTOBER 26   The Central Executive Committee of the Petrograd Soviet approves the creation of the Military-Revolutionary Committee to defend the city from an expected German attack.

OCTOBER 27   The Central Executive Committee of the Petrograd Soviet votes against a seizure of power.

OCTOBER 28   The Petrograd City Committee of the Bolshevik party meets with representatives of the city's re-

[1] All dates given here, in the introduction, and in the documents are "New Style," that is, they conform to the Gregorian calendar adopted in the West. The Julian calendar, used in Russia before 1918, was thirteen days behind.

gions to hear reports on the chances of a successful uprising.

OCTOBER 29   The Central Committee of the Bolshevik party meets with its regional and professional organizations; a three-member "military section" is appointed to direct the uprising.

OCTOBER 30   The Second All-Russian Congress of Soviets, scheduled to meet in Petrograd on November 2, is postponed to November 7.

OCTOBER 31   Trotsky, addressing the Petrograd Soviet in the name of the Bolsheviks, denies that the party intends to stage an uprising.

NOVEMBER 2   The Military-Revolutionary Committee of the Petrograd Soviet holds its first meeting.

NOVEMBER 3–4   At night a delegation sent by the Military-Revolutionary Committee demands that the District Military Staff of the Provisional Government submit for approval all its orders; the request is denied.

NOVEMBER 4   The Military-Revolutionary Committee declares the staff a "counterrevolutionary organ" and decrees only orders issued by the committee are to be obeyed by troops stationed in the city.

NOVEMBER 5   Commissars of the Military-Revolutionary Committee are dispatched to military units and garrisons.

NOVEMBER 6   The Military-Revolutionary Committee places all units on the alert. Trotsky persuades the garrison of the powerful Peter and Paul Fortress, with its arsenal, to subordinate itself to the committee. In the evening, Lenin, disguised, joins Trotsky at the Smolny.

NOVEMBER 7   In the early hours of the morning units of the Military-Revolutionary Committee take over strategic points and institutions. At 2:30 P.M. Trotsky opens the Second Congress of Soviets, announcing deposition of the Provisional Government and passage of power into the hands of the soviets. In the evening there is fighting over the Winter Palace, the seat of the Provisional Government.

NOVEMBER 8   At 2 A.M. the Winter Palace surrenders. At 5:30 A.M., after the Mensheviks and Socialists Revolutionaries leave in protest, the Congress of Soviets votes for passage of power to the soviets.

INTRODUCTION

T H E   E V E N T S of November 1917 which led in Russia to the establishment of the Soviet government can be studied with varying degrees of depth. They can be viewed as one phase in the modernization of an economically underdeveloped country; as a dramatic protest against Western influence and a reversion to pre-eighteenth–century institutions; as the first socialist revolution, the inauguration of a new era in world history; or as many other things. But all such interpretations should not obscure the fact that what happened in Petrograd on November 7, 1917, was the consequence of a deliberate act undertaken by a small group of persons for the purpose of seizing power. They had but a vague notion of what they would do with power once it was theirs, and certainly none of the interpretations which would subsequently attach themselves to their action. "First you engage yourself, and then you see," Lenin quoted Napoleon to his associates, who wanted a precise account of what he would do once he became head of government. All he knew was that he wanted power, and once it was his, nothing could wrest it from him.

The technique of power-seizure, with which this section is concerned, forms an important feature of Communism and all modern dictatorships. At bottom, the methods by which such different individuals as Napoleon, Lenin, and Hitler came to power were identical. All rose to prominence against a background of war and social unrest which had weakened the fabric of society and created a demand for firm authority. All took advantage of genuine social anxieties to hypnotize society with imaginary enemies—"Jacobins" in the case of Napoleon, "counterrevolutionaries" in the case of Lenin, "Jews and Communists" in the case of Hitler. By this means they gained power, ostensibly to suppress these enemies, but in fact to establish an irremovable dictatorship. The Bolshevik coup presents a classic example of this method, consciously devised and faultlessly carried out.

The Bolshevik seizure of power was made possible by the abdication in March 1917 of Nicholas II. The Emperor had resigned under the pressure of political and military leaders who felt that his removal from the scene was necessary if Russia was to stay in the war against Germany and Austria. This forfeiture of authority—one can hardly call it an overthrow—was at first greeted in the urban centers with wild enthusiasm. Indeed, the new regime, the Provisional Government, revitalized the war effort. But it was not long before insoluble problems began to arise. The imperial government was the pivot around which the country's political life had revolved for centuries. Its removal created a vacuum which the Provisional Government, short in both experience and personnel, could not fill. To make matters worse, radical intellectuals immediately took advantage of their newly won freedom to incite the population. With their encouragement, the peasants now began to call for more land, the workers for more pay, the national minorities for more autonomy. Such demands would have strained an established government in time of peace; pressed on a young government in time of war, they brought it to the verge of collapse.

At this point, the Provisional Government headed by Alexander Kerensky had two alternatives. It could have withdrawn from the war and concentrated on internal problems; or it could have kept on fighting but established a military dictatorship capable of suppressing the internal forces undermining its authority. For a variety of reasons, the government chose instead simultaneously to pursue the war and to carry out a social and political revolution at home. The result was both military stalemate and anarchy.

The government's predicament produced in the summer of 1917 two contenders for power. One was the generals, who, with the backing of conservative groups, wished to establish firm authority in the country and to mobilize all the available resources for the pursuit of the war. However, they lacked leadership, political experience, and even an articulated program. Their one effort—the so-called Kornilov uprising of early September 1917 —was so amateurish that to this day some historians are not quite certain whether it ever took place.

The second contender was the Bolsheviks, who placed all their hopes on the other alternatives: the withdrawal from war and promotion of social revolution. The Bolsheviks were a small party in terms of popular following, but they had two superb leaders. One, Lenin, was endowed with an indomitable will to power and an excellent sense of political realities. The other, Trotsky, was a marvelous orator capable of mesmerizing crowds (as Lenin was not), and a skillful manipulator of pseudoparliamentary institutions of the kind that revolution brings to the surface. Neither felt constrained by loyalty to the nation, as did the generals, or to democracy, as did the leaders of the other political parties. Their propaganda, directed primarily at the war-weary peasants in soldiers' and sailors' uniform, promised immediate peace and land. It had a powerful effect, and the Bolshevik ranks grew steadily. In mid-July they staged an abortive uprising against the Provisional Government, in consequence of which a number of their leaders were arrested or went into hiding. But they recovered their fortunes in the second week of September, when the government, believing itself to be menaced by General Kornilov and his followers, turned to them for help. At this time Trotsky was released on bail from prison. It may be noted that in their voluminous propaganda to the soldiers and sailors, the Bolsheviks never mentioned their one constant aim, which was the establishment of a one-party dictatorship; instead, they consistently put themselves forward as defenders from the generals and other alleged foes of the democratic institutions established since March.

Lenin, who had been hiding since July, decided by the end of September

that the time was ripe to stage another uprising and addressed a letter to
the party's Central Committee saying so (Document 1A). As the letter reveals, Lenin was very much afraid the world war would suddenly come to
an end, depriving the Bolsheviks of their main asset in the struggle for
power.

Lenin's colleagues, however, were hesitant. The July fiasco fresh in their
minds, they had no desire to jeopardize the growing party with another abortive coup which could cripple it once and for all. They were convinced
that time was working in their favor; in particular they attached much importance to their growing influence over the soviets. It was Trotsky who
more than anyone else saw the strategic advantages in fusing the Bolshevik
bid for power with the whole soviet movement.

The word *soviet* means no more than council. As semipolitical bodies
these councils first came into existence during the Revolution of 1905. Originally they were merely striking committees of industrial workers, operating
under worker direction. But radical intellectuals even then saw their political
potential and transformed them into instruments of political pressure. In
October 1905 the St. Petersburg Soviet, by organizing a general strike, played
a crucial role in forcing the imperial government to grant the country a constitution. Trotsky had been very active in these events, in the course of which
he acquired much skill in manipulating the soviets—a skill which was to be
of decisive importance to the Bolsheviks later on. The soviets reappeared
all over the country in 1917 as spontaneous institutions of popular self-rule.
Most of the pressure on the Provisional Government for internal reforms
was channeled through them. The socialist intellectuals, especially the Mensheviks, viewed the soviets as institutions expressing the general will, whose
task it was to keep the Provisional Government (a "bourgeois" government,
in their eyes) on the correct "democratic" path, in a regime resembling a
dyarchy. They did not think of them as capable of assuming full political
responsibility.

Lenin's attitude toward the soviets varied with the successes and failures
which the Bolsheviks experienced in them. In the spring of 1917, developing the theses first formulated by Trotsky, he advanced the slogan "All power
to the soviets." In this manner he hoped to weaken the authority of the
Provisional Government. But when the soviets, whose executive committees
were largely in the hands of Mensheviks and Socialists Revolutionaries,[2]
refused to back his slogan and helped the government to suppress the Bolshevik July uprising, he changed his mind. He now declared the soviets "nonenti-
ties, marionettes," and demanded that the party concentrate all its efforts
on organizing an armed uprising with its own forces. This demand met with
opposition from the majority of the Central Committee who, largely under

---

[2] The Mensheviks were Marxist socialists who tended to be more evolutionary and
democratic than the Bolsheviks. The Socialists Revolutionaries were socialists whose program emphasized agrarian democracy, socialization of land. and far-reaching political decentralization.

Trotsky's influence, persisted in exploring the possibilities of synchronizing the bid for power with the forthcoming All-Russian Congress of Soviets. Trotsky planned first to maneuver the Petrograd Soviet into giving him control of the city's military units, and then, on the day of the meeting of the Congress of Soviets, to take over the capital city in its name. He and most of the other members of the Central Committee were quite convinced (and probably correctly) that a direct attack on the government, advocated by Lenin, would spell disaster. Analyzing his actions several years later, Trotsky stated that "the preparation of the uprising and its realization under the cover of preparing the Second Congress of Soviets and under the slogan of defending it put in our [that is, Bolshevik] hands inestimable advantages" (Document 5). Lenin, however, was so infuriated by this strategy, behind which he suspected fear of action, that in a letter of October 12 (Document 1B) he offered his resignation from the Central Committee (a threat which he did not carry out). "First defeat Kerensky and then convene the Congress [of Soviets]," was his advice.

In the meantime, thanks to the relentless work of Trotsky and his colleagues on the Central Committee, the Bolsheviks were indeed gaining adherents in the great urban soviets. On October 8 they won a majority in the Petrograd Soviet, and Trotsky was elected its chairman. In this position he was superbly placed to carry through his plan of action. Lenin, apparently persuaded of the soundness of this procedure, wrote another letter on October 21, called "Counsel of a Bystander," in which he approved the fusion of the Bolshevik uprising with the assumption of power by the soviets, but warned that the passage of power could not be achieved peacefully, merely by voting, and offered advice on general principles of insurrectionary procedure (Document 1C).

The actual preparations for the coup began on October 22, when the Provisional Government gave Trotsky the chance for which he had been waiting. On that day the government ordered a number of military units stationed in Petrograd to leave the city and move to the front. The demoralized troops did not want to go, and the issue was raised in the soviet. The Bolsheviks now sounded the alarm, presenting this order as a counterrevolutionary move designed to surrender Petrograd to the Germans. To meet it, they proposed a resolution calling on the soviet to assume responsibility for the defense of the city, and providing for the creation of a "Revolutionary Committee of Defense" to direct it (Document 2A). This Committee the Bolsheviks had secretly decided to use as the instrument of seizing power. The Petrograd Soviet, confused by rapidly changing events and hypnotized by Trotsky's rhetorical fireworks, approved the Bolshevik resolution. The deception worked, and Trotsky afterwards claimed that the issue of power had been in effect settled on that day.

On October 23 Lenin, who had secretly made his way to Petrograd the preceding day, attended a clandestine meeting of the Central Committee. At this meeting it was formally voted to carry out an armed uprising. No date was set, although there are reasons to believe the participants thought either of November 2, when the Second All-Russian Congress had been scheduled to convene in Petrograd, or November 4, the national "Day of soviets."

Trotsky now developed in the press and from the speaker's rostrum an intensive campaign of propaganda in which he accused the Provisional Government in a variety of ways but with persistent vehemence of planning subversive action against the soviets and conspiring either with the Germans or with the Russian generals, or both, to abandon Petrograd and with it the achievements of the "revolution." Impressed by his speech (Document 2B), the members of the Bolshevik-sponsored "Congress of Soviets of the Northern Region" voted on October 26 in favor of the transfer of all power to the soviets (Document 2C; see also Document 2E). The Menshevik members of the Petrograd Soviet issued a formal protest in which they sought to explain the meaning of the Bolshevik strategy, but theirs was a voice in the wilderness. When, at the meeting of the Petrograd Soviet of October 31, a Menshevik deputy inquired whether there was any truth in the rumor that the Bolsheviks were planning an armed uprising against the wishes of the soviet, Trotsky flatly dismissed this charge as bourgeois calumny. "We conceal nothing. I declare in the name of the soviet that we have not ordered any armed uprising" (Document 2F). This denial calmed somewhat the fear of the soviet and the vigilance of the Provisional Government.

The Bolsheviks at this time concentrated their attention on the Military-Revolutionary Committee, whose membership, thanks to Trotsky's position as chairman of the soviet, they were able to determine. The soviet, disregarding the warnings of the Mensheviks, authorized this committee to establish contact with the military units located in Petrograd and to dispatch to them commissars in order "to protect certain institutions and depots." In this manner, the Bolsheviks, disguising their agents as legitimate representatives of the soviet, succeeded in placing their men in most of the military detachments of Petrograd and in assuming control over arsenals containing weapons and ammunition.

In the meantime, the Executive Committee of the All-Russian Congress of Soviets, dominated by Mensheviks and Socialists Revolutionaries, voted to postpone the Second All-Russian Congress of Soviets from November 2 to November 7 in order to allow the deputies more time for travel. This decision rather played into the hands of the Bolsheviks (though this was not apparent at the time) because their forces were not yet sufficiently organized for action. They now moved the date of the uprising to November 7.

The coup began to unroll on the night of November 3–4, when a delegation from the Military-Revolutionary Committee appeared before the District Military Staff of the Provisional Government, which was in charge of the city's garrison, and demanded that the staff henceforth submit all orders to the committee for approval. Agreement to this demand would have been tantamount to a surrender of authority to the committee, and the city's military commander rejected it in no uncertain terms. The Bolsheviks, acting through the Military-Revolutionary Committee, then issued a special order to the city's military units which declared that the staff had broken off relations with the soviets and become a tool of the counterrevolution. "Orders not signed by this [Military-Revolutionary] Committee are void," it stated (Document 3A). This order was followed by two others (Documents 3B and 3C) in which military units were alerted to defend the "revolution" and the soviets from an alleged attack by the Provisional Government, and reminded of their duty to take orders only from the Military-Revolutionary Committee and its commissars.

In fact, however, not only did the Provisional Government plan no offensive action against the soviet, but it failed to take the most elementary precautions for its own security. Prime Minister Kerensky was sublimely confident that another Bolshevik coup would permit him to liquidate the party, and he spent much of his time away at the army's headquarters in Mogilev. Even Lenin, still in hiding, was not well aware what Trotsky was up to. On November 6 Lenin wrote a fervent letter to the Central Committee in which he insisted that the uprising be staged immediately, it did not matter how and under what slogans, but without a moment's delay: revolutions are decided not by votes, he reminded his colleagues, even votes of soviets, but by force (Document 4A).

On November 6, while the delegates to the Second Congress were assembling, Trotsky made a speech in which he quieted whatever fears they may have had by asserting once more that all the military preparations undertaken by the Military-Revolutionary Committee were purely defensive. "The Revolutionary Committee," he said, "came into being not as an organ of an uprising, but on the basis of the self-defense of the revolution." It was created to prevent the surrender of the city. All its measures had only this purpose in mind.

On the night of November 6–7 the Military-Revolutionary Committee ordered the troops to occupy key points in the city and then to disarm units and patrols subordinated to the staff. The action proceeded quite peacefully —"like a change of guards," according to one eyewitness. Trotsky hoped to have the whole city in his hands by the time the Second Congress opened its first session in the afternoon of November 7. But some government units stationed in the Winter Palace, the center of the Provisional Government, resisted. While a certain amount of desultory shooting took place, the congress convened. The Mensheviks and Socialists Revolutionaries, protesting against the Bolshevik action as illegal and "counterrevolutionary," walked out of the congress (Document 4B). Lenin, who in the evening of November 6 had arrived in disguise at the Smolny Institute where the congress assembled, now made his first public appearance. Later that night the congress proclaimed the passage of all power to the soviets (Document 4C). In this proclamation, again, nothing was said of the Bolshevik party.

Trotsky thus succeeded in disguising the coup which was to place the

Bolsheviks in complete control over the country as a defense of the city of Petrograd and of the principle of rule by councils. The warning of the Mensheviks and Socialists Revolutionaries that the coup, organized by the Bolsheviks behind the back of the soviet, signified in fact not the beginning but the end of the whole principle of soviet authority was quite lost on the delegates, who for months had been accustomed to a dyarchy between the Provisional Government and the soviets. To most of them the events of November 7 probably simply meant a *de jure* recognition of the *de facto* situation: the Provisional Government collapsed; the soviets took over. The Bolsheviks naturally played along with this delusion, agreeing to call the new authority a "soviet government" and giving every appearance of a willingness to share power with other parties represented in the soviets. In fact, however, on November 7 they began to exert, behind the soviet façade, an unlimited one-party rule.

DOCUMENTS

1] Three Dispatches from Lenin, Fall 1917

> After the failure of the Bolshevik uprising in July 1917, the Provisional
> Government issued warrants for the arrest of the party's leaders. Lenin man-
> aged to elude arrest and to hide in Finland, which was then part of the
> Russian Empire. From there he kept irregularly in touch with the party's
> Central Committee, which maintained a clandestine existence in Petrograd.
> Its leading figures were Trotsky, Kamenev, and Zinovev, the latter two being
> resolutely opposed to an armed uprising. Lenin's letters were intended to prod
> the Central Committee into action. His advice was not heeded, and the Central
> Committee proceeded to seize power through the Petrograd Soviet and its
> Military-Revolutionary Committee.

A] THE BOLSHEVIKS MUST SEIZE POWER, SEPTEMBER 25–27 *

To the Central Committee and the Petrograd and Moscow Committees of
the Russian Social Democratic Labor party: [3]

With a majority in the Soviets of Workers' and Soldiers' Deputies in both
capitals, the Bolsheviks can and must seize power.

They can, because the active majority of the popular revolutionary elements in both capitals is sufficient to swing the masses, to overcome the
enemy's resistance and destroy it, to take power and hold it. By immediately
proposing a democratic peace, by immediately giving land to the peasants, by
restoring the democratic institutions and liberties which Kerensky has crushed
and destroyed, the Bolsheviks will establish a government that *no one* will
overthrow.

Most of the people are *for* us. This has been shown by the long and
arduous path followed from May 19 to September 13 and to September 25;
our majority in the Soviets of the capitals is the *result* of the movement of
the people *over to our side*. This is also demonstrated by the vacillations of
the SR's and Mensheviks and by the increased influence of the Internationalists among them.[4]

[3] The Russian Social Democratic Labor party was the main Marxist party. It was split
into a Bolshevik (Leninist) faction and a Menshevik faction. *Editor.*

[4] The Internationalists were Bolsheviks and other socialists opposed to the continuation
of the war. *Editor.*

* Translated by Daniel Mulholland from V. I. Lenin, *Sochineniia,* 3rd ed. (Moscow–
Leningrad, 1935), Vol. XXI, pp. 193–94.

The Democratic Conference[5] does *not* represent the majority of the revolutionary nation but *merely the conciliationist petty-bourgeois leadership.* One must not be deceived by election figures, since the question is not one of elections: compare the municipal elections of Petrograd and Moscow to those of the soviets. Compare the elections in Moscow to the strike there on August 25: these are the objective criteria that indicate where is the majority of revolutionary elements: at the head of the masses.

The Democratic Conference is deceiving the peasants since it gives them neither peace nor land.

Only a Bolshevik government will satisfy the peasants.

But why must the Bolsheviks seize power right *now?*

Because the imminent surrender of Petrograd will diminish our chances of success a hundredfold.

And we are not strong enough to prevent the surrender of Petrograd while Kerensky & Co. are at the head of the army.

Nor can we "wait for" the Constituent Assembly[6] since Kerensky & Co. *can break it up* at any time by the same device of surrendering Petrograd. Only our party, having taken power, can guarantee the convocation of the Constituent Assembly and then, having taken power, it will indict the other parties for procrastination and make the charge stick.

Only if we act quickly can we avert a separate peace between the English and German imperialists.

The people are tired of the vacillations of the Mensheviks and SR's. Only our victory in the capitals will rally the peasants to us.

The question is not one of the "day" or "moment" of the insurrection in a narrow sense. Only the general consensus of those in contact with the workers and soldiers, with the *masses,* can make that decision.

The point is that our party is virtually holding its *own* congress at the Democratic Conference, and this congress, whether it wants to or not, must decide *the fate of the revolution.*

The point is to make the *task* clear for the party, to make *armed insurrection* in Petrograd and Moscow (plus the district), the conquest of power, the overthrow of the government, the order of the day. We must consider *how* to agitate for this without expressing ourselves so in print.

[5] The Democratic Conference was one of the several meetings organized by the Provisional Government in an effort to win public support for its policies. It convened in September 1917. *Editor.*

[6] The Constituent Assembly, planned for January 1918, was to have been the representative body charged with the task of legislating Russia's fundamental political and social laws, and to have formed a new, permanent government replacing the Provisional Government. Despite Lenin's statement, it was not Kerensky but Lenin himself who broke it up. The elections, held on a broad franchise, gave the Bolsheviks only one-fourth of the seats, whereupon Lenin ordered it dissolved by force after it had held its first session. *Editor.*

We must remember and take to heart Marx's words on insurrection: "*Insurrection is an art,*" etc.[7]

It would be naive to wait for a "formal" Bolshevik majority: no revolution waits for *that*. Nor are Kerensky & Co. waiting—they are preparing the surrender of Petrograd. It is precisely the miserable vacillations of the Democratic Conference that must and will exhaust the patience of the workers of Petrograd and Moscow. History will not forgive us if we do not take power now.

We have no machinery of government? We do—the Soviets and democratic organizations. The international situation right at *this* moment, *on the eve* of a separate peace between the English and the Germans, is in *our* favor. To offer peace to the world right now is to *win*.

If we seize power at once in Moscow and Petrograd (it does not matter who begins, perhaps it can even be Moscow) we will win *unconditionally and indubitably*.

N. Lenin

B] THE CRISIS HAS RIPENED, OCTOBER 12

The selection that follows is from a letter written in protest against the Central Committee's opposition to Lenin's demand for an immediate armed uprising.*

What should be done? One must *aussprechen was ist*, "tell all," admit the fact that we have in the Central Committee and in the leadership of the party a tendency, an attitude which would *wait for* the Congress of Soviets, which *opposes* the immediate seizure of power, which opposes an immediate insurrection. We must overcome this tendency, this view.

Otherwise the Bolsheviks will *disgrace* themselves forever and *disintegrate* as a party.

Because to let the moment go by and "wait for" the Congress of Soviets is *complete idiocy* and *unmitigated treachery.*

It is unmitigated treachery to the German workers.[8] We cannot wait for their revolution to *begin*!! If we were to, even the liberdans [9] would give us their "support." But this revolution *cannot* begin while Kerensky, Kishkin,[10] & Co. are in power.

---

[7] Lenin refers to Marx's analysis in his *Revolution and Counterrevolution in Germany*, summarized below in Lenin's "Counsel of a Bystander." *Editor.*

[8] In the sense that (according to Lenin) the German workers were relying on the Russians to put an end to the war. *Editor.*

[9] A play on words on the names of Liber (real name M. I. Goldman) and F. I. Dan, two prominent Menshevik figures in the Soviet organization. *Editor.*

[10] N. M. Kishkin, a liberal, was a member of the Provisional Government. *Editor.*

* Translated by Daniel Mulholland from V. I. Lenin, *Sochineniia*, 3rd ed. (Moscow–Leningrad, 1935), Vol. XXI, pp. 240–41.

It is unmitigated treachery to the peasants. With the Soviets of both *capitals* behind us, to allow the suppression of the peasant revolt means to *lose*,
and *deservedly* so, all the confidence the peasant has in us; it means to fall
in the peasants' eyes to the level of the liberdans and the rest of the scoundrels.

To "wait for" the Congress of Soviets is complete idiocy because it means
to waste *weeks*, when weeks, and even days, decide now *everything*. This is
a cowardly refusal to take power, since by November 14–15 that will become
impossible (both politically and technically, since the Cossacks will be called
out on the day of any such stupidly "scheduled" [11] insurrection).

To "wait for" the Congress of Soviets is idiocy because the Congress *will
not produce anything, cannot produce anything.*

But what of the "moral" significance of the Congress? Amazing!! What
is the "significance" of resolutions and negotiations with the liberdans when
we know that the Soviets are *in favor* of the peasant and yet the peasant is
being *suppressed!!* By this means we will reduce the soviets to the role of
miserable windbags. First defeat Kerensky and then convene the Congress.

The Bolsheviks are *assured* right now of success in the insurrection because (1) we can [12] (if we do not "wait for" the Congress of Soviets) strike
unexpectedly from three directions, from Petrograd, Moscow, and the Baltic
fleet; (2) we have slogans that guarantee support for us: "Down with the
government that suppresses the peasant revolt against the landlords!" (3) we
have a majority *in the country;* [13] (4) the Mensheviks and SR's have gone
to pieces; (5) we have the technical means to seize power in Moscow (which
could even begin in order to paralyze the enemy with surprise); (6) we have
thousands of armed workers and soldiers in Petrograd who can seize instantly
the Winter Palace, the General Staff, the telephone exchange, and all the
major typographies; we cannot be ejected from these places, and agitation
in the *army* will then be such that it will be *impossible* to use it against a
government of peace, land for the peasant, etc.

If we should strike instantly, suddenly from three points, Petrograd, Moscow, and the Baltic fleet, the chances are 99 per cent that we will win with
fewer losses than we had during July 16–18, for *the troops will not come
out* against a government of peace. Even if Kerensky has *already* introduced
"loyal" cavalry, etc. into Petrograd, still, given a blow from two sides and
the sympathy of the army *for us*, Kerensky will be forced to *surrender*. If
we do not take power now, with all the chances on our side, all talk about
the power of Soviets is nothing but a *lie*.

Not to take power now, to "wait," to gibber in the Central Executive
Committee [of the Soviet], to confine ourselves to the "struggle for an or-

[11] To "convene" the Congress of Soviets on November 2 in order to decide to "take
power"—how can this be distinguished from a stupid "scheduling" of the insurrection?
Power can be seized now, while on November 2–11 they will not let you take it.
[12] What has the party done to *study* the disposition of troops, etc., to realize the
insurrection as an "art"? Nothing but talk in the Central Committee, etc.!!
[13] This statement had no basis in fact. *Editor.*

gan" [of the Soviet], the "struggle for the congress" [of Soviets], all this means the *ruin of the revolution.*

In view of the fact that the Central Committee has *not even answered* my entreaties in this spirit since the opening of the Democratic Conference, that the Central Organ *expunges* from my articles remarks on such howling blunders of the Bolsheviks as the shameful decision to participate in the Pre-Parliament [14] and the offer to the Mensheviks of a place in the soviet presidium, etc., etc., considering all this I must understand here a "subtle" hint that the Central Committee is unwilling even to consider this question, a subtle hint to shut my mouth, and an invitation to withdraw.

I must therefore *submit my request to resign from the Central Committee,* which I now do, reserving for myself the freedom of agitation *in the ranks* of the party and at the party congress.[15]

For it is my complete conviction that if we "wait" for the Congress of Soviets and let this moment slip by we are *ruining* the revolution.

October 12   N. *Lenin*

P.S. A series of facts indicates that *even* the Cossack troops will not march against a government of peace! And how many Cossacks are there? Where are they? Anyway, won't the army as a whole detail units to fight *for us?*

c] COUNSEL OF A BYSTANDER, OCTOBER 21 *

LETTER TO THE CENTRAL COMMITTEE

I am writing these lines on October 21 and there is little hope that it will reach you, Petrograd comrades, by the twenty-second. Possibly they will be outdated, since the Congress of Northern Soviets [16] is fixed for October 23. But still I will try to give the "counsel of a bystander" in the event the probable insurrection of the workers and soldiers of Petrograd and the entire environs is imminent but has not yet taken place.

It is clear that all power must pass to the soviets. It should be no less indisputable to every Bolshevik that the revolutionary proletarian power (or the Bolshevik power—they are one and the same now) will receive the greatest sympathy and complete support of all the toilers and exploited of the world in general, of the warring countries in particular, and especially of the

[14] The Pre-Parliament was another national conference convened by the Provisional Government to bolster its position. It met early in October. *Editor.*

[15] Lenin did not carry out his threat to resign. *Editor.*

[16] The Congress of Soviets of the Northern Region was a meeting organized by the Bolsheviks without authorization from the Central Executive Committee of the soviets. It was heavily Bolshevik in representation. See below Trotsky's speech and resolutions (Documents 2B and 2C). *Editor.*

* Translated by Daniel Mulholland from V. I. Lenin, *Sochineniia,* 3rd ed. (Moscow–Leningrad), 1935, Vol. XXI, pp. 319–20.

Russian peasantry. There is no need to dwell on these altogether well-known and long proven truths.

But it is necessary to dwell on one thing that is far from clear to all our comrades: that the transfer of power to the Soviets means now in practice an armed insurrection. This seems obvious, but not everyone has pondered it and thought it through. To reject now the armed insurrection would be tantamount to rejecting the principal slogan of Bolshevism (All Power to the Soviets) and all revolutionary proletarian internationalism in general.

But armed insurrection is a *special* form of political struggle, subject to special rules, which must be carefully pondered. Karl Marx expressed this truth with striking force when he wrote that armed *"insurrection, like war, is an art."*

Marx put forth among the main tenets of this art:

1. *Never play* with insurrection, but, once having started it, know firmly that it must *be carried through to the end.*

2. It is necessary to concentrate a *great superiority of force* in the decisive place, at the decisive moment, otherwise the enemy, being better prepared and organized, will destroy the rebels.

3. Once the insurrection is begun, one must act with the greatest resolution and absolutely, unconditionally take the *offensive.* "Defence is death to an armed insurrection."

4. One must try to surprise the enemy napping, to seize the moment when his troops are dispersed.

5. One must chalk up *daily* (or, in the case of a single city, even hourly) some kind of success, however small, buttressing at any cost the *"superiority of morale."*

Marx has summed up the lessons on armed insurrection for all revolutions with the words of "the greatest master of revolutionary tactics in history, Danton: 'Audacity, audacity, and once more audacity.' "

Applied to Russia and to October 1917 this means: a simultaneous attack on Petrograd with all possible surprise and speed, unconditionally from without and within, from the workers' districts and from Finland, Revel, and Kronstadt,[17] an attack by the *whole* fleet, the concentration of a *gigantic preponderance* of force against the fifteen to twenty thousand (possibly more) that our "bourgeois guard" (the Junkers), our "Vendean troops" (part of the Cossacks), etc. can muster.[18]

Our three main forces, the fleet, the workers, and the military units, must be combined absolutely to seize and hold, *regardless of the casualties,* (a) the telephone and (b) the telegraph exchanges, (c) the railroad stations, (d) the bridges most especially.

---

[17] Kronstadt is a Russian naval base on an island off Leningrad (Petrograd). *Editor.*
[18] Junkers were military cadets, generally favorable to the Provisional Government. "Vendean troops" refers to the Vendée, the center of royalist opposition during the French Revolution. *Editor.*

Separate the *most resolute* elements (our "shock troops" and *worker youth,* along with the best of the sailors) into small units for the occupation of the most vital points and *for their* participation everywhere in important operations, such as: [19]

To surround and isolate Petrograd, to seize it by the combined attack of the fleet, the workers, and army, such is the task which requires *artistry and triple audacity.*

We must set up units of the best workers, supplied with rifles and explosives, to attack and surround the enemy's "centers" (the Junker schools, the telegraph and telephone, etc.) under the motto: *"Death to all, but the enemy shall not get through."*

Let us hope that if the uprising is decided upon the leaders will successfully apply the great legacy of Danton and Marx.

The triumph of both the Russian and the world revolution depends on two or three days of struggle.

"Bystander"

2] Trotsky Takes the Offensive, October 22–25

A] THE FORMATION OF THE MILITARY-REVOLUTIONARY COMMITTEE

On the pretext of defending Petrograd from the advancing German armies, Trotsky persuaded the Petrograd Soviet to establish a Military-Revolutionary Committee with authority over the city's garrison and arsenals, which it did through the document that follows, the Resolution of the Petrograd Soviet of Workers' and Soldiers' Deputies on the Removal of the Petrograd Garrison. The Committee in fact prepared the forces for the Bolshevik *coup d'état.* [*]

At this moment of mortal peril to the people and the revolution the Petrograd Soviet of Workers' and Soldiers' Deputies declares: the Kerensky government leads the country to ruin. Having demonstrated its total inability to conduct war, it cannot bring itself to propose peace. In fact, however, the whole salvation of the country lies in a quick conclusion of peace. Together with the bourgeoisie, Kerensky is preparing to hand over Petrograd, the main citadel of the revolution, to the Germans. The Allied imperialists are clearly conniving in Wilhelm's advance on Petrograd.[20] The heroic sailors, perish-

---

[19] A passage seems to be missing here in the original. *Editor.*

[20] The charge that Kerensky and the allies were plotting with the Germans to surrender Petrograd is, of course, without foundation. *Editor.*

[*] Translated by Daniel Mulholland from K. Riabinskii, ed., *Revoliutsiia 1917 goda* (Moscow–Leningrad, 1926), Vol. V, p. 238.

ing, see in the Bonaparte-Kerensky not a friend but an enemy. The Petrograd Soviet of Workers' and Soldiers' Deputies cannot assume any responsibility before the army for the so-called strategy of the Provisional Government, and particularly for the removal of troops from Petrograd. The salvation of Petrograd and the country lies in the transfer of power to the soviets. The soviet government must propose an immediate armistice to all nations and, until peace is concluded, take in its own hands the task of assuring the fighting capacity of the army and of defending Petrograd and the country. At the same time the Petrograd Soviet of Workers' and Soldiers' Deputies calls on the garrison of Petrograd to take immediately all measures to develop and consolidate its combat readiness. The Petrograd Soviet charges the Executive Committee, jointly with the Soldiers' Section and representatives of garrisons connected with Petrograd, to organize a Revolutionary Committee of Defense, which is to concentrate in its hands all information concerning the defense of Petrograd and its approaches, as well as to take all steps to arm the workers and thus guarantee both the revolutionary defense of Petrograd and the security of the people from the attack which the military and civilian Kornilovites [21] are openly preparing.

B] Trotsky's Report to the So-Called Congress of Soviets of the Northern Region on the Activity of the Petrograd Soviet, October 24

At this Bolshevik-sponsored meeting Trotsky appeared as the representative of the Petrograd Soviet. The purpose of his speech was to justify a resolution calling for the transfer of all power to the soviets.*

We are the party which sets the tone of the soviets and if, despite the disappointment of our great initial hopes, we still have a strong soviet, this is because it is armed with a new program of merciless struggle with its class enemy. The Petrograd Soviet is waging an implacable struggle with the government and the parties which support it.

You know that when the danger from the front became sufficiently apparent the Provisional Government began to make efforts to move to Moscow. At its side were our "defensists," [22] who, having given up Petrograd without a fight, would continue to win good marks for their defensist policy in Moscow.

Hatred for revolutionary Petrograd has inspired this plan.

---

[21] The Kornilovites were followers of General Kornilov, a proponent of strong authority and leader of the so-called Kornilov uprising in September. *Editor.*

[22] The defensists, unlike the internationalists, favored Russian participation in World War I. *Editor.*

* Translated by Daniel Mulholland from L. D. Trotsky, *Sochineniia* (Moscow, n.d.), Vol. III, Part 2, pp. 5–6.

Our government can run away from Petrograd, but the revolutionary people of Petrograd will not leave: they will defend it to the last.

Petrograd, as the Bible says, is the "city on the mount," it is visible to all. Everyone knows our mood and our work.

And now the General Staff has offered a plan for removing from Petrograd two-thirds of its garrison. We were faced with this question. The soviet "authorities" [23] have decided to accede to the staff, even though they distrust those who undertake the removal [of troops].

The Baltic fleet has spoken otherwise. It has said that it does not believe a single word of the Provisional Government, this veritable government of national betrayal. And yet, nonetheless, the Baltic fleet dies defending the revolution.

The military authorities have demanded the removal of the troops; we do not know where to, but we do know where from—from revolutionary Petrograd. Before Kornilov's conspiracy an order was also issued for the removal of troops, and we were assured then, too, that this was necessary for strategic reasons.

We cannot say, as do the defensists (who, however, do not make the slightest effort to defend the revolution), "if the government orders, we must obey." The Petrograd Soviet does not and will not take on itself such a responsibility.

After all, this question will confront tomorrow every military unit of the Petrograd garrison, and we are aware of our responsibility to Russia and her people.

At issue is the fate of Petrograd, and we want to settle it jointly with you, the representatives of the provincial soviets.

We must take in our hands the defense of the country as a whole. The best defense of the country will be an immediate peace proposal to the peoples of the whole world, over the heads of their imperialist governments.

Dare we entrust the conduct of the war to people who can neither wage war nor conclude peace?

There is no one except the Soviet of Workers' and Soldiers' Deputies able to cope with this task because outside the Soviets there are only Kornilovites, or semi-Kornilovites, or political failures who have broken with the revolutionary people.

There is only one way out: the destiny of the nation must pass to the All-Russian Soviet of Workers' and Soldiers' Deputies.

---

[23] "Soviet 'authorities' " refers to the Central Executive Committee, controlled by anti-Bolshevik socialists (Mensheviks and Socialists Revolutionaries). *Editor.*

c] Resolution of the Congress of Soviets of the
Northern Region on the Report on the Current
Situation, October 25 *

The Northern Regional Congress of Soviets of Workers' and Soldiers' Deputies has met during the most critical days of the Russian revolution.

The army is being disorganized from above by the whole policy of the Provisional Government, most of all by its refusal to wage a struggle for peace and by the leading role played by the counterrevolutionary part of the officer corps which is openly preparing a new, more dangerous attempt at Kornilovism. Under these circumstances, all the ministerial programs for the democratization of the army and improvement of its combat readiness are empty words. The military stance of the nation inevitably deteriorates with every hour. There is no solution this way.

Russia lacks an independent foreign policy. The Allied imperialists, losing ground in their own countries, continue to dispose of the fate of the Russian people. The plan to send Skobelev to the Paris Conference,[24] supposedly on behalf of the Russian democracy, to collaborate diplomatically with the worst enemies of democracy, is an effort of futility and hypocrisy. The question of a fourth winter campaign is actually being decided for the Russian soldier on the stock markets of London and New York.

The ruling German plunderers, confronted by incipient insurrection in the German fleet, have moved their troops on Petrograd. The mighty English fleet remains passive in the face of the serious danger hanging over the capital of Russia, the center of her war industry. The Russian counterrevolutionaries are united with the English imperialists in their hatred toward revolutionary Petrograd and both find an actual accomplice in the bloody-handed German Kaiser.

The internal condition of the country is intolerable; marauding, speculation, and plunder prevail in all branches of the war economy. The worsening anarchy in food supply arouses the indignation of the starving masses. The selfishness of the landlords, backed by the agrarian policy of the Provisional Government, has driven the desperate peasants to launch an agrarian revolt. The working class, including the railroad, postal, and telegraph workers, find themselves in a tightening noose of inflation, lockouts, unemployment, and starvation. The financial policy of the Provisional Government knows one precept only: "After us, the deluge."

Handpicked by the defensists-conciliationists, the impotent Pre-Parliament

---

[24] The Paris Conference of the Allied powers was scheduled for November 1917 for the purpose of discussing and coordinating war activities. Skobelev, a Menshevik and member of the Petrograd Soviet, was sent there as representative of the Provisional Government and the soviets with a mandate calling for general peace. *Editor.*

* Translated by Daniel Mulholland from L. D. Trotsky, *Sochineniia* (Moscow, n.d.), Vol. III, Part 2, pp. 11–13.

only serves as camouflage for the policy of the bourgeoisie, of Kerensky, of the military leadership and Allied diplomacy—the policy of counterrevolutionary conspiracy and the inevitable disruption of the Constituent Assembly.

The coalition regime [25] has disorganized, bled, and tormented the country. The so-called Democratic Conference has ended in pitiable bankruptcy. The workers, soldiers and [class-]conscious peasants have indignantly rejected the ruinous and treacherous policy of alliance with the bourgeoisie.

The nation can be saved only by an immediate transfer of all power to the organs of the revolution, the Soviets of Workers', Soldiers', and Peasants' Deputies, in the center and locally.

The Soviet government will immediately offer, in the name of Russia, an armistice on all fronts and an honorable democratic peace to all nations.

The Soviet government will immediately give all land of the nobility to the peasants without compensation.

The Soviet government will proceed immediately to demobilize the industry and to satisfy the peasants' needs.

The Soviet government will convene the Constituent Assembly at the appointed time.

The Provisional Government is ruining the country and survives only by force. But the country wants to live and the Provisional Government must stand aside. The soviets have not only justice on their side but force as well. The time for talk has passed. The hour has come when only the resolute, unanimous action of all soviets can save the country and the revolution and solve the problem of central authority.

D] MENSHEVIK PROTEST, PETROGRAD SOVIET, OCTOBER 29 *

Broido, speaking in the name of the Mensheviks, announced that the question under discussion was bound up with the defense of the capital. None of us, he said, "questions that the taking of Petrograd by the Germans is a death blow to the revolution. But we should do nothing which would interfere with unity of effort directed toward the defense of Petrograd. The defense of Petrograd is the task of the staff of the Petrograd Military District. The Revolutionary Committee is a Bolshevik idea, but the Bolsheviks have no men capable of resolving the issues connected with the defense of the city. Comrades, we are passing through an unusually serious time. Petrograd is threatened not only by the Germans, but also inside Petrograd agitation is being carried on, inciting the masses to come out in the streets with the slogan, 'All Power to the Soviets.' Under these circumstances, the Revolutionary Committee may become something else, something dangerous and threatening.

[25] The Provisional Government. *Editor.*

* Translated by Daniel Mulholland from *Izvestiia* (No. 199, October 17/30, 1917).

"Until now the Bolsheviks have failed to answer the question put to them by Dan: Whether they are going to take part in uprisings and whether they regard such uprisings as beneficial, whether they are calling on the masses to come on the street to seize power?

"Your refusal to answer may be explained either by your faint heart or by doubts of your own strength. If your vacillation is caused by doubt, then I bless you for your doubts. . . . Such an uprising, we are deeply convinced, would be the funeral of the revolution. The Revolutionary Committee which has been projected here is nothing else than an organization of a revolutionary staff for the seizure of power. We are against it and will not join it. . . . We have information from many sources that the masses are not in favor of an uprising. . . ."

Trotsky followed Broido: "In answering the question of Comrade Broido, whether the Bolsheviks are preparing an armed uprising, I should like to know in whose name he is asking it: that of Kerensky, the counterintelligence, the secret police, or other such institutions? . . ." In concluding his speech, Trotsky insisted on the necessity of taking power out of the hands of the irresponsible leaders of the country by a unanimous demonstration of the power of the democracy, and called for a protest against the removal of the troops from Petrograd.

E] TROTSKY, "THE THREAT TO PETROGRAD AND THE STRUGGLE FOR PEACE," OCTOBER 30

The following is an article written by Trotsky for a Bolshevik newspaper.*

The war has gone on now for thirty-nine months, and the end is not yet in sight. The bourgeoisie demand the prosecution of the war—"to victory." In August, at the Moscow Conference, Kerensky said, "Damn anyone who talks about peace now." The allies of our bourgeoisie, the capitalists of England, America, France, and Italy call for war "to the end." But where is this end? It is not visible. Are we closer to peace now than at the beginning of the revolution? Has our military position really improved? No; it has become immeasurably worse. The criminal offensive begun by Kerensky on July 1 brought a retreat, the surrender of Riga, and the great danger now hanging over Petrograd.

Three and a quarter years of war have not given security to our capital. What is there to assure any improvement in the future? If we lose Petrograd, we lose almost half of our defense industry. It would be impossible to evacuate factories to the provinces and get them working again soon enough.

---

* Translated by Daniel Mulholland from L. D. Trotsky, *Sochineniia* (Moscow, n.d.), Vol. III, Part 2, pp. 18–21.

This would take months. Consequently, the surrender of Petrograd would deal an irremediable, quite mortal blow to our military supplies. And yet the government, which openly reckons on the possibility of surrendering Petrograd to the Germans, does nothing to bring the war to an end.

With the first news of the danger of a German attack on the capital, the ministry began to talk about moving to Moscow. The Kerensky government has frequently, even before this, tried to get away from revolutionary Petrograd where it feels as if on a red-hot iron. Now it hastens to justify its flight to Moscow with "strategic" reasons.

The garrison and workers of Petrograd stirred anxiously. What is all this about? The government openly admits that after thirty-nine months of war it is unable to defend the capital. But instead of taking decisive steps to conclude peace while there is still time, the irresponsible and criminal government of the bourgeoisie prepares to abandon Petrograd to its fate. The Soldiers' Section of the Petrograd Soviet at once struck at the treacherous plot of the counterrevolutionaries and Bonapartists. The garrison deputies posed the issue thus: the government, unable to defend the capital, must either conclude an immediate peace or, if it is incapable of so doing, it must go hence and make way for a truly popular government. The Petrograd Soviet has agreed with this proposition of its Soldiers' Section, and added that the bourgeoisie gladly reconciles itself to the destruction of the revolutionary capital. The calculation of the counterrevolutionaries is clear: Wilhelm will seize the strongest bastion of the revolution, red Petrograd, and the Kornilovites will use the occasion to eradicate the conquests of the people.

The government obviously became frightened of the indignation which its plan to desert to Moscow had aroused. In the so-called Pre-Parliament, Mr. Kerensky explained that he should not be so misunderstood, that he had been "slandered," and that just now the government has no intention of leaving. "Surrender Petrograd," exclaim the "patriotic" Cadets,[26] the teachers and patrons of Kerensky, "the thought has not even occurred to us!"

But unfortunately for the Petrograd counterrevolutionaries, their Muscovite accomplices are rather more candid. Rodzianko,[27] the ex-president of the state Duma and the generally acknowledged spokesman of the whole landlord and bourgeois counterrevolution, openly declared in the commercial circles' newspaper, *Russkoe utro*:

"Petrograd is in danger. . . . Well, too bad for Petrograd. . . . Some people are concerned that the central institutions (i.e., the Soviets, etc.) will perish in Petrograd. But I must say that I, for one, would be quite glad if all these institutions were to disappear since they have done nothing but inflict harm on Russia."

"Too bad for Petrograd," says the patriot Rodzianko, speaking for bour-

---

[26] "Cadets" was a popular name for the Constitutional Democrats, the Russian liberal party. *Editor.*

[27] M. V. Rodzianko was a conservative statesman who, at the time of the abdication of Nicholas II, directed the Russian parliament (Duma). *Editor.*

geois Russia. And he feels precisely the same way about the Baltic fleet. "With the loss of Petrograd," he confesses, "the fleet will be lost, anyway." But there is no cause to mourn: "Some of the ships there are thoroughly debauched."

Thus, it is the clear intention of the bourgeoisie to hand over Petrograd and the Baltic fleet to Wilhelm. Rodzianko quite precisely explains why he finds this necessary. "After the loss of Riga," he says, "the city became more orderly than it had ever been; ten trouble-maker leaders were shot; the metropolitan police returned; the city has become completely safe."

The patriot Rodzianko is extending his hand to the German Kaiser; perhaps they are already striking a bargain through third persons for the simultaneous throttling of the Baltic fleet and Petrograd. But Kerensky in the Pre-Parliament complains of "slander" and sputters about the salvation of Petrograd. But who believes Kerensky? First, in August, Kerensky himself had made a deal with Kornilov to send the Third Cavalry Corps to Petrograd for the "pacification" of the proletariat and the garrison. Secondly, Kerensky is retained in the government now mainly to talk. The real decisions are made behind the scenes. There the Rodziankos, Miliukovs, Guchkovs, Riabushinskiis, and Kaledins [28] impatiently wait for Wilhelm, who is to introduce in Petrograd the same sort of order he brought to Riga.

The bourgeoisie needs the war to continue, not to gain victory (in which they no longer believe), but to uproot the revolution. To surrender the Baltic fleet, Kronstadt, and Petrograd to the Germans, to exhaust completely the army, to break its spirit, to divide and strangle the peasants—such is the diabolical plot of the propertied classes. Every worker, soldier, sailor, and peasant must have a clear understanding of this.

The Baltic sailors declared at the recent Northern Regional Congress of Soviets, through their president, Comrade Dybenko, "Only a soviet government, by offering immediate peace to all nations, can save the Baltic fleet, Petrograd, and the revolution."

The same voice came to us from the trenches. Daily, delegations from the army, from regiments and corps, come to us, to the soviet, and with one voice say:

"The army can wait no longer. It has no shoes, no clothing, no food. Winter is coming. The soldiers have lost faith in the deceitful phrases of the bourgeois and defensist "patriots," behind whose back the Rodziankos are in command. The soldiers demand peace because in peace alone lies their salvation. There is a limit to the trials which the army's patience will bear. What will happen if the army in a fit of despair should desert the front? This would spell the end of the revolution. There is only one way out: propose an immediate armistice on all fronts."

But the present government cannot, will not, wants not to take this way

---

[28] P. N. Miliukov was an eminent historian and leader of the Constitutional-Democratic party, A. I. Guchkov a conservative statesman, P. P. Riabushinskii a wealthy industrialist, and A. M. Kaledin a general. *Editor.*

out: it acts on the orders of the Russian and Allied Rodziankos. It is not responsible to the people but to the stock brokers. "The Kerensky government," the Petrograd Soviet has declared, "leads the country to ruin." This is the terrible truth. Every day brings us closer to destruction. After Petrograd falls it will be too late to talk of rescue; if the head is lost, one does not mourn the hair. The time to act is now, before it is too late. The soviets must take power. The All-Russian Congress of Soviets of Workers' and Soldiers' Deputies, which meets on November 2, must propose an immediate armistice in the name of the army, the proletariat, and the revolutionary peasants. The domestic situation in all countries is tense to the extreme. Everywhere the armies and masses have been seized by the desire for immediate peace. A winter campaign hangs like a dreadful specter over Europe. Under these circumstances the voice of the revolutionary soviet power will have decisive meaning. It will be impossible for the governments of Europe to continue the war after Russia has proposed peace.

Soldiers, workers, peasants! The government of the counterrevolutionary bourgeoisie is ruining the country. Only the All-Russian Congress of Soviets can save it. It must propose peace. This proposal you will give your vigorous support. This is a matter of life and death. Our nation wants to live. All that drives it to death and destruction must be mercilessly cast aside!

F] Trotsky Denies Bolsheviks Plan an Insurrection (Declaration to the Petrograd Soviet, October, 31)

In view of mounting rumors in and out of the Petrograd Soviet that the Bolsheviks were planning an uprising, Trotsky made a declaration at the soviet in the name of the Bolshevik party formally denying the charge. The following account, partly verbatim, partly summary, is reproduced as it appeared in a contemporary Bolshevik newspaper.*

"During the last few days all the newspapers have been filled with news, rumors, and articles about the coming insurrection; the insurrection is attributed sometimes to the Bolsheviks, sometimes to the Petrograd Soviet.

"The resolutions of the Petrograd Soviet are public. The soviet is an elective institution; each of its members is responsible to the workers and soldiers who have elected him. This revolutionary parliament of the proletariat and the revolutionary garrison cannot make decisions unknown to the workers and soldiers.

"We conceal nothing. I declare in the name of the Soviet that we have not ordered any uprising. But if, in the course of things, the soviet were

---

* Translated by Daniel Mulholland from L. D. Trotsky, *Sochineniia* (Moscow, n.d.), Vol. III, Part 2, pp. 31-33.

obliged to order an uprising, the workers and soldiers would follow its call like one man.

"The bourgeois newspapers have indicated November 4 as the day of the rising. This 'subtle' prophecy has made the rounds of all the papers. But November 4 had been fixed unanimously by the Executive Committee [of the soviet] as the day of agitation, propaganda, the rallying of the masses around the soviet banner, and donations for the benefit of the soviet.

"Further, reference is made to the requisition of five thousand rifles from the Sestroretskii factory which I signed. Yes, I have signed it, by virtue of the decision passed back during the Kornilov affair for the arming of a workers' militia. And the Petrograd Soviet will in the future continue to organize and arm the workers' guard.

"But all this information, all these 'facts' are suppressed by the paper *Den'*." [29]

Comrade Trotsky read out the "plan" published in yesterday's *Den'* of a Bolshevik insurrection which was supposed to have taken place the previous night. In the "plan" were indicated in detail the routes by which the Bolshevik armies were to have proceeded and the points they were to have seized. Included in it were even instructions that the insurgents from the Novaia Derevnia region take along "shady elements" (laughter in the hall).

"I beg you to listen so you will learn which route each army was to have taken . . ." (laughter).

"Comrades, this report needs no commentary, any more than the newspaper in which it appeared needs description.

"The purpose of this campaign is clear.

"We are now in a conflict with the government which can take an extremely sharp turn. The question concerns the removal of troops. Now the bourgeois press wants to create an air of hostility and suspicion around the Petrograd soldiers and workers, and incite at the front hatred toward the Petrograd soldiers.

"Another acute problem is that of the Congress of Soviets. Government circles know our point of view on the role of the Congress of Soviets. The bourgeoisie knows that the Petrograd Soviet will propose to the congress that it take power into its hands, offer a democratic peace to the warring nations, and give the peasants land. They are trying, therefore, to disarm Petrograd by removing its revolutionary garrison; and they are hastening to arm and dispose everyone under their control by the beginning of the congress, so as to be able to throw their forces to break up the representative gathering of workers, soldiers, and peasants. Just as an artillery barrage opens an attack against an army, so the present campaign of lies and slander is the prelude to an armed attack on the Congress of Soviets.

"We must be on the alert. We have entered a period of sharpest conflict. An attack from the counterrevolution must be expected at all times.

[29] *Den'* was a Menshevik newspaper. *Editor.*

"But at the first attempt from its side to disrupt the Congress of Soviets, at their first attempt at an offensive we shall reply with a merciless counter-offensive which we intend to follow through to the end."

3] The Military-Revolutionary Committee Begins the Uprising, November 4–5

A] Telegram from the Committee to the Petrograd Garrison, November 4 [*]

At its meeting on November 3 the revolutionary garrison of Petrograd united around the Military-Revolutionary Committee of the Petrograd Soviet of Workers' and Soldiers' Deputies as its directive organ.

In spite of this, the staff of the Petrograd Military District refused, during the night of November 3–4, to recognize the Military-Revolutionary Committee, declining to transact business with the representatives of the Soldiers' Section of the soviet. By this act the [military] staff has broken off relations with the revolutionary garrison as well as with the Petrograd Soviet of Workers' and Soldiers' Deputies. Having broken with the organized garrison of the capital, the staff becomes a tool of the counterrevolutionary forces.

The Military-Revolutionary Committee declines all responsibility for the acts of the staff of the Petrograd Military District.

Soldiers of Petrograd! It is for you, under the direction of the Military-Revolutionary Committee, to defend the revolutionary order against counter-revolutionary attempts. Orders not signed by the Military-Revolutionary Committee are invalid. All directives issued by the Petrograd Soviet for this day, the day of the Petrograd Soviet of Workers' and Soldiers' Deputies, remain in full force. Every soldier is obliged to maintain strict vigilance, firmness, and absolute discipline. The revolution is in danger! Long live the revolutionary garrison!

B] The Appointment of Military Commissars by the Military-Revolutionary Committee, November 5 [†]

To the population of Petrograd. For the information of the workers, soldiers and all citizens of Petrograd, we proclaim:

[*] Translated by Daniel Mulholland from *Krasnaia letopis'*, No. 8, 1923, p. 17.
[†] Translated by Daniel Mulholland from *Listovki petrogradskikh bol'shevikov, 1917–1920* (Leningrad, 1957), Vol. III, p. 103.

In the interest of defending the revolution and its conquests from the assaults of the counterrevolution, we have appointed commissars to military units and to especially critical points of the capital and its environs. Orders and directives reaching these points are to be obeyed only when confirmed by these authorized commissars. The commissars, as representatives of the soviet, are inviolable. Resistance to the commissars is resistance to the Soviet of Workers' and Soldiers' Deputies. All steps have been taken by the soviet to preserve revolutionary order from counterrevolutionary and pogromist assaults. All citizens are requested to give the fullest support to our commissars. In case of disturbances citizens should contact the commissars of the Military-Revolutionary Committee of the nearest military unit.

The Military-Revolutionary Committee of the Petrograd
Soviet of Workers' and Soldiers' Deputies

c] THE MOBILIZATION ORDER, NOVEMBER 6 *

PETROGRAD SOVIET OF WORKERS' AND SOLDIERS' DEPUTIES—*Soldiers! Workers! Citizens!*

The enemies of the people have gone during the night on the offensive. The Kornilovites on the staff are trying to smuggle in Junkers and shock battalions from the suburbs. The Junkers in Oranienburg and the shock troops in Tsarkoe Selo have refused to move.[30] A treacherous blow against the Petrograd Soviet of Workers' and Soldiers' Deputies is being planned. The newspapers *Rabochii put'* and *Soldat* have been closed down, their presses sealed.[31] The campaign of the counterrevolutionary conspirators is directed *against the All-Russian Congress of Soviets* on the eve of its opening, *against the Constituent Assembly, against the people.* The Petrograd Soviet of Workers' and Soldiers' Deputies defends the revolution. The Military-Revolutionary Committee is in charge of repulsing the attack of the conspirators. The entire garrison and the whole proletariat of Petrograd are ready to deal a crushing blow to the enemies of the people.

The Military-Revolutionary Committee decrees:

1. All regimental, company, and staff committees, together with the commissars representing the soviet, all revolutionary organizations must *sit in continuous session,* collecting all information on the plans and activities of the conspirators.

[30] Oranienburg and Tsarkoe Selo are localities in the vicinity of Petrograd. *Editor.*
[31] One of the few active measures of self-defense taken by the Provisional Government on the eve of the Bolshevik coup was to order the closing of two Bolshevik newspapers. The order was countermanded by the Bolsheviks, and the presses were reopened. *Editor.*
* Translated by Daniel Mulholland from *Listovki petrogradskikh bol'shevikov, 1917–1920* (Leningrad, 1957), Vol. III, pp. 106–07.

2. No soldier can absent himself without the permission of his unit committee.

3. Two representatives of every [military] unit and five from every regional soviet must be sent at once to the Smolny Institute.[32]

4. All activities of the conspirators must be reported at once to the Smolny Institute.

5. All members of the Petrograd Soviet and all delegates to the All-Russian Congress of Soviets are asked to report immediately to the Smolny Institute for an emergency session.

The counterrevolution has raised its criminal head.

A great danger threatens all the conquests and aspirations of the soldiers, workers, and peasants. But the forces of the revolution are incomparably stronger than those of its enemies.

The people's cause is in strong hands. The conspirators will be crushed. No hesitancy, no doubts. Firmness, steadfastness, endurance, resolution. Long live the revolution!

The Military-Revolutionary Committee

4] The Seizure of Power, November 6–7

A] LENIN'S LETTER TO THE CENTRAL COMMITTEE, NOVEMBER 6

In his hideaway in Petrograd, where he had moved earlier in the month from Finland, Lenin was not able to keep abreast of the quick flow of events. In fact, he was unaware that the uprising was already in progress when he wrote this alarmed letter to the Central Committee.*

Comrades,

I am writing this in the evening of the sixth, when the position is extremely critical. It is perfectly clear that right now in truth any delay in the insurrection is deadly.

I assure you with all my might that everything hangs by a thread now, the tasks of the day are matters which cannot be decided by conferences or congresses (not even by the Congress of Soviets) but solely by the people, by the masses, by the struggle of armed masses.

The bourgeois pressure of the Kornilovites and the firing of Verkhovskii [33]

---

[32] The Smolny Institute was the seat of the Petrograd Soviet. *Editor.*

[33] A. I. Verkhovskii was the Minister of War of the Provisional Government. He was removed from his post for having suggested peace negotiations with the Germans. *Editor.*

* Translated by Daniel Mulholland from V. I. Lenin, *Sochineniia*, 3rd ed. (Moscow–Leningrad, 1935), Vol. XXI, pp. 362–63.

show that it is impossible to wait any longer. We must at all costs this evening, tonight, arrest the government, disarm the Junkers, etc. (defeating
them if they show resistance).

We cannot wait!! Everything may be lost!!

The price of taking power immediately is to defend the people (not the
Congress [of Soviets], but the people, the army, and the peasants most of
all) from the Kornilovite government which has driven out Verkhovskii and
formed a second Kornilovite conspiracy.

Who should take power?

That is unimportant now; let the Military-Revolutionary Committee or
"another institution" take it, which will declare it will hand power over only
to the true representatives of the people's cause, the cause of the army (an
immediate peace proposal), the cause of the peasants (the land must be
seized at once and private property in it abolished), the cause of the hungry.

All regions, all regiments, every force must be mobilized at once to send
delegations to the Military-Revolutionary Committee and to the Bolshevik
Central Committee, insistently demanding from them that in no case, under no circumstances, can Kerensky & Co. be left in power until the seventh;
this business must be decided this evening or during the night.

History will not forgive revolutionaries for procrastinating—revolutionaries
who could win today (and certainly will win today) but who risk losing much
tomorrow, risk losing everything.

Taking power today, we would do so not against the Soviets but on their
behalf.

The business of the insurrection is to seize power; its political purpose
will become clear after power has been seized.

It would be a catastrophe or a formality to wait for the chancy voting of
November 7; the people are justified and obliged to resolve questions of this
kind not by voting but by force; the people are justified and obliged at critical moments of the revolution to force the hands of their representatives,
even the best of them, and not simply to wait for them.

The history of all revolutions proves this and it would be an appalling
crime if revolutionaries would let slip the moment, knowing that on them
depends the *salvation of the revolution*, the offer of peace, the salvation of
Petrograd, the prevention of famine, the transfer of land to the peasants.

The government is shaking. We must finish it off, no matter what!

Any delay in the insurrection is deadly.

B] Protest of Menshevik and Socialist Revolutionary
Deputies to the Second All-Russian Congress of
Soviets, November 7

The Menshevik and Socialist Revolutionary deputies who had assembled in
Petrograd for the Second Congress of Soviets, outraged by the Bolshevik seizure

of power, in the name of but without a mandate from the soviets, issued separate declarations of protest, and, followed by jeers of the Bolsheviks, walked out of the meeting.*

DECLARATION OF THE MENSHEVIKS

In view of the fact,

1. that the military conspiracy was organized and carried out by the Bolshevik party in the name of the soviets behind the backs of all other parties and fractions represented in the soviets;

2. that the seizure of power by the Petrograd Soviet on the eve of the Congress of Soviets is an act of disorganization, a disruption of the whole soviet organization, which has undermined the significance of the congress as the plenipotentiary representative of revolutionary democracy;

3. that this conspiracy throws the country into internecine war, breaks up the Constituent Assembly, threatens military disaster, and paves the way for the triumph of the counterrevolution;

4. that the only feasible peaceful way out of the situation lies in negotiations with the Provisional Government for the formation of a regime based on all strata of the democracy;

5. that the Russian Social Democratic Labor party (United) considers it its duty to the working class not only to deny all responsibility for the actions of the Bolsheviks, who wrap themselves in the soviet banner, but also to warn the workers and soldiers against this adventurist policy, so disastrous to the country and the revolution.

Therefore, the Russian Social Democratic Labor party (United) fraction quits the present congress and invites all other fractions that also reject responsibility for the actions of the Bolsheviks to meet at once to consider the situation.

DECLARATION OF THE SOCIALIST-REVOLUTIONARY FRACTION

The Socialist-Revolutionary fraction of the All-Russian Congress of Soviets of Workers' and Soldiers' Deputies, in agreement with the Central Committee of the Socialist Revolutionary party, declares:

1. The seizure of power carried out by the party of Bolsheviks and by the Petrograd Soviet of Workers' and Soldiers' Deputies on the eve of the Constituent Assembly and on the day preceding the opening of the All-Russian Congress of Soviets of Workers' and Soldiers' Deputies is a crime before the motherland and the revolution; it means the beginning of civil war and the

---

* Translated by Daniel Mulholland from K. G. Kotel'nikov, ed., *Vtoroi vserossiiskii s'ezd sovetov rabochikh i soldatskikh deputatov* (Moscow–Leningrad, 1928), pp. 37–38.

breakup of the Constituent Assembly; it threatens the collapse of the revolution.

2. Anticipating an outburst of popular indignation, inevitable in view of the unavoidable fiasco of Bolshevik promises, which are known beforehand to be incapable of realization, the Socialist Revolutionary fraction calls on all the revolutionary forces of the country to organize themselves to guard the revolution so that when the coming catastrophe occurs they will take charge of the country's fate in their hands and prevent the triumph of the counterrevolution, thus being in a position to achieve a quick conclusion of a general democratic peace, the convocation of the Constituent Assembly at its appointed date, and the socialization of land.

3. Stating the fact of the seizure of power by the Bolshevik party and the Petrograd Soviet of Workers' and Soldiers' Deputies led by it, the Socialist Revolutionary fraction lays at their door all the responsibility for the results of this senseless and criminal step, and leaves the congress, because this action has made it impossible to work in common with them. In addition, the Socialist Revolutionary party considers this congress unauthorized because the front and many of the soviets are inadequately represented in it.

c] Resolution of the Second Congress of Soviets Proclaiming the Overthrow of the Provisional Government, November 7–8 *

To the workers, soldiers and peasants:

The Second All-Russian Congress of Soviets of Workers' and Soldiers' Deputies has opened. The overwhelming majority of soviets are represented in it. A number of delegates from the peasants' soviets are also present at the Congress. The authority of the conciliationist Central Executive Committee has ended.

Relying on the will of the overwhelming majority of workers, soldiers, and peasants, relying on the victorious insurrection of the workers and garrison in Petrograd, the congress takes all power in it hands.

The Provisional Government is overthrown. Most members of the Provisional Government are already under arrest.

The soviet government will propose an immediate democratic peace to all nations and an immediate armistice on all fronts. It guarantees the transfer, without compensation, of all noble, crown, and monastic lands to the disposition of the peasant committees. It will defend the soldiers' rights and carry through the complete democratization of the army. It will establish workers' supervision over production. It will ensure the timely convocation

* Translated by Daniel Mulholland from K. G. Kotel'nikov, ed., *Vtoroi vserossiiskii s'ezd sovetov rabochikh i soldatskikh deputatov* (Moscow–Leningrad, 1928), pp. 93–94.

of the Constituent Assembly. It will concern itself with the supply to the cities of bread and to the villages of goods of prime necessity. It will assure all the nationalities inhabiting Russia the right to real self-determination.

The congress decrees: All power in the localities passes to the Soviets of Workers', Soldiers', and Peasants' Deputies, which must ensure real revolutionary order.

The congress appeals to the soldiers in the trenches to maintain vigilance and steadfastness. The Congress of Soviets is confident that the revolutionary army will be able to defend the revolution from all the encroachments of imperialism until the new government achieves the conclusion of a democratic peace which it will propose directly to all the nations.

The new government will take all steps to supply the revolutionary army with all the necessities by a decisive policy of requisitions and taxation of the propertied classes, and it will also improve the situation of soldiers' families.

The Kornilovites—Kerensky, Kaledin, and the others—are trying to lead troops against Petrograd. Some units, which Kerensky had put into action by fraud, have come over to the side of the revolutionary people.

Soldiers! Fight against the Kornilovite Kerensky. Be on your guard!

Railroad workers, stop all detachments sent by Kerensky against Petrograd!

Soldiers, workers, employees—the fate of the revolution and the fate of a democratic peace are in your hands.

Long live the revolution!

> *The All-Russian Congress of Soviets of Workers' and*
> *Soldiers' Deputies. Delegates from the Peasants' Soviets.*

5] Trotsky, "Lessons of October"

Shortly after Lenin's death, which occurred in 1924, Trotsky found himself locked in a life-and-death struggle with Stalin and his associates. In an attempt to discredit their rival by showing that Trotsky was not the rightful heir of Lenin's authority, Stalin's party brought out every disagreement which Trotsky had had with Lenin. In the course of the polemic Trotsky wrote an essay called "Lessons of October" in which, with remarkable candor, he explained why he had insisted, against Lenin's will, on synchronizing the Bolshevik uprising with the Second All-Russian Congress of Soviets. These remarks provide a unique insight into the techniques of the power seizure and shed light on the contemporary documents cited above.*

All these letters [of Lenin],[34] where every phrase has been hammered on the anvil of the revolution, are of exceptional interest, both for their character-

[34] Trotsky is referring to the letters of Lenin cited above (Documents 1A–C and 4A). *Editor.*

* Translated by Daniel Mulholland from L. D. Trotsky, *Sochineniia* (Moscow, n.d.), Vol. III, Part 1, pp. xlviii–li, lii, liv.

ization of Lenin and for their estimate of the situation. Their fundamental, pervasive idea is dismay, protest, indignation against any fatalistic, temporizing, Social-Democratic, Menshevik view of the revolution as some kind of endless tape. If time is in general an important factor in politics, its significance grows a hundredfold in war and revolution. By no means all that can be done today can be done tomorrow. To revolt, to overthrow the enemy, to seize power may be possible today, but not the next day. But, after all, to seize power is to turn the rudder of history; can such an event really depend on an interval of twenty-four hours? Yes, it can. When matters have come to an armed insurrection, events are not measured by the long yardstick of politics, but by the inch-tape of war. To let slip by a few weeks, a few days, sometimes even one day, is equivalent, under certain circumstances, to the surrender of the revolution, to capitulation. Without Lenin's anxiety, his pressure, his criticism, his intense and passionate revolutionary mistrust, the party very likely would not have fallen into line at the crucial moment, for opposition at the top was very strong, and the staff always plays a major role in warfare, including civil war.

But at the same time it is quite clear that the preparation of the uprising and its realization under the cover of preparing the Second Congress of Soviets and under the slogan of defending it, put in our hands inestimable advantages. From the moment when we, the Petrograd Soviet, invalidated the order of Kerensky transferring two-thirds of the garrison to the front, we had already passed in fact into a state of armed insurrection. Lenin, living outside Petrograd, failed to appreciate the full significance of this fact. So far as I can remember, not a word is said in any of his letters of the time about this circumstance. And yet the outcome of the insurrection of November 7 already had been three-quarters (if not more) predetermined at the moment we resisted the removal of the Petrograd garrison, formed the Military-Revolutionary Committee (October 29), appointed our commissars to all military units and institutions, and in this way isolated not only the staff of the Petrograd military district but the government as well. Essentially this *was* the armed insurrection—an armed although bloodless revolt of the Petrograd regiments against the Provisional Government—under the leadership of the Military-Revolutionary Committee, and under the slogan of preparing the defense of the Second Congress of Soviets, which was to decide the fate of power. Lenin's advice to begin the insurrection in Moscow, where he reckoned on a bloodless victory, arose precisely from the fact that in his hideaway he was unable to appreciate that fundamental break which had occurred not only in the morale but also in the organizational cohesion of the whole military system, in the entire military chain of command and hierarchy after the "quiet" insurrection of the capital's garrison at the end of October. From the moment when the battalions, obeying the order of the Military-Revolutionary Committee, refused to leave the city, and stayed put, we had in the capital a victorious uprising, just barely disguised at the top by the remains of the bourgeois-democratic statehood. The insurrection of November 7 had merely a supplementary character. Precisely for this reason it was so pain-less. In Moscow, on the contrary, the conflict had a much more protracted and sanguinary quality, although in Petrograd the authority of the Council of People's Commissars had been already assured. Quite obviously, if the insurrection had begun in Moscow before the uprising in Petrograd it would have been still more protracted and its outcome highly questionable. And failure in Moscow would have had a dismal effect on Petrograd. To be sure, victory was not out of the question also in this way. But the path events actually took turned out much more economical, more advantageous, and more decisive.

We were able more or less to synchronize the seizure of power with the Second Congress of Soviets only because the "quiet," almost "legal" armed insurrection, at least in Petrograd, had been already three-quarters, if not nine-tenths, an accomplished fact. We call this insurrection "legal" in the sense that it developed and grew out of the "normal" conditions of dual power.[35] Even when the conciliationists had dominated the Petrograd Soviet it often happened that the soviet examined or corrected governmental deci-sions. This became, as it were, an integral part of the constitution of that regime which has entered history under the name of "Kerenskyism." After we had come to power in the soviet,[36] we Bolsheviks merely continued and deepened the methods of dual power. We took it upon ourselves to revise the order removing the garrison. Thus, by the traditions and legal measures of dual power we disguised the actual uprising of the Petrograd garrison. Moreover, by formally synchronizing in our agitation the question of power with the opening of the Second Congress of Soviets, we developed and deep-ened those traditions of dual power which had already succeeded in emerg-ing, preparing the framework of soviet legality on a national scale for the Bolshevik insurrection.

We did not lull the masses with soviet constitutional illusions, because under the slogan of the struggle for the Second Congress [of Soviets] we won and organizationally consolidated behind ourselves the bayonets of the revolutionary army. At the same time we succeeded better than could have been hoped in luring our enemies, the conciliationists, into the trap of so-viet legality. To be politically cunning, particularly during revolution, is al-ways dangerous; you may fail to deceive the enemy but succeed in deceiv-ing the masses following you. If our "cunning" was one hundred per cent successful this was only because it was not an artificial concoction of smart-alecky strategists wishing to avoid civil war, but because it flowed naturally from the conditions of the disintegration of the conciliationist regime, from their glaring contradictions. The Provisional Government wanted to get rid

[35] "Dual power" refers to the sharing of the power between the Provisional Govern-ment and the soviets which the Mensheviks and Socialists Revolutionaries had advocated and in effect achieved. *Editor.*

[36] That is, the Petrograd and Moscow Soviets, where the Bolsheviks obtained majorities in September 1917. *Editor.*

of the garrison; the soldiers did not want to go to the front. We gave this natural reluctance a political expression, a revolutionary purpose, a "legal" disguise. By this means, we assured an extraordinary unity within the garrison, and closely tied it with the Petrograd workers. On the contrary, our opponents, given the hopelessness of their position and the confusion in their minds, were inclined to accept the soviet disguise at face value. They wanted to be deceived, and we gave them fully the opportunity to do so. . . .

It is one thing to organize an armed insurrection under the slogan of a naked seizure of power by a party, but it was quite another to prepare and then to carry out the insurrection under the slogan of defending the rights of the Congress of Soviets. Thus, the synchronization of the seizure of power with the Second Congress of Soviets implied no naive hope whatever that the congress could by itself resolve the problem of power. Such fetishism of the soviet form was quite alien to us. All the necessary work for the seizure of power, not only political but also organizational and military in the technical sense, proceeded at full steam. But the legal camouflage for this work remained the very same appeal to the coming congress, which was to resolve the problem of power. Launching an offensive on all fronts, we preserved an appearance of defensiveness. On the contrary, the Provisional Government, if only it had found the courage seriously to defend itself, would have had to encroach on the Congress of Soviets, forbid its convocation, and thereby provide our side with most convenient grounds for the armed insurrection. Moreover, we had not only placed the Provisional Government in a politically disadvantageous position, but we deliberately lulled further its already lazy and moribund senses. These people believed in all seriousness that we were primarily concerned with soviet parliamentarism. . . .

In order that this whole broad, mist-wrapped maneuver should have succeeded, it was necessary for several quite exceptional circumstances, large and small, to coincide. Above all, it was imperative to have an army which was no longer willing to fight. The whole course of the revolution, especially in its first period, from February through October inclusively . . . would have been entirely different if we had not had at the time of the revolution a defeated and discontented army of millions of peasants. Only under these conditions was it possible successfully to carry off the experiment with the Petrograd garrison, which had predetermined the November victory. This unique combination of a "dry," almost imperceptible insurrection with the defense of Soviet legality from the Kornilovites can by no means be elevated to the status of a general law [of revolutions]. On the contrary, it can be said with confidence that in this form this experience will never again be repeated anywhere. But it must be studied carefully. It will broaden the outlook of every revolutionary by revealing to him the variety of methods and means that can be brought into play providing there is clarity in the posited goal, a correct assessment of the situation, and determination to see the struggle through to the end.

CONCLUSION

W ILLIAM J AMES spoke of habit as a faculty which permits man to automatize many activities and thereby conserve energy for responsibilities requiring deliberation and an effort of the will. Much the same may be said of societies. The habits of political responsibility are acquired in the process of self-rule; once ingrained, they allow society to concentrate its attention on matters of policy—this is, on matters which demand decisions. Like an individual, a society that has acquired them does not collapse from the burden of excessive decision-making.

Unfortunately for herself, Russia had not been given an opportunity to acquire such habits. In March 1917, after several centuries of rule by an autocratic-bureaucratic government, the nation was suddenly confronted with responsibilities of the very broadest kind, all of which called for decisions. The country had to develop a new political and administrative system to replace the defunct imperial one, to redistribute property, and to settle the matter of war and peace and many issues of equal gravity. At first Russians met this challenge with enthusiasm, but it was not long before they became worn out by the sheer responsibility of making decisions. By autumn 1917 something like a paralysis of the will overcame a large part of the country. Few had expected freedom to involve such an effort.

Lenin and Trotsky sensed this and realized that Russia was ready for the re-establishment of an authoritarian government prepared to assume responsibility for the numerous problems confronting the country. But they also knew that the nation would not agree to surrender its newly won democratic rights. Hence they concealed their seizure of power and one-party rule behind a façade of "soviet democracy." In this way the country had both the illusion of democracy and absolution from democracy's responsibilities.

A country with democratic habits would not necessarily have been immune to such a deception, but it would certainly have been less vulnerable to it. It would have had institutions to which it was accustomed and practices that were beyond debate. It would have had some sense of what was possible and what was not. It would, therefore, have been able to concentrate its attention on the most pressing foreign and domestic issues facing the country, leaving more fundamental questions to be solved after peace had been re-established. As a result, it would have been less easily seduced by the preposterous charges and promises made by the Bolsheviks in full cognizance of the country's political immaturity.

The Bolshevik seizure of power provided a model which has much influenced subsequent totalitarian leaders and parties. The use of it has been effective wherever social disintegration has undermined the traditional politi-

cal system. In this sense, the events which took place in Petrograd in November 1917 are of worldwide historical significance.

STUDY QUESTIONS

1] What was Lenin's strategy for an uprising? How did it
   differ from Trotsky's?
2] What arguments did the Bolsheviks employ to persuade
   the soviet and the soldiers to entrust authority to the
   Military-Revolutionary Committee?
3] What were the advantages of disguising the Bolshevik
   seizure of power as an assumption of authority by the
   Second Congress of Soviets?
4] What differences can be perceived between the private
   (intraparty) and the public pronouncements of the Bolshevik leaders?

RECOMMENDED READINGS

PRIMARY

BUNYAN, J. AND H. H. FISHER. *The Bolshevik Revolution, 1917–1918* (Stanford,
    Cal., 1934).
GOLDER, F. A. *Documents of Russian History, 1914–1917* (New York, 1927).
SUKHANOV, NIKOLAI N. *The Russian Revolution, 1917: A Personal Record*, ed.,
    abr., and trans. by Joel Carmichael (London and New York, 1955).
TROTSKY, LEON. *The History of the Russian Revolution*, trans. by Max Eastman,
    3 vols. in 1 (Ann Arbor, Mich., 1957).

SECONDARY

CHAMBERLIN, WILLIAM H. *The Russian Revolution, 1917–1921*, 2 vols. (New
    York and London, 1952).
DEUTSCHER, ISAAC. *The Prophet Armed: Trotsky, 1879–1921* (London and New
    York, 1954).
SCHAPIRO, LEONARD. *The History of the Communist Party* (New York, 1959).

The Destruction of German Democracy: The Rise of Nazism, 1928–34

JAMES J. SHEEHAN

NORTHWESTERN UNIVERSITY

CONTENTS

D] The Theory of the Fuehrer State
(Schmitt, *Positionen und Begriffe im Kampf mit Weimar-Genf-Versailles, 1923–1939*)

CHRONOLOGY

1918

NOVEMBER 9   The German republic is proclaimed at a time of national defeat and internal disorder.

1923

NOVEMBER 8–9   Hitler unsuccessfully attempts to overthrow the Bavarian government. He is arrested and sentenced to five years in prison, but is released after less than one year.

1925

APRIL 26   Paul von Hindenburg is elected president of the republic.

1928

MAY 20   Reichstag elections.

JUNE 13   The formation of a coalition government under the leadership of the Social Democrats.

1929

OCTOBER   The stock market crash in the United States heightens the growing economic crisis in Germany.

DECEMBER 22   The Young Plan is accepted by referendum.

1930

MARCH 27   The coalition government ends and on the following day Heinrich Brüning is made Chancellor.

JULY 16   The Reichstag is dissolved. Brüning promulgates the necessary legislation by means of presidential decree.

SEPTEMBER 14   Reichstag elections.

1931

MAY 11   The fall of the Credit Anstalt, an important Austrian bank, marks the beginning of financial collapse throughout central Europe.

1932

APRIL 10   Von Hindenburg is re-elected president.

MAY 30   Brüning is forced to resign and is replaced by Franz von Papen.

JULY 20   Von Papen removes the Socialist government of Prussia.

JULY 31   Reichstag elections.

AUGUST 13   Negotiations between Hitler and Papen break down because Hitler refuses to accept anything but the Chancellorship.

NOVEMBER 6 Reichstag elections.

DECEMBER 2 Von Papen is replaced by General Kurt von Schleicher.

1933

JANUARY 30   Hitler is made Chancellor.

FEBRUARY 27–28 The Reichstag building is burned. The Nazis declare a state of national emergency, blame the fire on the Communists, and issue a decree suspending individual liberties.

MARCH 5   Reichstag elections.

MARCH 21   The Reichstag opens at a ceremony in Potsdam.

MARCH 24   The Reichstag passes the so-called Enabling Act.

MARCH–JULY   All political organizations are dissolved and replaced by Nazi-run bodies.

1934

JUNE 30   After an alleged attempt at revolt, the leaders of the SA are brutally murdered on Hitler's orders.

AUGUST 2   President von Hindenburg dies and Hitler assumes sole executive power.

INTRODUCTION

T HE D O M I N A N T theme in the political history of Europe between the world wars is the decline of parliamentary democracy. In 1919 the war "to make the world safe for democracy" had been won and democratic governments were established throughout most of Europe. By 1939 only a few European nations retained viable democratic institutions. On the Iberian peninsula, in Italy, and in most of central and eastern Europe, parliamentary rule was replaced by authoritarian regimes. Perhaps the most significant failure of parliamentary government occurred during the last years of the German republic. Here the victory of antidemocratic forces was complete and the results of this victory were tragic, for Europe and for the world.

Although the collapse of the German republic must be seen as part of a process present in all of Europe, its origins lie in the historical background and development of German democracy itself. From its establishment in 1918, the German republic was weakened by the fact that it was founded at a time of national defeat and humiliation. Many Germans sought a scapegoat for their defeat and accused the leaders of the republic of betraying the German armies. Moreover, there was no strong democratic tradition in Germany. Important elements in German society were suspicious of political parties and parliamentary institutions. Throughout the life of the republic these people longed for what they felt had been the splendor and discipline of the monarchy. Finally, the republic was threatened by the presence of strong antirepublican feelings in the army, judiciary, and bureaucracy. In 1918 the republican government had felt obliged to form an alliance with these groups in order to save Germany from a Communist revolution. Thereafter, the democratic leaders never felt willing or able to strike against these strongholds of antirepublicanism.

In 1924, after five years of crisis and disorder, the republic entered a period of relative stability. The return of prosperity led people to hope that the economic dislocations of the early twenties were over. However, political problems remained. Even during the mid-twenties the political parties were unable to achieve a stable coalition government with a coherent program. This inability was to prove fatal during the years after 1929.

The first indication that the period of stability was over appeared in the summer of 1929. The occasion was the conflict which erupted in Germany over the Young Plan, a proposal to settle the long-standing and explosive issue of German war reparations. The right-wing parties opposed the plan because of the financial burdens it imposed upon Germany and also because acceptance of the plan seemed to involve acceptance of the justice of the Versailles peace treaty. The parties on the right mobilized in opposition to the Young Plan and injected into German politics the violence and bitterness which were to be the hallmarks of the republic's last years. The republican leaders were able to carry the fight over the Young Plan to a successful conclusion, but even as they were doing so the first effects of the world economic crisis were felt in Germany. By the winter of 1929–30 three million Germans were unemployed; during the next three years this figure was to increase to over six million. In the face of the deepening depression, the parties in the coalition government found it increasingly difficult to work together. Finally, in March 1930, the parties which supported the government declared themselves unable to agree on a relatively minor issue and the Chancellor and his ministers were forced to resign. This failure to compromise ended the last democratically based government of the Weimar republic.

Field Marshall Paul von Hindenburg, the aged war hero who had been elected President of the republic in 1925, then named Heinrich Brüning to the Chancellorship. Brüning wanted to form a government based on a coalition of the moderate and conservative parties. He was prepared, however, to rule without the Reichstag (the legislative assembly) should that prove necessary. Until July 1930 Brüning was supported by a narrow majority in the Reichstag. On July 16 a negative coalition of all the groups opposed to Brüning was able to defeat a fiscal measure which he had proposed. Brüning responded by promulgating the law on the authority of article 48 of the constitution, which provided for rule by presidential decree during times of national emergency. Brüning then dissolved the Reichstag and called for new elections.

The elections held in September 1930 resulted in a serious defeat for the moderate, pro-republican parties. The republic's radical opponents on the left and right captured almost 40 per cent of the Reichstag seats. Thus in the autumn of 1930 parliamentary government in Germany was threatened not only by Brüning's willingness to govern with article 48 but also by the disruptive presence in the Reichstag of violent and intransigent antidemocratic groups.

The most dramatic gains in the elections of September 1930 were made by Adolf Hitler's National Socialist party, which captured 107 seats. During the twenties the Nazis were a small, violent group on the fringes of the right wing antirepublican movement. In the elections of 1928 they had elected only twelve delegates to the Reichstag. In 1929, however, they made an alliance with the conservative German National People's party during the struggle over the Young Plan, an alliance which provided them with financial support and with a "respectability" hitherto denied them. By the autumn of 1930 the Nazis had replaced the German National People's party as the most significant and dynamic of the right wing, antidemocratic parties.

It is impossible to explain the appeals of National Socialism in terms of any single social group or any one ideological statement. Like every mass movement, the Nazis appealed to different people for different reasons. To those Germans who were shocked and bitter because of the defeat of 1918, the Nazis promised a revival of German power and a revision of the peace treaties. To those distrustful of the republic, they promised an authoritarian government, above the parties. To those whose economic and social position had been undermined by the financial crises of the twenties, they promised a revitalization of the economy and a restoration of the old social order. To the industrialists, who were increasingly fearful of the growing Communist movement, they promised vigorous anti-Communist activity.

The keystone of the Nazi program was anti-Semitism. It was through propaganda against the Jews that the tangled, even somewhat contradictory threads of the ideology were unified: thus the traitors who had caused the defeat of the German armies were supposed to be Jews, as were the hidden powers behind the Weimar "system." The Nazis believed that the economic crisis had been caused by Jewish international financiers and also that the Jews were in control of the Communist movement. Hitler considered race to be the essential factor in history. National regeneration could be achieved, therefore, only when the Jews were excluded from German life. In the unstable and violent years after 1929, an increasing number of Germans seemed willing to listen to this explanation for their discontent and to accept this vision of the future.

As the number of Hitler's followers grew, some of his associates urged him to seize power violently. However, Hitler remained committed to a course of semilegality. He encouraged his followers to use any means necessary to disrupt the life of the republic, but at the same time he sought to become the legally appointed Chancellor of Germany.

After the elections of September 1930, Brüning continued to rule Germany by means of presidential decree. The moderate parties, fearful of the growth of left and right, agreed to tolerate though not to join the Brüning government. It was clear, however, that Brüning's power actually rested on the continued confidence of eighty-four–year-old President Hindenburg, whose authority was necessary for the use of article 48. The first sign that the President's confidence in Brüning was waning appeared in the autumn of 1931. During the next six months many of Hindenburg's closest friends and advisers intrigued against the Chancellor. As a result of these intrigues, Brüning was forced to resign in May 1932. One more step away from democratic government had been taken: the Chancellorship no longer depended upon the support—or even the toleration—of the Reichstag, but on the machinations of the men around the almost senile President.

Brüning was replaced by Franz von Papen, a wealthy aristocrat who hoped to reconstitute the government on the basis of pre-1918 authoritarianism. Papen believed that it would be possible to domesticate the Nazis and to include them in a conservative government. In July 1932 the Chancellor called new elections. The results proved disastrous for Papen's plans. The Nazis received 230 seats (37.8 per cent) and showed no signs of allowing themselves to be dominated by the Chancellor. Equally important, the democratic majority which had tolerated the Brüning government was destroyed.

Aside from the support of a handful of conservatives in the Reichstag, Papen's government rested entirely on the authority of the President.

Ten days before the elections of July 1932, the democratic cause in Germany suffered another serious defeat. On July 20 Papen forcibly removed the socialist government in Prussia, the largest of the German federal states. Papen's action was clearly illegal. Had the pro-democratic forces in society joined in a vigorous action against Papen's violation of the constitution, the will to resist might have been restored to the republican camp. However, Papen's coup met protests, but nothing else. This lost opportunity deepened the defeatism and despair among the moderates and left them ill prepared to face the challenges of the next months.

In the autumn of 1932 Papen resolved to make one more attempt to broaden the basis for his government. In September he again dissolved the Reichstag. In the elections held that November there appeared the first signs that the strength of the Nazi movement had passed its peak. Furthermore, the party was beset by internal divisions and financial difficulties. Papen, however, still had no basis for support in the Reichstag. He was determined, therefore, to ignore the parliament and to introduce an authoritarian regime. At this point Papen, like Brüning, became the victim of intrigues within President Hindenburg's circle of advisers. In December 1932 General von Schleicher announced that Papen's plans to alter the constitution would lead to civil war and that the army would be unable to keep order should this occur. Hindenburg reluctantly dismissed Papen, and Schleicher himself became Chancellor.

During December 1932 and January 1933 both Schleicher and Papen sought a way to include the Nazis in a coalition government. Schleicher wanted to take advantage of the divisions within the Nazi movement and lure some of the dissident elements into a government under his control. Meanwhile, Papen negotiated with Hitler in the hope that he might still find a way to include the Nazis in a conservatively oriented coalition. Toward the end of January 1933 Papen's efforts showed signs of success. Hitler continued to insist that he be made Chancellor, but he seemed willing to compromise on most of the other ministries. On January 27 Schleicher was forced to admit that his efforts had failed. Like Papen eight weeks earlier, Schleicher now wanted to suspend the constitution and rule without the Reichstag. Hindenburg, mindful of the arguments that Schleicher himself had used in December 1932, refused to support the Chancellor's plan. Three days later, on January 30, 1933, the government arranged by Papen was established with Hitler as Chancellor.

Papen was convinced that he could control the Nazis even with Hitler as Chancellor. He planned to use Hitler's talents as an agitator to gain support for a government dominated by the same alliance of industrialists and landowners which had ruled pre-1918 Germany. During his first months in power, Hitler was willing to preserve the illusion that his movement was part of a "national revival" based on the traditions of the German past. Such an illusion was an important aid in gaining the support of Hindenburg and of the conservative elements which dominated the army and bureaucracy. At the same time, Hitler took steps to insure the support of the business community by assuring German industrialists that their interests would be protected in a National Socialist state.

Despite his talk about a "national revival," Hitler had no intention of being a pawn in the hands of Papen. The Nazis used their ministerial positions to gain control of the police and they also secured the support of the war ministry. This control over the instruments of effective force enabled the Nazis to carry out a vigorous campaign of terror and intimidation against their enemies. However, Hitler realized that it was necessary to conceal the violence which accompanied the extension of Nazi power behind a mask of legality. On February 28, 1933, the legal basis for the persecution of anti-Nazi forces was laid by a presidential decree suspending constitutional rights and the autonomy of the state governments. After a terror-filled electoral campaign, elections for the Reichstag were held on March 5. The Nazis received 44 per cent of the vote and with their conservative allies commanded a majority. Three weeks later the Reichstag was forced to pass the so-called Enabling Act which formally excluded the parliament from German affairs. Only the Social Democrats had the courage to defy Nazi threats and vote against the bill.

In the weeks following the passage of the Enabling Act Hitler gradually widened the circle of Nazi power. On March 31 the autonomy of the federal states was destroyed. One week later a decree was issued which removed all Jews and "politically unreliable" persons from the bureaucracy. In June and July the political parties were dissolved and the National Socialists became the only legal political organization. Similar action was taken against trade unions, which were replaced by a Nazi-sponsored "Labor Front."

By the summer of 1933, therefore, the police, parliament, political parties, and bureaucracy were either destroyed or in Nazi hands. President von Hindenburg's health was deteriorating and Hitler was able to neutralize his influence. Hitler now had to face a potential source of opposition within the Nazi movement itself. After January 30, 1933, the storm troopers of the Nazis' paramilitary organization (the SA) had become increasingly disappointed with Hitler's failure to achieve what they considered to be the goals of the Nazi revolution. The SA wanted to absorb the army into their own organization and to make radical changes in German society. Hitler, on the other hand, was willing to compromise with the army and to leave the present social order intact in return for the support of the bureaucracy and business community. In the spring of 1934, Hitler felt it was necessary to curtail the power of the SA in order to maintain absolute control over the Nazi movement and to insure the backing of the army, bureaucracy, and business community. On June 30, 1934, Hitler struck. He accused the leaders of the SA of planning a coup against the government and had them murdered. His action cleared the way for the final consolidation of his regime.

On August 2, 1934, Hindenburg died and Hitler combined the offices of Chancellor and President. The army formally acknowledged their support of this move by swearing an oath of "unconditional obedience to the Fuehrer of the German Reich and Volk, Adolf Hitler."

In August 1934 the Nazis' control of German public life was complete. Hitler's power was as absolute as that of any tyrant in history. Hitler's ambitions, however, exceeded those of traditional dictatorships. He desired total domination of German society, domination of the private as well as the public sectors of human life. Using all the power of modern technology, Hitler and his followers sought to direct every aspect of German life toward the fulfillment of the Nazi ideology. The press, the universities, science and art, work and leisure were all regimented. The Nazis employed a carefully planned combination of terror and indoctrination to transform the individual into an obedient and enthusiastic cog in the machinery of party and state. Thus Hitler was able, without effective opposition, to lead his nation on a campaign of aggression and barbarity unmatched in the history of modern Europe.

DOCUMENTS

1] The Nazi Program

A] THE PARTY PROGRAM OF 1920

The first program of the National Socialist party contains many elements that were to form the basis for Hitler's campaign against the republic. It should be noted, however, that Hitler de-emphasized the social and economic aspects of this program when he began to find support from the leaders of German industry.*

The program of the National Socialist German Workers' party is a time program. The leaders decline, after achievement of the purposes laid down in the program, to set up new goals only for the purpose of making possible the continuance of the party through the artificially stimulated dissatisfaction of the masses.

1. We demand the union of all Germans in one Great Germany by the right of self-determination of peoples.

2. We demand the equality of the German nation with all other nations and abrogation of the Treaties of Versailles and St. Germain.

3. We demand land and territory (colonies) for the feeding of our people and for the settlement of our surplus population.

4. Only those who are members of the nation can be citizens. Only those who are of German blood, without regard to religion, can be members of the German nation. No Jew can, therefore, be a member of the nation.

5. He who is not a citizen shall be able to live in Germany only as a guest and must live under laws governing foreigners.

6. The right to decide on the leadership and on the laws of the state may belong only to citizens. Therefore we demand that every public office, of whatever sort, whether of the Reich, of the states, or of the communes, shall be filled only by citizens. We fight against the corrupting parliamentary system of filling offices with people chosen because of their party viewpoint without regard to character and ability.

7. We demand that the state be obliged, in the first instance, to provide the possibility of work and life for the citizen. If it is not possible to feed the entire population of the state, the subjects of foreign states (non-citizens) must be expelled from the Reich.

* From James K. Pollock and Harlow J. Heneman, eds., *The Hitler Decrees* (Ann Arbor, Mich.: George Wahr, 1934), pp. 1–3. Reprinted by permission of the publishers.

8. All further immigration of non-Germans is to be prevented. We demand that all non-Germans who have immigrated to Germany since the second of August, 1914 shall be compelled to leave the Reich immediately.

9. All citizens must possess the same rights and duties.

10. The first duty of every citizen is to work productively with mind or body. The activities of individuals must not transgress the interests of the community but must be for the common good.

Therefore we demand:

11. The elimination of income which is acquired without labor or effort.

12. Out of regard for the frightful sacrifice in goods and blood which every war demands from the nation, personal enrichment through war must be designated as a crime against the nation. We demand, therefore, summary confiscation of all war profits.

13. We demand the nationalization of all trusts.

14. We demand profit-sharing in large concerns.

15. We demand a large scale extension of the old-age pension system.

16. We demand the creation of a sound middle class and its maintenance, immediate communalization of large department stores and their rental at low cost to small merchants, the strictest control of all small merchants in their dealings with the national government, the states or the communes.

17. We demand land reform adapted to our national needs, the enactment of a law for the uncompensated expropriation of land for public purposes, the elimination of land interest and the prevention of land speculation.

18. We demand the most ruthless campaign against everyone who injures the public interest by his actions. Those who commit crimes against the people, usurers, profiteers and so forth, must be punished by death, without respect to religion or race.

19. We demand the substitution of Germanic common law for the materialistic international Roman law.

20. In order to make possible the attainment of higher education for every capable and industrious German and thereby the entrance into a leading position, the state has the responsibility of providing for a fundamental extension of our entire educational system. The teaching plans of all educational institutions must be adapted to the demands of practical life. An understanding of national consciousness must be taught to the children at the earliest possible age. We demand the education at state expense of especially gifted children of poor parents without regard to profession or position.

21. The state must care for the improvement of the people's health through the protection of mother and child, through the forbidding of child-labor, through development of physical capability by means of legislative provision of a gymnastic and sports duty and through the greatest support of all associations engaged in physical education of youth.

22. We demand the abolition of the mercenary army and the formation of a people's army.

23. We demand legislative action against conscious political lies and their propagation through the press. In order to make possible the creation of a German press, we demand that:

> a. All editors and contributors of newspapers which appear in German must be citizens,
>
> b. Non-German newspapers must have the special permission of the state in order to be published. They shall not be allowed to be published in the German language,
>
> c. Every financial participation in German newspapers or the influencing by non-Germans is to be forbidden and we demand as punishment for violation the closing of such newspaper plant, as well as the immediate expulsion from the Reich of the participating non-German.
>
> Newspapers which work against the public welfare are to be forbidden. We demand legislative action against an artistic and literary tendency which exerts a destructive influence over our national life and the closing of institutions which conflict with these demands.

24. We demand the freedom of all religions in the state in so far as they do not endanger its welfare or offend against the morals and sense of decency of the German race.

The party as such represents the standpoint of a positive Christianity without binding itself to a particular belief. It fights the Jewish materialistic spirit within and without and is convinced that a permanent convalescence of our nation can only succeed from within on the foundation of: public interest before private interest.

25. For the carrying out of all these we demand: The creation of a strong central power in the Reich, absolute authority of the political central parliament over the entire Reich and all its organizations.

The formation of professional and trade chambers for the carrying out of the general laws of the Reich in the individual federal states.

The leaders of the party promise to work ruthlessly for the carrying out of the points above set forth even to the extent of risking their lives for the program.

Munich, February 24, 1920   *Adolf Hitler*

B] SELECTIONS FROM HITLER's *Mein Kampf*

Hitler wrote *Mein Kampf* in 1924 while he was in prison. The book is part autobiography, part polemic, part pseudo-scientific tract. It gives, with chilling candor, Hitler's program for foreign and domestic policy.

The first of the following selections describes Hitler's discovery of the "Jewish menace." The second states his conception of the Jewish conspiracy to take over the world.*

* From Adolf Hitler, *Mein Kampf* (New York: Reynal and Hitchcock, 1941), pp. 75–76, 78, 84, 448–51. Reprinted by permission of Houghton Mifflin Company.

Nothing gave me more cause for reflection than the gradually increased insight into the activities of Jews in certain fields.

Was there any form of filth or profligacy, above all in cultural life, in which at least one Jew did not participate?

When carefully cutting open such a growth, one could find a little Jew, blinded by the sudden light, like a maggot in a rotting corpse.

The Jews' activity in the press, in art, literature, and the theater, as I learned to know it, did not add to their credit in my eyes. All unctuous assertions were of little or no avail. It was sufficient to look at the bill-boards, to read the names of those who produced these awful works for theaters and movies if one wanted to become hardened for a long time. This was pestilence, spiritual pestilence with which the people were infected, worse than the Black Death of former times! And in what quantities this poison was produced and distributed! Of course, the lower the spiritual and the moral standard of such an art manufacturer, the greater his fertility, till such a fellow, like a centrifugal machine, splashes his dirt into the faces of others. . . .

Now I did not evade the discussion of the Jewish question any longer; no, I sought it out. As I learned to look for the Jew in every field of our cultural and artistic life, I suddenly bumped against him in a place where I had never suspected.

The scales dropped from my eyes when I found the Jew as the leader of Social Democracy. This put an end to a long internal struggle. . . .

If, with the help of the Marxian creed, the Jew conquers the nations of this world, his crown will become the funeral wreath of humanity, and once again this planet, empty of mankind, will move through the ether as it did thousands of years ago.

Eternal Nature inexorably revenges the transgressions of her laws.

Therefore, I believe today that I am acting in the sense of the Almighty Creator: By warding off the Jews I am fighting for the Lord's work.

.   .   .

For hours the black-haired Jew boy, diabolic joy in his face, waits in ambush for the unsuspecting girl whom he defiles with his blood and thus robs her from her people. With the aid of all means he tries to ruin the racial foundations of the people to be enslaved. Exactly as he himself systematically demoralizes women and girls, he is not scared from pulling down the barriers of blood and race for others on a large scale. It was and is the Jews who bring the negro to the Rhine, always with the same concealed thought and the clear goal of destroying, by the bastardization which would necessarily set in, the white race which they hate, to throw it down from its cultural and political height and in turn to rise personally to the position of master.

For a racially pure people, conscious of its blood, can never be enslaved by the Jew. It will forever only be the master of bastards in this world.

Thus he systematically tries to lower the racial level by a permanent poisoning of the individual.

In the political sphere, however, he begins to replace the idea of democracy by that of the dictatorship of the proletariat.

In the organized mass of Marxism he has found the weapon which makes him now dispense with democracy and which allows him, instead, to enslave and to "rule" the people dictatorially with the brutal fist.

He now works methodically towards the revolution in a twofold direction: economically and politically.

Thanks to his international influence, he ensnares with a net of enemies those peoples which put up a too violent resistance against the enemy from within, he drives them into war, and finally, if necessary, he plants the flag of revolution on the battlefield.

In the field of economics he undermines the States until the social organizations which have become unprofitable are taken from the State and submitted to his financial control.

Politically he denies to the State all means of self-preservation, he destroys the bases of any national self-dependence and defense, he destroys the confidence in the leaders, he derides history and the past, and he pulls down into the gutter everything which is truly great.

In the domain of culture he infects art, literature, theater, smites natural feeling, overthrows all conceptions of beauty and sublimity, of nobility and quality, and in turn he pulls the people down into the confines of his own swinish nature.

Religion is ridiculed, customs and morality are presented as outlived, until the last supports of a nationality in the fight for human existence in this world have fallen.

Now begins the great, final revolution. The Jew, by gaining the political power, casts off the few cloaks which he still wears. The democratic national Jew becomes the blood Jew and the people's tyrant. In the course of a few years he tries to eradicate the national supporters of intelligence, and, while he thus deprives the people of their natural spiritual leaders, he makes them ripe for the slave's destiny of permanent subjugation.

The most terrible example of this kind is offered by Russia where he killed or starved about thirty million people with a truly diabolic ferocity, under inhuman tortures, in order to secure to a crowd of Jewish scribblers and stock exchange robbers the rulership over a great people.

2] German Politics, 1928–33

A] Elections to the Reichstag

The results of the last five elections to the German Reichstag (shown in the chart on page 252) suggest the increasing radicalization and polarization of German politics.*

B] The Violence of Political Life

Albert C. Grzesinski was a leading Social Democrat who took charge of the Berlin police in November 1930. These comments are from the autobiography which he wrote after being forced into exile by the Nazis.†

Bloody clashes and violent street fighting between the members of the radical parties were on the increase. Nazi and communist propaganda was responsible for grave disorders. Ordinary brawls had given way to murderous attacks. Knives, blackjacks and revolvers had replaced political argument. Terror was rampant. Carefully prepared alibis helped the terrorists on both sides to escape conviction. In my efforts to deal with the incipient civil war, I availed myself of a law dating back as far as 1850 and authorizing the police to take disturbers of the peace into *Schutzhaft*—temporary custody. These measures were sharply criticized and denounced by the republican press. Their criticism did not deter me.

Rowdiness and political degeneracy had already reached appalling proportions. A surprise police raid of a secret radical meeting netted over fifty revolvers, daggers, brass knuckles and weapons of every description which I placed as visual demonstration before the Prussian Diet. One might have expected signs of disgust and revulsion on the part of the people's representatives, but this was not so. On the contrary, they laughed at the exhibition and showed their obvious incapacity to grasp the true meaning of portents.

The terrorist methods of both Nazis and communists were essentially the same. Communist terrorist groups, consisting of four men, operated in districts where they were unknown. The number of these groups never exceeded twenty, but despite a reward of 20,000 Reichsmark, approximately $5,000, the police were unable to make arrests. Numerous police officers were killed in these years. The most outrageous case was the murder of two police

* From Wilhelm Mommsen, ed., *Deutsche Parteiprogramme* (Munich: Isar Verlag [now: Günter Olzog Verlag], 1960), pp. 795–96. Reprinted in English by permission of the publishers.

† From the book *Inside Germany* by Albert C. Grzesinski. Copyright, 1939, by E. P. Dutton & Co., Inc. Reprinted by permission of the publishers. [Pp. 130–32.]

ELECTIONS TO THE REICHSTAG, 1928/1933

	Communist Party	Social Democratic Party	Democratic Party [1] (State Party)	Economic Party [2]	German People's Party [3]	Center Party [4]	Bavarian People's Party [5]	German National People's Party [6]	National Socialist Party
MAY 20, 1928									
Million	3.265	9.153	1.506	1.397	2.680	3.712	.946	4.382	.810
Seats	54	153	25	23	45	62	16	73	12
Percentage	10.6	29.8	4.9	4.5	8.7	12.1	3.1	14.2	2.6
SEPT. 14, 1930									
Million	4.592	8.578	1.322	1.362	1.578	4.128	1.059	2.458	6.410
Seats	77	143	20	23	30	68	19	41	107
Percentage	13.1	24.5	3.8	3.9	4.5	11.8	3	7	18.3
JULY 31, 1932									
Million	5.283	7.960	.372	.147	436	4.589	1.193	2.177	13.746
Seats	89	133	4	2	7	75	22	37	230
Percentage	14.6	21.6	1.0	.4	1.2	12.5	3.2	5.9	37.4
NOV. 6, 1932									
Million	5.980	7.248	.337	.110	.662	4.231	1.095	2.959	11.737
Seats	100	121	2	1	11	70	20	52	196
Percentage	16.8	20.4	.9	.3	1.8	11.7	3.1	8.8	33.1
MARCH 5, 1933									
Million	4.848	7.182	.334	0	.432	4.425	1.074	3.137	17.277
Seats	81	120	5	0	2	73	19	52	288
Percentage	12.3	18.3	0.9	0	1.1	11.2	2.7	8.0	43.9

[1] The Democratic Party was a moderate, pro-republican party. In 1930 it was replaced by the State Party.
[2] The Economic Party was a splinter group composed mainly of members of the German National People's Party. It professed to represent the interests of the middle class.
[3] The German People's Party was based upon an uneasy coalition of those who supported the republic and those who looked for an alliance to the right.
[4] The Center was a Catholic party which contained a wide variety of political viewpoints. After 1928, the party was oriented towards the right.
[5] The Bavarian People's Party was the Bavarian wing of the Center.
[6] The German National People's Party was a conservative, largely monarchist party. After 1928 it was dominated by Alfred Hugenberg, a radical antirepublican. [The preceding footnotes are the editor's.]

captains on August 9, 1931, near the Karl Liebknecht house, Communist Party headquarters, at the Buelow Square in east Berlin. The two were ambushed on the day the plebiscite on an early dissolution of the Prussian Diet was held. This plebiscite had been demanded by the Nationalists and the Nazis and was actively supported by the communists. . . .

In May of the same year a series of political murders was unloosed with the murder of the communist Heimburger by Nazis. Other assassinations followed in quick succession and within a short time the number had risen to twenty-nine. Twelve communists, six Nazis, one member of the Nationalist Stahlhelm, two Social Democrats, four police officers and four men with unknown party affiliations were killed. Thirteen murders had been committed by communists, nine by Nazis. Large stores of arms were found by the police in their periodical searches of radical hide-outs; 618 revolvers and 12,000 rounds of ammunition, not to speak of a motley collection of other weapons, were confiscated early in 1931.

The number of major political crimes was increasing so rapidly that I decided to go before the public. In a press interview, I made the facts known and insisted that the governments of the Reich and Prussia take strong measures to put an end to this state of affairs. In March, 1931, the long overdue emergency decree was passed. It provided the police authorities with new powers to strike at the political underworld. It came too late. These measures were only temporarily successful. The political crisis could no longer be solved by ordinary means. Public safety became more and more insecure. From June 1 to July 20, 1932, 461 political riots occurred in Prussia. Eighty-two persons were killed and 400 seriously wounded.

c] Hitler and German Industry

The following description is by Fritz Thyssen, a powerful industrialist forced into exile in 1939. Thyssen's memoirs are not always accurate, but they do provide some valuable information and an insight into the political attitudes of big business in Germany.*

I did not become a member of the National Socialist party until December, 1931. This was after my collaboration in a great mass meeting in Harzburg, at which Alfred Hugenberg, as leader of the German National People's party, and Hitler, as leader of the German National Socialist Labor party, announced the co-operation of the two parties. . . . I personally had worked zealously for the German Nationals, but finally had fallen out with their leader. Even while I was a member of the German National party, the National Socialists were congenial to me. I considered them to be sensible

* From *I Paid Hitler* by Fritz Thyssen. Translated by César Saerchinger. Copyright 1941 by Cooperation Publishing Co., Inc. Reprinted by permission of Holt, Rinehart and Winston, Inc. [Pp. 97–104.]

and rational. . . . I came to know Adolf Hitler in Munich, when I was still a member of the German National party. I did not enter into closer relationship with him until sometime later on, and even then we never became very intimate.

.   .   .

But I did in fact bring about the connection between Hitler and the entire body of Rhenish-Westphalian industrialists. It is common knowledge that on January 27th, 1932—almost a year before he seized power—Adolf Hitler made a speech lasting about two and a half hours before the Industry Club of Düsseldorf. The speech made a deep impression on the assembled industrialists, and in consequence of this a number of large contributions flowed from the resources of heavy industry into the treasuries of the National Socialist party.

The preliminaries to this "historic" speech are worth noting. It was not my original intention to let Hitler speak to this gathering. In fact, no provision had been made for the delivery of a National Socialist address. On the contrary, the committee of the Industry Club had given permission to a Social Democrat to make a speech, with the result that the members became greatly excited, and many threatened to resign. At a very stormy session of the committee I said there was only one way of making good this mistake, and that was to invite a National Socialist to address the assembly as well. This proposal was adopted.

. . . I asked Gregor Strasser to make the speech at the Düsseldorf Club. But shortly after this I accidentally met Adolf Hitler in Berlin. When I mentioned to him the projected address before the Düsseldorf Industry Club he said, "I think it would be better if I came myself." I duly agreed; and it was actually through this invitation that Hitler first became properly known in the Rhineland and in Westphalia. So far as I was concerned the origin of the invitation had no political significance. But Hitler, no doubt, immediately saw the political value of the opportunity which was thus offered to him.

I have personally given altogether one million marks to the National Socialist party. Not more. My contributions have been very much overestimated, because I have always been rated the richest man in Germany. But after all, what does it mean to own factories? It does not follow that a man has a lot of cash to spare. In any case, Hitler had other sources of money besides me. In Munich, for instance, there was Herr Bruckmann, the well-known printer; and in Berlin there was Carl Bechstein, the worldrenowned piano manufacturer, who also contributed large sums. Aside from this, Hitler did not receive many subsidies from individual industrialists.

It was during the last years preceding the Nazi seizure of power that the big industrial corporations began to make their contributions. But they did not give directly to Hitler; they gave it to Dr. Alfred Hugenberg, who placed about one-fifth of the donated amounts at the disposal of the National Socialist party. All in all, the amounts given by heavy industry to the Nazis

may be estimated at two million marks a year. It must be understood, however, that this includes only the voluntary gifts, and not the various sums
which the industrial enterprises were obliged to provide for the party's
numerous special manifestations.

.   .   .

But Hitler's relations did not extend to industrialists in general. In fact,
besides old Kirdorf, who was not really an owner of heavy industrial works,
I was the only one of that ilk who freely exposed himself in this connection.
The case of Herr Krupp von Bohlen und Halbach, head of the famous
munition works, was the reverse of mine. Until Hitler's seizure of power,
Herr von Krupp was his violent opponent. As late as the day before President
von Hindenburg appointed Adolf Hitler chancellor he urgently warned the
old field-marshal against such a course. But as soon as Hitler had the power,
Herr von Krupp became one of his most loyal party adherents. I am not
saying this in order to reflect on Herr von Krupp in any way. In any case, this
would not minimize my own mistake. And I candidly confess that I did
make a great mistake when I trusted Adolf Hitler. Only it would be much
better if Herr von Krupp could get himself to confess his mistake as well.

In making this confession I must emphasize again and again—not as a
complete excuse, but by way of extenuation—that the trouble with the Nazis
was not the party itself but certain individuals in it.

3] Hitler Comes to Power, January 1933

From the summer of 1941 until the end of 1944 a stenographer recorded the
long and rambling monologues which Hitler directed to his intimate circle.
Although Hitler's memory was not always reliable, these conversations provide
important information on Hitler's career. In these reminiscences of the events
leading to January 30, note the emphasis Hitler placed on the necessity for
legality.*

When I roundly refused [August 1932] to consider any compromise and accept the Vice-Chancellorship in a von Papen Cabinet, and after the vain
and treacherous attempts of General Schleicher, supported by Gregor Strasser, had failed to split the solid unity of the Party, political tension reached
its zenith. Not only did Schleicher fail to win over a log-rolling majority in
the Reichstag, but as a result of his go-slow policy as regards national economy, the number of unemployed rose, during the first fifteen days of his
regime, by no less than a quarter of a million. In January 1933—one month,
that is, after his assumption of office—Schleicher saw no other alternative

* Reprinted from *Hitler's Secret Conversations, 1941–1944,* ed. by H. R. Trevor-Roper,
by permission of Farrar, Straus & Giroux, Inc. [and Weidenfeld & Nicolson, Ltd.]. Copyright 1953 by Farrar, Straus & Young, Inc. [Pp. 402–05.]

but to dissolve the Reichstag and form a military Cabinet, upheld solely by the support of the President of the Reich.

But the idea of a military dictatorship, in spite of his great personal confidence in General Schleicher, filled old von Hindenburg with the liveliest apprehension. . . .

Faced with this situation of extreme political tension, von Hindenburg, through the intermediary of von Papen, approached me, and in the famous Cologne conversations explored the ground.[1] For myself, I had the impression that all was going well for me. I made it quite clear, therefore, that I would not hear of any compromise, and threw myself, heart and soul, personally into the Lippe electoral campaign.

After the electoral victory at Lippe—a success whose importance it is not possible to over-estimate—the advisers of the Old Gentleman [Hindenburg] approached me once more. A meeting was arranged at Ribbentrop's house with Hindenburg's son and Herr von Papen. At this meeting I gave an unequivocal description of my reading of the political situation, and declared without mincing words that every week of hesitation was a week irretrievably wasted. The situation, I said, could be saved only by an amalgamation of all parties, omitting, of course, those fragmentary bourgeois parties which were of no importance and which, in any case, would not join us. Such an amalgamation, I added, could be successfully assured only with myself as Reich's Chancellor.

At this juncture I deliberately neglected my work within the Party in order to take part in these negotiations, because I considered it of the highest importance that I should legitimately take over the Chancellorship with the blessing of the Old Gentleman. For it was only as constitutionally elected Chancellor, obviously, and before undertaking any measures of reconstruction, that I could overcome the opposition of all the other political parties, and avoid finding myself in constant conflict with the Wehrmacht [i.e., the army]. My decision to attain power constitutionally was influenced primarily by my knowledge of the attitude of the Wehrmacht vis-à-vis the Chancellorship. If I had seized power illegally, the Wehrmacht would have constituted a dangerous breeding place for a coup d'état . . . by acting constitutionally, on the other hand, I was in a position to restrict the activities of the Wehrmacht to its legal and strictly limited military function—at least until such a time as I was able to introduce conscription. Once that was accomplished, the influx into the Wehrmacht of the masses of the people, together with the spirit of National Socialism and with the ever-growing power of the National-Socialist movement, would, I was sure, allow me to overcome all opposition among the armed forces, and in particular in the corps of officers.

On 24th January 1933—the day after the SA assault on the Karl Liebknecht-Haus in Berlin had resulted in a tremendous loss of prestige for the

---

[1] In fact, von Papen seems to have been operating on his own initiative. *Editor.*

Communist Party and caused great indignation in Berlin—I was again invited by von Papen to a conference. Von Papen told me at once that Schleicher had formally asked the Old Gentleman for the plenipotentiary powers to set up a military dictatorship, but that the latter had refused and had stated that he proposed inviting Adolf Hitler, in the rôle of leader of a national front, to accept the Chancellorship and to form a Government, with the proviso that von Papen should be nominated Vice-Chancellor.

I replied that I took cognisance of the offer, and, without permitting any discussion of detail, stated the conditions under which I was prepared to accept. These were the immediate dissolution of the Reichstag and the organization of new elections. Under the pretext that I should be away from Berlin, I avoided a tentative suggestion that I should have a ten-minute talk with the Old Gentleman. Mindful of the experiences of the previous year, I was anxious to avoid giving rise to any undue optimism within the Party, such as was invariably the case whenever I was received by the Old Gentleman.

I took the opportunity in this conversation with Herr von Papen of pressing home my advantage and carrying a step further the negotiations started by Göring for the tentative formation of a Government. It was with the German Nationalists that the negotiations proved most difficult, for Geheimrat Hugenberg displayed a greed for portfolios out of all proportion to the strength of his party, and, because he feared that he would probably lose a great number of votes in any new elections, he would not hear of an early dissolution of the Reichstag. On 27th January, after a short absence from Berlin, I had a personal conference with Hugenberg, but we were unable to agree.

The negotiations for the formation of a Government were further complicated by General Schleicher and his clique, who did all in their power to wreck them. General von Hammerstein, Schleicher's most trusted colleague and Commander-in-Chief of the Army, was even stupid enough to have the impertinence to ring me up and tell me that "under no circumstances would the Wehrmacht sanction my acceptance of the Chancellorship!" If Herr Schleicher and his friends really imagined they could shake my determination with puerilities of this sort, they were grievously mistaken. My only reaction was to impress emphatically on Göring to accept as Minister of the Reichswehr only a General who enjoyed my confidence, such as General von Blomberg, who had been recommended to me by my friends in East Prussia.

On 28th January the Weimar Republic finally collapsed. Schleicher resigned, and von Papen was instructed to sound the various parties with a view to the formation of a new Government. For my own part, I at once declared that any half-measures were now unacceptable to me. The 29th, naturally, was buzzing with conferences, in the course of which I succeeded in obtaining Hugenberg's agreement to the dissolution of the Reichstag in return for the promise to give him the number of seats in the new Government which he had originally demanded for his Party, convincing him that with the Reichstag in its present form, it would be impossible to achieve anything.

The next afternoon Göring brought me the news that on the morrow the Old Gentleman proposed officially to invite me to accept the Chancellorship and the task of forming the Government. . . .

By eleven o'clock on the morning of 30th January, I was able to inform the Old Gentleman that the new Cabinet had been formed, and that the majority in the Reichstag required by constitution to enable it to function had been acquired. Shortly afterwards I received at the hands of the Old Gentleman my appointment as Chancellor of the German Reich.

At the beginning my task as the head of this Cabinet was the reverse of simple. With the exception of Frick, I had initially not one single National-Socialist member of the Cabinet. It is true that some of the others, like Blomberg and Neurath, had promised me their support but the remainder were quite determined to go their own way. Gereke, the Commissioner for Labour, who a little later was arrested and found guilty of embezzlement, was from the beginning my most persistent opponent. . . .

Apart from the difficulties inherent in the formation of a Government, I very quickly realised that the Old Gentleman had called upon me to accept the Chancellorship only because he could see no other constitutional way out of the political impasse. This was obvious from the number of conditions he imposed. He informed me, for instance, that all questions connected with the Reichswehr, the Foreign Office and overseas appointments remained in his hands. He further decided that von Papen must be present whenever he received me officially; and it was only after much hesitation and the intervention of Meissner, that the Old Gentleman was pleased to sign the order for the dissolution of the Reichstag, which I had managed to rattle through during the session of 31st January.

Within a week or so, however, my relations with Hindenburg began to improve.

4] The "Legal" Revolution

A] THE DECREE OF FEBRUARY 28, 1933

Just as Hitler stressed the legality of his rise to power, he also sought legal sanctions for the extension of his control over Germany after January 30. On the night of February 27 the Reichstag building burned. The Nazis blamed the Communists and issued the "Decree for the Protection of the People and State," presented below. Following it is a selection from the instructions sent to the German Police on the implementation of the decree.*

* From the "Decree of the Reich President for the Protection of the People and State, February 28, 1933," *Nuremberg Documents*, 1390 PS.
"Execution of Ordinance for Security of People and State," *Nuremberg Documents*, 2371 PS.

THE DECREE

In virtue of Section 48 (2) of the German Constitution, the following is decreed as a defensive measure against Communist acts of violence endangering the state:

Article 1

Sections 114, 115, 117, 118, 123, 124, and 153 of the Constitution of the German Reich are suspended until further notice. Thus, restrictions on personal liberty, on the right of free expression of opinion, including freedom of the press, on the right of assembly and the right of association, and violations of the privacy of postal, telegraphic, and telephonic communications, and warrants for house-searches, orders for confiscations as well as restrictions on property, are also permissible beyond the legal limits otherwise prescribed.

Article 2

If in a state the measures necessary for the restoration of public security and order are not taken, the Reich Government may temporarily take over the powers of the highest state authority.

Article 3

According to orders decreed on the basis of Article 2, by the Reich Government, the authorities of states and provinces, if concerned, have to abide thereby.

Article 4

Whoever provokes, or appeals for or incites to the disobedience of the orders given out by the supreme state authorities or the authorities subject to them for the execution of this decree, or the orders given by the Reich Government according to Article 2, is punishable—insofar as the deed is not covered by other decrees with more severe punishments—with imprisonment of not less than one month, or with a fine from 150 up to 15,000 Reichsmarks.

Whoever endangers human life by violating Article 1 is to be punished by sentence to a penitentiary, under mitigating circumstances with imprisonment of not less than six months and, when violation causes the death of a person, with death, under mitigating circumstances with a penitentiary sentence of not less than two years. In addition the sentence may include confiscation of property.

Whoever provokes or incites to an act contrary to public welfare is to be punished with a penitentiary sentence, under mitigating circumstances, with imprisonment of not less than three months. . . .

This decree enters in force on the day of its promulgation.

Berlin, 28 February 1933   The Reich President   *von Hindenburg*
                              The Reich Chancellor   *Adolf Hitler*
                              The Reich Minister of the Interior   *Frick*
                              The Reich Minister of Justice *Dr. Guertner*

ITS EXECUTION

As a defense against the criminal, communistic activities and a means of ruthless suppression of this source of peril, whose extremely dangerous scope has been revealed at the last minute, the Reich president decided on 28 Feb. 1933 to proclaim the decree for the protection of the people and the State.

For the actual application of the measures authorized in this decree, I give the following directions:

1. Sect. 1 of the decree not only suspends temporarily Articles 114, 115, 117, 118, 123, 124, and 153 of the Constitution; it rather eliminates all other Reich and State limitations in this matter, as far as this is necessary or practical in order to reach the aims of this decree. . . . Conforming to the aim and purpose of the decree, the additional permissible actions will be directed primarily against the communists, but also against all those working with the communists or even indirectly supporting or promoting their criminal aims. To avoid any blunder, I remind you that the Decree for the protection of the people and State, dated 28 Feb. 1933, should be used against members or institutions other than communistic, anarchistic, or social democratic parties or organizations, when such measures serve for the defense of such communistic tendencies in their broadest meaning.

B] Hitler's Address to the Reichstag, March 23, 1933

The road to a complete Nazi dictatorship was cleared by the Enabling Act passed by the Reichstag on March 24. The following selection is from the speech with which Hitler introduced this bill. Note how Hitler skillfully combined threats and promises of moderation.*

In order to place themselves in a position to fulfil the tasks . . . the Government have had the Enabling Bill introduced in the Reichstag by the National Socialist and German National parties. Part of the proposed measures require the majority necessary for constitutional amendments. The carrying out of these tasks is necessary. It would be contrary to the spirit of the national renaissance and not meet the necessities of the case if the Government were to negotiate and ask for the sanction of the Reichstag to their measures in each case. But in promoting this bill the Government are not actuated by the intention of doing away with the Reichstag as such. On the contrary, they reserve for themselves in future the opportunity of informing the Reichstag regarding their measures of obtaining its sanction.

* From James K. Pollock and Harlow J. Heneman, eds., *The Hitler Decrees* (Ann Arbor, Mich.: George Wahr, 1934), p. 72. Reprinted by permission of the publishers.

But the authority and the fulfilment of the aforesaid tasks would suffer if doubt were to arise among the people as to the stability of the new regime. The Government of the Reich consider a further meeting of the Reichstag impossible in the nation's present state of profound agitation. Hardly ever has a revolution on such a large scale been carried out in so disciplined and bloodless a fashion as this renaissance of the German people in the last few weeks. It is my will and firm intention to see to it that this peaceful development continues in future.

Yet it is all the more necessary that the National Government should be given that sovereign position which, at such a time, is the only one suited to prevent a different development. The Government will only make use of these powers in so far as they are essential for carrying out the vitally necessary measures. Neither the existence of the Reichstag nor that of the Reichsrat are menaced. The position and rights of the President of the Reich remain unaffected. It will always be the foremost task of the Government to act in harmony with his aims. The separate existence of the federal States will not be done away with. The rights of the churches will not be modified. The number of cases in which an internal necessity exists for having recourse to such a law is in itself a limited one. All the more, however, the Government insist upon the passing of the law. They prefer a clear decision in any case. They offer the parties in the Reichstag the possibility of a peaceful settlement and, consequently, of an understanding to be arrived at in the future. But the Government are equally resolved and ready to meet the announcement of refusal and thus of resistance.

It is for you, Gentlemen, now to decide for peace or war!

c] GOERING ON LEGALITY

In a speech to a Nazi gathering on March 3, 1933, Goering gave a view of legality which stands in marked contrast to the apparent concern for legalism which was present in more official statements.*

Fellow Germans, my measures will not be crippled by any judicial thinking. My measures will not be crippled by any bureaucracy. Here I don't have to give Justice, my mission is only to destroy and exterminate, nothing more! This struggle, fellow Germans, will be a struggle against chaos and such a struggle I shall not conduct with the power of any police. A bourgeois state might have done that. Certainly, I shall use the power of the state and the police to the utmost my dear Communists, so that you won't draw any false conclusions but the struggle to the death, in which my fist will grasp your necks, I shall lead with those down there—those are the brown shirts.

* From a speech entitled "We Bear the Responsibility," given on March 3, 1933. Reprinted in *Nazi Conspiracy and Aggression*, Vol. V (Washington, D.C.: U.S. Government Printing Office, 1946), p. 496.

D] THE SA TERROR

The series of decrees which established the Nazi domination of Germany tell
only part of the story of Hitler's first months in power. At the same time
Hitler was promising moderation and legality his followers were terrorizing the
population. The following firsthand account is by Hans Bernd Gisevius, later
one of the leaders of the German opposition to Hitler.*

Foremost among the children of the Revolution were the storm troopers.
They were the incarnation of the Revolution. . . .

For fifteen months Adolf Hitler let the SA run things. It was only natural that the storm troopers should feel themselves the real victors. But now
they wanted to taste the full fruits of their triumph.

For years they had filled themselves with their own bloodthirsty songs of
hatred. At all their "storm" meetings the dream of their revolutionary vengeance, the so-called "night of the long knives," had been painted for them
in glowing colors. Is it any wonder that these starvelings—morally degener-
ate from years of unemployment, roused to fever-pitch by countless speeches
at innumerable meetings, their "heroism" proved in a hundred brawls—should
now begin to live and to react in their own fashion? Fundamentally, this
private army of the SA put into practice after the seizure of power only
what Joseph Goebbels had persuaded them would be their merited glory as
the Brown nobility of the Third Reich. This extraordinary fraternity took
in all those who came to it voluntarily, and knocked down all who resisted.

The ancient and eternally new intoxication that comes from possession
of power proved as heady as ever. The SA, in accord with the Party plat-
form, though with very little deliberation, had been appointed an auxiliary
police force. Very well, then it would really play the part of a police force.
. . . Before long they were leaving the policeman behind at headquarters
and roaming the streets alone in search of "enemies of the state."

The SA conducted large-scale raids. The SA searched houses and offices.
The SA made confiscations. The SA conducted hearings of witnesses. The
SA imprisoned. In brief, the SA established itself as a permanent auxiliary
police force and laughed at the administrative and judicial principles which
dated from the days of the "system," of the Weimar Republic. The worst
feature of all, so far as the helpless government authorities were concerned,
was that the SA would not release its prey. Woe to the unfortunate who
was caught in the clutches of the storm troopers.

At this time there arose the "bunkers," those dreadful private jails of the
SA. It was the duty of every good SA unit to have at least one of these.
"Taking away" unfortunate persons became a customary right of the SA.
The efficiency of a leader was judged by the number of his prisoners, and

* From Hans Bernd Gisevius, *To the Bitter End* (Boston: Houghton Mifflin, 1947),
pp. 102–04. Reprinted by permission of Fretz and Wosmuth, Zurich.

the reputation of an SA tough depended on the strength of arm with which he conducted a prisoner's "education." The Movement could no longer offer the attraction of *Saalschlachten*, those rousing brawls that had so often taken place at Nazi meetings before the seizure of power. Nevertheless, the "battle" continued; the difference was that beatings were handed out for the purpose of feeling the reality of power.

The first opponent, of course, was Communism; but it was in reality only the first. Once the strong-armed heroes had been appointed auxiliary policemen in defense of their imperiled government, a reign of terror in the streets began which had nothing to do with the struggle against Bolshevism.

The sort of violence that went on in our large cities in those first months during and after the struggle for totality is almost beyond belief. The beast in men was let loose with a vengeance; the basest instincts came to the fore. Blindly the old fighters and the newer and newest fighters struck out against the enemy.

The enemy was first alleged, as we have noted, to be Communism. Then it was—somewhat more generally—Marxism. Later the limits were extended —reaction. And—always—it was the Jew. But names meant nothing at all. All had their turn, of course—the men of the Red Front, the Social Democratic functionaries, others whose political color was not brown, and the Jews. But as the SA developed its taste for sadism, the concept of "enemy of the state" was extended to unpleasant neighbors, the club treasurer, to the troublesome landlord and the impolite creditor. People who had never harmed anyone were horribly abused. Innocents who had been picked up by chance were beaten half to death.

All these excesses are typical mass orgasms, familiar in all times of revolutionary turbulence. It was the unleashed masses who howled, plundered, tortured, and killed in those days. The best proof of that is the fact that within a few months the enormously expanded SA consisted, at least a third of it, of former adherents of the old parties of the Left. It is well known that in June and July of 1933 there were some SA units which were almost entirely Communist. The popular phrase for them was "Beefsteak Nazis"— Brown on the outside, Red inside. These noble fellows were by no means any gentler with folk of their own kind. They were even worse.

In that first decisive year more cases of manslaughter were presented before Reich Minister of Justice Guertner than his office had previously dealt with in a whole decade. He was compelled, no matter what he may privately have thought, to pardon all those outrages as committed "in excess of zeal for the National Socialist Revolution." It was these officially sanctioned bestialities of the first months that later emboldened the sadists of the concentration camps. The generalized brutalization that extended far beyond the realm of the Gestapo toward the end of the Revolution was the inescapable consequence of that early practice of condoning the Brown violence.

5] National Socialism and the "National Revival"

A] HINDENBURG AND HITLER AT POTSDAM, MARCH 21, 1933

During his first months in power, Hitler sought to win the support of the conservative sectors of society by stressing the relationship between Nazism and the traditions of German history. The most dramatic instance of this tactic was the Reichstag meeting held at the Garrison Church in Potsdam where the tomb of Frederick the Great recalled the greatness of the Prussian past. Notice how Hitler tried to use his relationship with Hindenburg as the symbol for the cooperation of the old and new Germanies.*

Hindenburg:

. . . Many and arduous are the tasks which you, Herr *Reichskanzler,* and you, gentlemen, Members of the Cabinet, have before you. Both in home and foreign politics, in our own household as in the world, there are difficult problems to solve and important decisions to be made. I am convinced that Chancellor and Government will attack these problems with firm determination, and I trust that you, the members of the newly formed Reichstag, will take your stand behind the Government in a full appreciation of the state of affairs and the measures which are necessary, and that you for your part will do all in your power to support the work of the Government.

The place in which we are assembled today summons up memories of the Prussia of former days which became great in the fear of God by devotion to duty, unfailing courage and selfless patriotism, which principles have welded the German peoples into one nation. May the spirit of this hallowed spot inspire the men of today, may it free us from selfish concerns and party strife and join us together in a feeling of devotion to the best of our national traditions and spiritual renewal for the service of a proud, free and united Germany.

With this desire in my heart, I extend my greetings to the Reichstag at the beginning of its new term of office and call upon the Chancellor to address the assembly.

Hitler:

. . . The National Government, conscious that they have the will of the nation behind them, demands from the parties and the representatives of the nation that, after fifteen years of misery in Germany, they raise themselves above the doctrinaire conceptions of party politics and recognize the

* From James K. Pollock and Harlow J. Heneman, eds., *The Hitler Decrees* (Ann Arbor, Mich.: George Wahr, 1934), pp. 57–72. Reprinted by permission of the publishers.

inevitable necessity of cooperation which has been laid upon us by the needs of the times and their threatening consequences.

The task, which fate has demanded that we fulfill, makes it our bounden duty to rise high above the petty considerations of everyday party politics.

We are determined to restore once more unity of spirit and of determination to our people.

We are determined to protect the eternal foundations of our national life, the strength and the virtues which are our birthright.

We are determined to raise once more to the guiding principles of organisation and government those ideas without which no nation and no country can rise to greatness.

We are determined to combine trust in the sound and natural instincts of life with a steady development of inner and foreign policy.

We are determined to constitute a government which, instead of constantly wavering from side to side, shall be firm and purposeful, and restore to our people a source of unshakable authority.

We are determined to profit from all those experiences which in past centuries have proved of value to mankind, politically and economically, both to the individual and to the community.

We are determined to restore politics to that level which shall enable them to act as the reorganizing and guiding principles of national life.

We are determined to make use of all the truly vital forces in the nation which shall serve to ensure the future of Germany, to gather together all men of good will under our banner, and to deprive those who wish to harm our nation of the power to do so.

We are determined to create a new community out of the German peoples—a community formed of men of every status and profession and of every so-called class, which shall be able to achieve that community of interests which the welfare of the entire nation demands. All classes must be welded together into a single German nation.

This nation shall take under its protection for all time our faith and our culture, our honour and our freedom.

In our relations to the world we wish, having clearly before our eyes the sacrifices of the War, to be the champions of a peace which shall finally heal those wounds from which all are suffering.

The Government of the national renaissance is determined to fulfill the task which they have undertaken before the German nation. They stand today before the German Reichstag with the earnest desire to receive from it the support necessary for the fulfilling of their mission. May you, the elected representatives of the nation, recognise the meaning of this epoch and join with us in the great work of national restoration.

There is among us today a grand old man. We rise to salute you, Herr Generalfeldmarschall.

Three times you have fought on the field of honour for the existence and the future of our nation.

As lieutenant in the army of the King of Prussia, you fought for the unity of Germany; under him who afterwards became the first German Kaiser . . . you fought for the glorious founding of the German Empire and, as our supreme leader, you fought in the greatest War of all time for the existence of the Reich and for the freedom of our people.

You were present when the German Empire came into being, you beheld the work of the Great Chancellor, the glorious rise of our nation, and you have led us in those momentous times in which fate has allowed us to play our part.

Providence has willed it, Herr Generalfeldmarschall, that you should be present here today as the patron of the renaissance of our nation. Your marvellous career is a symbol for us all of the indestructible forces which are latent in the German nation. The youth of Germany and, indeed, the whole nation is filled with gratitude to you and that you have lent your approval and given your blessing to the rehabilitation of the German nation. May these forces give strength also to the newly elected representatives of the people.

May Providence at the same time grant us that courage and perseverance of which this spot, hallowed for every German, reminds us and give us who stand here at the tomb of our greatest monarch the strength to fight for the freedom and greatness of our people.

B] Goebbels on the Historical Position of National Socialism

In a speech of February 21, 1933, Joseph Goebbels suggested his view of the relationship between the Nazi regime and German history. Contrast Goebbels' remarks with Hitler's speech at Potsdam.*

I believe that there is no one in Germany today who doubts that on January 30 a new epoch in German historical development began.

National Socialism did not take over power for fun; it knows how to use it.

National Socialism is an ideology [Weltanschauung] and the problem now is to realize theories for which we fought in the opposition for fourteen years. Before, ministers came and went. They all operated on the same principles. National Socialism, however, proclaims a new ideology. It is not disposed to bind up wounds but to cauterize them radically. We want to undertake a basic change and we are ready to carry through a reform of [the national] mind and body.

We shall complete our work.

* Translated by Jacqueline Strain from Joseph Goebbels, *Revolution der Deutschen. 14 Jahre Nationalsozialismus*, 1933, pp. 125–26.

That was the fateful error of the November governments [i.e., the Republican governments]. They believed that make-shift measures would suffice; they did not see that the German crisis was a moral crisis, that it was necessary to go to its roots, and that these roots did not lie in economics or politics but in the innermost depths of the German people themselves.

We National Socialists have not only represented these principles since the seizure of power. In fact, the people brought us to power because since our political debut we have left no doubt that we intend basically to eliminate the German sickness.

The other parties also knew that we are not of their kind. I believe that no political movement has striven harder . . . for power than we National Socialists. Were our contemporaries, the political forces which we replaced, convinced that we would take over power only [in order] one day to give it up then perhaps we would have come to power one or two years earlier.

But one thing was clear to them: to give Hitler power would be a fundamentally decisive action.

January 30 produced a change in systems. Though power was, so to say, given to us as a gift, nevertheless a vast assortment of work was in store for us. When we were in the opposition, however, we had already won the support of the people for our objectives, and [as a result] we can now set to work immediately.

We have not drawn up a short-term program of promises. Our plans are long-term ones, and those whom we cannot win over by words we will convince by our deeds in the coming months and years.

6] The Establishment of a Totalitarian State

A] Goebbels on the Role of Propaganda, March, 13, 1933

The following selection is from a speech given by Goebbels on the day he was named the first Minister for Propaganda and Public Enlightenment.*

The new ministry [of Propaganda] has no other purpose than to unite the nation behind the idea of the national revolution. When this goal has been attained, my methods may be condemned. That, however, will be of little consequence, for the ministry by that time will have achieved its objective. . . .

. . . We are conducting the political struggle at home through a popular

* Translated by Jacqueline Strain from Joseph Goebbels, *Revolution der Deutschen. 14 Jahre Nationalsozialismus*, 1933, pp. 139–41.

movement which stands behind us and with the power of the state which stands above us. No one can doubt that it is pointless to form either a moderate or radical opposition against this government. This government will not fall; it is determined to remain [in power]. It will, however, also accomplish its objective of finding the necessary sympathy among the masses.

In the course of time revolutionary changes in all fields, especially technology, have taken place. Today we are living in the age of the radio and of great mass demonstrations. Mass marches of one hundred, two hundred, or three hundred thousand people are no longer impossible for us.

The most important tasks of this ministry must be the following: First, all the propaganda institutions . . . on the Reich and state levels must be centralized in the hands of one person. It must also be our task to instill a modern impulse into these propaganda institutions and to bring them into harmony with the present. It must not be left for technology to forge ahead of the Reich; rather, the Reich must keep pace with technology. Only the most modern is good enough. We are living now in an age in which the masses must support politics. The National Socialist movement and the present government of the national revolution which it heads are based exclusively on the principle of personality. The principles of the masses and of personality do not need to be contradictory. On the contrary, the true personality will never subordinate itself to the masses; rather, the reverse relationship will exist. The modern leaders of the people . . . must understand the masses.

b] The Duties of the Propaganda Minister

The following decree was issued on June 30, 1933, in order to define the responsibility of the newly created Propaganda Ministry. The matter-of-fact legal terminology should not obscure the immense implications of this decree for every aspect of national life.*

Based upon the order of the Reich President of 13 March 1933, I decree in agreement with the Reich Minister of Foreign Affairs, the Reich Minister of the Interior, the Reich Minister of Economics, the Reich Minister of Nutrition and Agriculture, the Reich Postminister, the Reich Minister of Transportation, and the Reich Minister of Public Enlightenment and Propaganda as follows:

The Reich Minister of Public Enlightenment and Propaganda has jurisdiction over the whole field of spiritual indoctrination of the nation, of propagandizing the state, of cultural and economic propaganda, of enlightenment of the public at home and abroad; furthermore, he is in charge of the administration of all institutions serving these purposes.

* From the "Decree Concerning the Duties of the Reich Ministry for Public Enlightenment and Propaganda, June 30, 1933," *Nuremberg Documents, 2030 PS.*

Therefore, the Reich Minister of Public Enlightenment and Propaganda takes over the following jurisdictions:

1. From the jurisdiction of the Foreign Office: News services and enlightenment in foreign countries; art; art exhibitions; moving pictures and sport abroad.

2. From the jurisdiction of the Reich Ministry of the Interior: General Domestic enlightenment, Academy of Politics, establishment and celebration of national holidays and of state celebrations in conjunction with the Reich Minister of Interior, Press, (including the Institute for Journalism), Radio, National anthem, German Library in Leipzig, Art, Music, including the Philharmonic Orchestra, Theater, Moving Pictures, Campaign against lewd and obscene literature.

3. From the jurisdiction of the Reich Minister of Economics and of the Reich Ministry for Nutrition and Agriculture: Propaganda in the field of business, exhibitions, fairs and commercial publicity.

4. From the jurisdiction of the Reich Postministry and of the Reich Ministry of Transportation: Propaganda for tourism.

Furthermore, there are transferred from the Reich Postministry all radio matters with the exclusion of the technical administration; the administration of the buildings of the Reich Radio Corporation and the Radio Corporation is not included in that exception. However, the Reich Minister of Public Enlightenment and Propaganda must participate in the technical administration to the extent necessary for the execution of his own duties, especially in fixing the conditions for renting radio installations and the regulation of fees.

The representation of the Reich in the Reich Radio Corporation is entirely transferred to the Reich Ministry of Public Enlightenment and Propaganda.

In the areas designated, the Reich Minister for Public Enlightenment and Propaganda has the predominant jurisdiction, including legislation. The general regulations are valid so far as the other Ministers of the Reich have to participate.

Berlin, 30 June 1933   The Reich Chancellor   *Adolf Hitler*

c] HITLER ON THE SA PURGE OF JUNE 30, 1934

In a speech of July 13, 1934, Hitler accepted full responsibility for the events of June 30. He declared that he had been forced to act as Germany's highest judge in order to crush this alleged danger to the state.*

* From Norman Baynes, ed., *The Speeches of Adolf Hitler*, 2 vols. (Oxford: Oxford University Press [under the auspices of the Royal Institute of International Affairs], 1942), Vol. I, pp. 320, 322, 324.

If disaster was to be prevented at all, action must be taken with lightning speed. Only a ruthless and bloody intervention might still perhaps stifle the spread of the revolt. And then there could be no question that it was better that a hundred mutineers, plotters, and conspirators should be destroyed than that ten thousand innocent SA men should be allowed to shed their blood. For if once criminal activity was set in motion in Berlin, then the consequences were indeed unthinkable. . . . I gave the order to shoot those who were the ringleaders in this treason, and I further gave the order to burn out down to the raw flesh the ulcers of this poisoning of the wells in our domestic life and of the poisoning of the outside world. And I further ordered that if any of the mutineers should attempt to resist arrest, they were immediately to be struck down with armed force. The nation must know that its existence —and that is guaranteed through its internal order and security—can be threatened by no one with impunity! And everyone must know for all future time that if he raises his hand to strike the State, then certain death is his lot. And every National Socialist must know that no rank and no position can protect him from his personal responsibility and therefore from his punishment. I have prosecuted thousands of our former opponents on account of their corruption. I should in my own mind reproach myself if I were now to tolerate similar offences in our own ranks. . . .

The penalty for these crimes was hard and severe. Nineteen higher SA leaders, thirty-one leaders and members of the SA, were shot, and further, for complicity in the plot, three leaders of the S.S., while thirteen SA leaders and civilians who attempted to resist arrest lost their lives. Three more committed suicide. Five who did not belong to the SA, but were members of the Party, were shot for taking part in the plot. Finally there were also shot three members of the S.S. who had been guilty of scandalous ill-treatment of those who had been taken into protective custody.[2]

d] The Theory of the Fuehrer State

The following selection is from a pamphlet written by the leading Nazi political theorist Carl Schmitt immediately after Hitler's speech of July 13, 1934. Schmitt's remarks suggest not only the enormity of Hitler's power, but also the extent to which the Nazis deviated from the traditions of political and legal philosophy dominant in Europe since the Enlightenment.[*]

The Führer protects justice from the most dire misuse when in the moment of danger he, by virtue of his leadership as the highest judge, directly creates

---

[2] It has been estimated that the number killed was actually double, perhaps even triple the figure Hitler admitted. Not only SA leaders were murdered; many others, such as General von Schleicher, were also shot. *Editor.*

[*] Translated by Mary Schubert from Carl Schmitt, "Der Führer schütz das Recht," *Positionen und Begriffe im Kampf mit Weimar-Genf-Versailles, 1923–1939* (Hamburg: Hanseatische Verlagsanstalt, 1940), pp. 199–203.

the law. "In this hour I was responsible for the destiny of the German nation and was therefore the highest judge of the German people" [Hitler said on July 13, 1934]. The true leader is always also a judge. From the position of leadership emanates judicial authority. . . .

In truth, the deed of the Führer was genuine jurisdiction. It was not subordinate to the judiciary but was itself the highest judiciary. It was not the action of a republican dictator who works in a legal vacuum, while the law closes its eyes for a moment so that thereafter the fiction of flawless legality can be retained. The judicial authority of the Führer springs from the same source of law from which all judicial authority of every nation originates. At the point of greatest distress this supreme justice proves itself and appears as the highest . . . realization of this law. All law stems from the nation's right to exist. Every governmental statute, every legal judgment contains only as much legality as flows to it from this source. The rest is not law but a "positive web of compulsory norms," of which a clever criminal is contemptuous. . . .

In sharp contrast the Führer emphasized the difference between his government and the state [*Staat*] and the state and governments of the Weimar system: "I did not want to deliver the young nation to the destiny of the old one." "On January 30, 1933, there was not for the nth time a new government formed, but a new regime pushed an old and sick age aside." When the Führer demands with such words the liquidation of a gloomy section of German history, then that is also of judicial significance for our legal thinking, for the practice of law and the interpretation of law. We must test anew our prevailing methods and trains of thought, the prevailing dogmas and the prior judgments of the highest courts in all areas of law. We must not hold blindly to the judicial concepts, arguments, and prejudices which an old and sick age brought forth. Many a sentence in the opinions of our courts is, indeed, to be understood as a justified resistance to the corruption of the system of that time; but even this, thoughtlessly carried on, would mean the opposite today and would make the judiciary the enemy of the present-day state. When in June of 1932 the Supreme Court of Justice saw the meaning of judicial independence in "the protecting of citizens in their legally recognized rights against possible governmental caprice," then that was spoken from a liberal-individualistic attitude. "The judicial authority is regarded as being above not only the head of the state and the government but also above all administrative organs." This is comprehensible within the framework of that time. But today the duty falls to us to establish with the greatest decisiveness the new meaning of all public legal institutions, also of the judiciary. . . .

Again and again the Führer reminds us of the collapse of the year 1918. From that point our present situation is determined. Whoever wants to evaluate correctly the serious events of the thirtieth of June must not extract the events of this and the two following days from the context of our total political situation, isolating and incapsulating them according to the manner of certain penal methods, until the political substance is driven out of them and only a purely judicial "fact-situation" or "non-fact-situation" remains. With such methods one cannot do justice to any highly political process. However, it belongs to the poisoning of the nation [*Volksvergiftung*] of the last decades and is a long-practiced skill of Germanophobic propaganda to establish precisely this isolation process as solely constitutional [*rechtsstaat-lich*]. . . .

In the face of the deed of Adolf Hitler, many enemies of Germany . . . will find it shocking that the present-day German state has the strength and the will to distinguish between its friends and its enemies. They will promise us the praise and the applause of the whole world if we again, as then in the year 1919, collapse and sacrifice our political existence to the idols of liberalism. Whoever sees the powerful background of our total political situation will understand the admonitions and warnings of the Führer and arm himself for the great spiritual battle in which we must uphold our just cause.

CONCLUSION

IN OFFICIAL Nazi historiography Hitler's coming to power was viewed as the result of an irresistible popular movement. Certainly National Socialism's impact on the German people should not be underestimated, but it should also be remembered that before 1933 the Nazis never received more than 37.4 per cent of the vote. Hitler's regime was not inevitable; it could have been prevented. Hitler succeeded not only because of his ability to capture the allegiance of millions of Germans and his own instinct for power, but also because the anti-Nazi forces in society were confused and divided. For example, men like Papen and Schleicher did not want a Nazi-dominated government. However, they helped bring Hitler to power in large measure because they misjudged their own ability to control the Nazis and use Hitler for their own ends. On the other side of the political spectrum, the Communists also misjudged the Nazi movement. The Communists did nothing to assist the republic because they were confident that, after a brief Nazi interlude, Germany would be ripe for a Communist revolution. Even the moderate, pro-republican parties did not fully grasp the threat posed by Nazism. The inability of these parties to save the coalition government in March 1930 illustrates their inability to see the extent of the crisis facing German democracy. After January 30, 1933, these parties clung to the illusion that legal opposition to Hitler was still possible. Even as late as March 1933, all the parties but the Social Democrats voted for the Enabling Act because they believed—or at least pretended to believe—that Hitler would keep his promises of moderation. These divisions and delusions among Hitler's opponents greatly facilitated his assumption of control over the German state. In the twelve years after 1933 Germany was to pay a ghastly price for these failures of intellect and will.

STUDY QUESTIONS

1] What was the relationship between National Socialism and the German conservatives?
2] To what extent was Hitler justified in stressing the legality of his assumption of power?
3] Was the Nazi seizure of power really a revolution?
4] Who bears the main responsibility for the destruction of German democracy?
5] What is to be learned about the role of the individual in history from the events leading to the formation of the Hitler government?

RECOMMENDED READINGS

PRIMARY

BAYNES, NORMAN, ed. *The Speeches of Adolf Hitler, 1922–1939*, 2 vols. (Oxford, 1942).

GOEBBELS, JOSEPH. *My Part in Germany's Fight* (London, 1935).

HITLER, ADOLF. *Mein Kampf* (Boston, 1943).

Nazi Conspiracy and Aggression, 8 vols. (Washington, 1946).

POLLOCK, JAMES AND HARLOW HENEMAN, eds. *The Hitler Decrees* (Ann Arbor, Mich., 1934).

TREVOR-ROPER, H. R., ed. *Hitler's Secret Conversations, 1941–1944* (New York, 1953).

SECONDARY

ARENDT, HANNAH. *The Origins of Totalitarianism* (New York, 1951).

BRECHT, ARNOLD. *Prelude to Silence* (New York, 1944).

BULLOCK, ALAN. *Hitler: A Study in Tyranny* (New York, 1961).

CRAIG, GORDON. *The Politics of the Prussian Army, 1640–1945* (New York and Oxford, 1955).

EYCK, ERICH. *History of the Weimar Republic*, 2 vols. (Cambridge, Mass., 1962–64).

HALPERIN, S. WILLIAM. *Germany Tried Democracy* (New York, 1946).

HEIDEN, KONRAD. *The Fuehrer* (London, 1944).

KOGON, EUGEN. *The Theory and Practice of Hell* (New York, 1958).

MAU, HERMANN AND HELMUT KRAUSNICK. *German History, 1933–1945* (New York, 1963).

MEINECKE, FRIEDRICH. *The German Catastrophe* (Boston, 1963).

NEUMANN, FRANZ. *Behemoth* (New York, 1944).

SEABURY, PAUL. *The Wilhelmstrasse: A Study of German Diplomats Under the Nazi Regime* (Berkeley, 1954).

WHEELER-BENNETT, J. W. *Hindenburg: The Wooden Titan* (London, 1936).

The Moral Dilemma
of Nuclear Warfare

THEODORE ROSZAK

CALIFORNIA STATE COLLEGE AT HAYWARD

CONTENTS

CHRONOLOGY

1945

AUGUST 5 The United States drops the first atomic bomb on Hiroshima; 100,000 are killed.

AUGUST 7 The United States drops an atomic bomb on Nagasaki.

1946

JUNE The United States places the Baruch Plan before the UN Atomic Energy Commission, the first comprehensive plan for the control of atomic energy.

JULY The United States opens the Bikini atomic testing series.

1949

SEPTEMBER President Truman announces the first Russian atomic bomb explosion.

1950

JANUARY President Truman directs the Atomic Energy Commission to begin research on a hydrogen bomb.

1952

JANUARY The UN sets up the Disarmament Commission to deal with both nuclear and conventional weapons.

NOVEMBER The United States opens the first hydrogen bomb test series at Eniwetok; the series includes an explosion of a 15-megaton bomb.

1953

AUGUST Russia explodes its first hydrogen bomb.

1954

MARCH The second United States hydrogen bomb test series is conducted at Bikini.

1957

MAY Great Britain explodes its first hydrogen bomb at Christmas Island.

AUGUST   Russia claims development of a multi-stage intercontinental ballistic missile (ICBM), beginning
the East-West competition in delivery systems.

OCTOBER 4   Russia launches Sputnik I.

1958

JANUARY 31   The United States launches Explorer I.

JULY   The opening of an eight-nation conference of scientists at Geneva on the detection of nuclear
tests, the first step toward a partial test ban.

NOVEMBER   The United States fires its first ICBM, the Atlas
missile with a range of 5–9,000 miles.

1960

JULY   The first underwater firing of the United States's
Polaris missile, having a range of 1,300 miles.

1962

OCTOBER   Russia explodes the largest of all hydrogen
bombs: 60 megatons, the explosive equivalent of
3,000 Hiroshima bombs.

1963

MARCH 19   France explodes its first nuclear device.

AUGUST 5   The United States, Great Britain, and Russia sign
a partial nuclear test ban.

1964

OCTOBER 16   China explodes its first nuclear device.

INTRODUCTION

THE MORALS of extermination weighed upon the conscience of mankind well before the first atomic bomb was detonated over Hiroshima on August 5, 1945. Indeed, the advent of nuclear weapons might be seen as only a technological elaboration of a moral crisis that was already well advanced in the years just before and during World War II, when the wars men fought were, by the standards of destruction we now use, "limited." As early as 1937 the Japanese bombardment of Nanking and the destruction that same year of the Spanish town of Guernica by dive-bombers the Nazis had loaned to General Franco revealed the fearful vulnerability of civilian populations to the new weapons of aerial warfare. Perhaps the Western democracies expected no better of Hitler than that he should resort to a strategy of obliteration bombing at the very outset of World War II—as indeed he did, with the devastation of Warsaw in 1939 and Rotterdam in 1940. But clearly the allied leaders set themselves a higher standard of conduct. When America entered the war in 1941, President Roosevelt, who had denounced the bombing of Nanking as "contrary to the principles of law and humanity," pledged that the United States "shall in no event, and in no circumstances, undertake the bombardment from the air of civilian populations or of unfortified cities." And, early in the war, the British government, under Winston Churchill's leadership, proclaimed that "His Majesty's Government have made it clear that it is no part of their policy to bomb non-military objectives, no matter what the policy of the German Government may be. In spite of the wanton and repeated attacks by the German Air Force on undefended towns . . . , His Majesty's Government steadily adhere to this policy."

But, as so frequently happens, the best intentions of the most principled political leaders weigh lightly in the scales against what is perceived to be military necessity. By 1942 the Royal Air Force had begun the "area bombing" of German cities, devoting 60 per cent of its bomb tonnage to the devastation of urban centers. "Our plans," Prime Minister Churchill now declared, "are to bomb, burn, and ruthlessly destroy in every way available to us the people responsible for creating this war." And by early 1945 the United States, which had already undertaken saturation bombing in Germany the year before, was carrying out obliteration fire-raids upon Japanese cities. These allied attacks were directed primarily against civilian populations and, as in the cases of the massive American assaults upon Tokyo and Hamburg, accounted for the deaths of as many as 100,000 people in a single raid. At the same time, the Nazis, in Eastern Europe, were cruelly multiplying their toll of civilian victims in the course of their program of Jewish and Slavic genocide.

All of these policies were, of course, pursued by what we now regard as "conventional means" of warfare: the blockbuster, the machine-gun squad, the napalm bomb, the gas chamber. It was not until a radically new weapon —the first atomic bomb—accomplished at Hiroshima in the space of thirty seconds on the morning of August 5, 1945, the death and damage which had required ten days and nights of steady allied bombardment at Hamburg that the massively and indiscriminately destructive nature of modern weapons of war, nuclear and conventional alike, was dramatized sufficiently to provoke significant public discussion. In the years since Hiroshima, to be sure, the atomic arsenals of the world have acquired thermonuclear, chemical, radiological, and biological weapons that multiply a thousandfold the destructiveness of the original atomic bomb. Among the biologicals alone, a few pints of botulinus toxin, which both the United States and Russia are producing in quantity, would be deadly enough to kill off the entire population of the earth, if the toxin could be widely enough distributed. As Herman Kahn, one of the leading American military strategists of the postwar period, has pointed out, the major world powers now undergo a revolution in weaponry regularly every five years. With each of these revolutions —both in the means of destruction and in the means of its delivery—decent men everywhere have found their consciences the more painfully challenged by the unfolding horrors of their own technological genius.

The crisis of conscience we find ourselves in resides in the fact that the military means presently at the disposal of the great powers, and increasingly available to lesser powers, are of such destructive magnitude that they deny man the capacity to apply force discriminately for the achievement of well-defined political objectives. Governments have thus lost the capacity to restrict with any dependability the damage that military operations can do to noncombatants. Increasingly, the devastation of war reaches out to destroy the enemy's civilian population and the social fabric that supports its life. It is this inability of modern weaponry to be applied "counter-forces" rather than "counter-people" that makes the moral dilemma of war in our time as poignant for nations whose intentions are purely defensive as for those that harbor aggressive ambitions. In the cold war, both East and West possess the same weapons. And whether used defensively or offensively, modern weapons of war strike as massively and cruelly at civilians as at military personnel. For this reason, modern war, whatever the immediate *casus belli*, whatever the ultimate designs of either side, threatens always to become total war: a genocidal conflict between whole populations.

And yet military force has traditionally been the final arbiter of international conflict. It remains today, in the view of many, the only source of power that can defend the interests and promote the policies of nations— a source of power that cannot be compromised by any nation unless all nations agree to reduce or surrender their arms together. Such a mutual reduction of armaments has been the goal of the various disarmament conferences held since the last world war. The first of these conferences, designed to control the building and use of atomic reactors, was inaugurated in June 1946 when America laid the famous Baruch Plan before the United Nations Atomic Energy Commission. Bold and generous in conception, the plan was nonetheless perceived by the Soviet Union as an effort on the part of the West to monopolize the promising economic potentialities of atomic energy and was thus rejected.

The course of disarmament negotiations since 1946 has been in keeping with this inauspicious beginning. Indeed, the partial test-ban treaty of August 1963 remains the only progress to date in the direction of the ambitious goal of "complete and universal disarmament" which the General Assembly of the United Nations endorsed unanimously in 1959. And while the partial test ban is a hopeful beginning (despite the fact that neither France nor mainland China is a party to it), it is nonetheless a very meager measure of disarmament. For by now the arms race has, as far as the United States and the Soviet Union are concerned, passed the point at which further large-scale nuclear testing is critical. The competition between the great powers, both possessing immense nuclear arsenals and capable of multiplying indefinitely the megatonnage of their bombs, has moved on to the perfection and proliferation of delivery systems like the intercontinental ballistic missile and the nuclear submarine.

And so the arms race and the balance of terror continue to structure the relations of East and West in the cold war. As long as this remains true, the problem of illimitable violence and its relationship to the ideals and interests of nations will stand as the basic moral challenge of our time.

What follows are five contrasting efforts to confront that challenge. The selections range in ethical scope from the militant and war-ready anticommunism of the Foreign Policy Research Institute to the Gandhian pacifism of Mulford Sibley. In each case it should be remembered that the author's discussion of nuclear weapons is related to his general vision of what his society's total foreign policy should be—a vision we cannot do full justice to here. War is what General Clausewitz called it: an extension of politics by other means. Our conception of the enemy and his intentions, our understanding of our own interests, our relationship to allies and neutrals: all these must go into a thorough analysis of military policy and disarmament.

DOCUMENTS

1] The Morals of Deterrence

Walter Stein, a British Catholic teaching at the University of Leeds, has contributed significantly to the ethical analysis of thermonuclear warfare both
within his church and in the religious community generally. His discussion here
of the morals of deterrence is from "The Defense of the West"; it is a closely
argued statement of the just-war tradition, which requires that acts of war be
governed by strictly defined ethical limitations.*

The primary job of a soldier is to defend the community against a particular form of attack—direct physical violence. In order to fulfill this important and honorable purpose he may use certain extreme measures; for example, he may, of course, kill enemy troops if this is the only practicable way
of protecting the community against them. It is important to see that the
right to kill is not something that belongs to a soldier because he has a uniform but because he has a certain job to do. Troops may be used for many
other purposes—quelling riots, or policing a conquered country, for example: in these circumstances they do not have the same right to use extreme
measures. Similarly, the man who may be killed is not just any man who
wears an enemy uniform but a man who cannot otherwise be prevented
from carrying out his present activity of violence; thus to shoot prisoners of
war who are not engaged in hostilities is just ordinary murder. If we may
not kill a man simply because he wears an enemy uniform, still less may we
kill him simply because he belongs to the enemy country or subscribes to
the enemy's religion or political ideology. On the other hand, if a man is
directly engaged in hostilities against the community, we may prevent him
by killing, whether or not he is wearing a uniform. Any such man, in or out
of uniform, is for the time being a combatant; he ceases to be a combatant
as soon as he presents no immediate danger of physical violence.

Now, of course, the line between combatants and noncombatants is one
of those which it is difficult to fix exactly, particularly is it difficult to draw
it in the heat of action; yet, nevertheless, there are large areas which unquestionably lie on either side of the line. If it is right to kill enemy troops,
what about civilians supplying their weapons? If it is right to kill munitions-
workers, what about those supplying the forces with food? What, moreover,
of all those who—in coal mines or steel plants or laboratories—stand behind

* From *Nuclear Weapons: A Catholic Response* edited by Walter Stein, © 1961 by
Merlin Press, Ltd., published by Sheed & Ward, Inc., New York. [Paperback edition
by Burns & Oates, Ltd.]

the immediate war-suppliers? And of those who, simply by performing the most unaggressive jobs, right down to hospital nursing and haircutting, keep the economy in being and thereby assist the war-effort? Is "totality" not implicit in modern societies?

At this point it is only necessary to repeat that difficulties about the drawing of lines do not dispense from conscientiousness; to suggest that, when all has been said, there remains a qualitative abyss between a pilot's or munitions-worker's job and a barber's; and that a high proportion of any population consists of children, full-time mothers, pensioners and sick people. Of course, if someone is so inclined, he can reply that mothers rear children and are good for their husbands, that children will one day be workers or even soldiers—and are, in fact, already knitting socks for the troops—that pensioners can do all sorts of things in a crisis, and that sick people frequently get well again. Moralizing can have its moments.

Here we should perhaps pause to observe that the legitimate killing of combatants is something horrible. War would be full of horrors even without the murder of noncombatants. It is important to say this because many people suppose that the objection to killing noncombatants is simply that the horrors of war ought to be kept within some conventional bounds. But the objection to murdering noncombatants is not simply that it makes war a degree more horrible, but that it is wicked. The killing of combatants is indeed a necessary evil—something ghastly which we may find ourselves bound to do; the killing of noncombatants is a *moral* evil, something which we have never the right to do.

Even when we have drawn some kind of line between combatants and noncombatants, there remains a further problem. Granted that we may never deliberately seek to kill an innocent man, must we always refrain from killing combatants if there is a danger of killing noncombatants as well? Clearly not. I may sink an enemy submarine even though I am sure there are prisoners on board. I may destroy an enemy arms dump even if I am sure that nearby civilians will be killed. In such cases I have a definite and justifiable military purpose and it is this that I seek to achieve. I do not deliberately try to kill the noncombatants; their death is a circumstance attendant upon the achieving of my purpose. In the case of combatants, on the other hand, I do *deliberately seek their death as a means* for protecting the community. It seems, then, that I may sometimes take action which issues in the death of noncombatants, provided that their death is *merely a circumstance attendant upon the thing I am trying to do.*

But, clearly, the consequences of an act can be "unintentional" in this sense only (i) if there is a reasonable proportion between the intended good and the unintended evil, (ii) if the evil effects do not become too vast in themselves (for there comes a point when sheer scale must deprive the concept of "unintended effects" of meaning), and (iii), above all, if the evil effects do not constitute a foreseen *means* of the *good ones* (for, of course, if they did, they themselves must needs be intended). And to intend an evil is evil, whatever the ultimate aim: the end does not justify the means.

.   .   .

Let it be quite clear what we are *not* saying. We are not saying that war can never, in principle, be justified. Nor that there are not powerful motives in justice—and even charity—to protect our countries against communist aggression. We can envisage situations in which, other things being equal, we *ought* to defend our countries—our liberty, our institutions—by force, even at enormous sacrifice. The point is that other things are not equal: their name is "massive nuclear bombardment" and "virtual annihilation."

These names are not of our invention; they are the names, respectively used by the 1958 British Government White Paper on Defense and by President Eisenhower, in his State of the Union Message of 9 January 1958, which —in spite of important modifications, intended to make the "ultimate deterrent" more genuinely *ultimate*—continue to define the basis of Western defense policy in the Kennedy era.

.   .   .

For the most part, however, participants in this discussion do not deny the claim that a total nuclear war would be immoral. Instead, those who nevertheless defend the stockpiling of nuclear weapons tend to base themselves on a distinction between "using" and "possessing" these weapons, or between a possible "total war" and the actuality of "nuclear deterrence."

This position is important because of the wide, and at times highly authoritative, support it commands. It usually relies on one of three arguments —or a combination between these arguments—which might be called: (i) the argument from bluff, (ii) the argument from military targets, and (iii) the argument from the enforcement of peace.

i. *The argument from bluff* simply asserts that, if it came to the point, Western governments would not in fact make good their threats, so that nuclear deterrence does not imply a conditional commitment to total war. Thus it is one thing to "have" these bombs; quite another to "use" them. And, immoral as it may be to engage in total nuclear war, there is nothing immoral about nuclear deterrence.

But are there any grounds at all for assuming that governments are merely bluffing? (And if there were, would the deterrent be a deterrent?) Was it not, in fact, Western governments who initiated the atomic era with Hiroshima and Nagasaki—and never expressed any regret about these acts? Are we to discount the categorical statements of our statesmen and soldiers, and credit them with the certainty of being liars? And even if it should, in spite of everything, turn out that all this apparatus of bombs and threats was vain, can we, as voters in democratic states, underwrite their commitment to admittedly wicked acts, in the hope that this commitment might perhaps be dishonored?

. . .

But the policy of deterrence not only involves genocidal threats by civil and military leaders, which we have every reason to think express real intentions—and involves acceptance of genocidal risks, even if the immediate purpose were simply to bluff: it also requires that those who actually operate the deterrent must, *at this moment,* be ready, if called upon, to carry out acts of genocide. As Air Commodore Magill said at the British Official Secrets Trial, in February 1962, in reply to the question "Would you press the button you know is going to annihilate millions of people?": "If the circumstances demanded it I would." Quite apart from such solemn public confessions, it is clear that anyone involved in the operation of the deterrent, however humble his job, must be similarly ready to contribute toward mass-annihilation: bomber and missile crews could not fulfil their functions without a constant, split-minute readiness to perform unhesitatingly whatever acts of genocide may be commanded.[1] Such a readiness—as insistent as it is dreadful—to be instantly available for automatic genocidal responses, presupposes a long-matured resolve to acts of mass-annihilation "if the circumstances demanded it." Can such Eichmann-like commitments—imposed by governments and peoples upon thousands of their servants—be meaningfully reduced to the language of bluff?

ii. One must take much more seriously *the argument from military targets,* if only because it is so often taken seriously. . . . There are several important expositions of this argument. Here I shall rely on an article by Fr. Paul Crane, S.J., from *The Month,* October 1959.[2] The article submits that we cannot assume

that the use of nuclear weapons by a just defendant is necessarily to be identified with the direct massacre of the innocent through the indiscriminate hydrogen bombing of an unjust aggressor's cities and towns. It need not be, for there are now in existence controlled nuclear devices which can be restricted to military targets. At the same time, one can conceive of military targets on which a certain type of nuclear bomb could be used whilst remaining discriminate in its effects: such, for example, could be a fleet at sea. One concludes . . . that nuclear war is not necessarily indiscriminate war and that, in consequence, the use of nuclear weapons by a just defendant is not necessarily immoral.

. . .

[1] Cf. N. M. L. Wharton, *The Tablet,* 18 November 1961, and the subsequent correspondence.
[2] Cf. Dr. L. L. McReavy's formulation in *The Tablet,* 29 March 1958 and the *Clergy Review,* February 1960. Cf. also "Falconer's" articles, "Should We Disarm?" in *The Catholic Times,* 17 February–10 March 1961.

In a sense this argument is absolutely invulnerable. It is proof against objection, in the same sense in which it would be unobjectionable to assert
that the mass-production of pornographic photographs need not necessarily
be identified with the direct debauchery of the public, since one can conceive of persons who would find a certain type of pornography of indubi-
table professional value: such, for example, could be a moral theologian.
One certainly might thus conclude that pornography is not necessarily pornographic and that, in consequence, the mass-reproduction of dirty pictures
by a patriotic company is not necessarily immoral.

Such arguments are unanswerable. All one can do, perhaps, is to mention
a few relevant considerations. One might, for instance, indicate that whilst
"controlled nuclear devices" are no doubt very ingenious inventions, it is
difficult to restrict governments to controlled nuclear devices. This, one
might add, would seem all the more important where governments have in
fact categorically proclaimed "to any potential aggressor the prospect of virtual annihilation of his own country." Then there is that "fleet at sea" (it
is remarkable how this fleet keeps turning up in this connection): one has
to admit, "a certain type of nuclear bomb" *could* be used against it—and
used with impressive efficiency—whilst remaining discriminate in its effects;
though this still leaves the question how many of these fleets, or armies concentrating in deserts, perhaps, are likely to be about. What we do, on the
other hand, know with some directness is that many hundreds or thousands
of "a certain type of bomb," and many thousands or ten-thousands of bombs
of other types (not necessarily negligible) are accumulating in various parts
of the globe. We do know that, already in April 1957, Admiral Burke, United
States Chief of Naval Operations, felt confident that "enough nuclear weapons for 'complete destruction' of the Soviet Union" were available in the
United States.[8] And we do know that American civil defense specialists have
found it convenient to give a new word—a unit—to our language: "mega-
corpse": one million dead bodies.

.   .   .

iii. The last of these three arguments, *the argument from the enforcement
of peace,* is sometimes associated with one or the other, or both, of the preceding arguments, sometimes it is offered by itself. It is the most popular of
all these arguments, being also the standard *secular* apologia for "deterrence."
. . . Rightly or wrongly, the maintenance of "the deterrent" is thus held to
be not only necessary for Western defense but necessary for present peace
—as also for the establishment of international arrangements that would secure the peace of the future.

In its own terms, this is a strong argument. . . . But even if, for discussion's sake, we assume that, on balance, the deterrent may support peace,
this would not necessarily justify it. It would justify it *if, and only if, in*

---

[8] Philip Noel-Baker, *The Arms Race*, p. 174; Stevens (London), 1958.

employing this threat, we were not already involved in immoral risks—and in immoral hypothetical decisions. The two preceding arguments purport precisely to meet this condition; they are meant to demonstrate that no evil *need* attach to the threat of nuclear war. If this could indeed be shown, then the goods of security and peace might undoubtedly justify the maintenance of the deterrent—and indeed might oblige us to maintain it. As we have seen, the arguments fail to support their claims. And nothing, not even the alleged interests of peace itself, can save murderousness from evil.

2] Military Strategy, Power, and Policy

The Foreign Policy Research Institute of the University of Pennsylvania, headed by Robert Strausz-Hupé, is among the foremost advocates of what is often called "hard line" diplomacy. Working from the assumption that the Soviet Union poses an implacable threat to the freedom of the West, the Institute urges in this selection (from *A Forward Strategy for America*) that the United States be prepared to support its interests and values, wherever challenged, by a forthright and unambiguous application of military power. Wielded with courage and discrimination, the Institute argues, armed force can be the best deterrent to the outbreak of major war; thus "the sooner we accept the fact that atomic munitions are here to stay and will in due course become a normal element of military force just as gunpowder did in its day, the safer the world will be." *

Wars, including general nuclear war, are fought to achieve objectives that lie beyond war. We must presume that the strategic dialogue between the U.S. and the U.S.S.R. is governed by rationality. If it were not, strategy would be a child's tale told by an idiot. Hence we have little choice but to preface our strategic planning with an act of faith. The U.S. and the U.S.S.R. leaders will seek to preserve the value of their respective societies and will strive to limit war to conditions under which both sides can not only survive, but also attain those objectives that lie beyond war. There is, however, an area of doubt: Do the United States and the Soviet Union place the same value on human life? We do not know the degree of damage which the Soviets might accept in order to bring about a conclusive settlement consonant with their objectives. We do know, however, that their current military literature stresses the importance of preparations for a long war and for fighting a nuclear war to a victorious conclusion.

The nature of a nation's commitment to human values will largely determine its selection of a strategy, the composition of its forces for defense and attack, and the way in which it uses its military power. American strategy does and must assign primacy to the contingency of thermonuclear exchange in a general war, the most frightful aspect of a future conflict. Yet war has many faces. To shy away from one is to withdraw into the illusion that war comes in pieces. War is an organic whole. If we must fight a war, its course will be governed by the contingency of thermonuclear exchange, no matter whether nuclear weapons will be used or not. If we do not go to war, nuclear power-in-being will weigh heavily in the scales of peace.

Hence, the capability for waging general nuclear war is the keystone of American defense. To base our strategy on the idea that nuclear war is "unthinkable" is to make such a war more likely. If, however, we cleave to the idea that nuclear war is possible, it will probably never occur. This is the paradoxical "logic of the feedback." To make timely provision for the most distasteful contingency in order to avoid it—this is the basic law of survival in the nuclear age.

.   .   .

The U.S. is caught inescapably in an "arms race" with the Soviet Union, whether it wishes to recognize this deadly competition or not. Contrary to general belief, such a race need not work against world stability and peace. It could serve as the most effective means to bring the communist rulers to reasonable terms. *For the Free World can far better afford such a competition than the communist bloc.* The economic resources of the Free World are so much greater than those of the communist bloc that, combined with a masterful exploitation of technology, a strategy based on overwhelming military means is well within our reach.

.   .   .

It is fallacious to assume that any power equation remains constant. The pace of change—military, economic, technological, political and psychological—makes it impossible to assume an absolute power advantage at any given time on the part of either the communist bloc or the Free World. To the simple question, "Who is militarily the stronger, we or the Soviets?" no categoric answer can be given. Missiles, nuclear weapons, submarines and army divisions are typical of some of the tangibles that enter into such a consideration. While measuring the known elements of the power balance as rationally and intelligently as we can, we must bear in mind that the nuclear age has introduced a unique uncertainty into the calculus of relative power. It is necessary to assess the strategic look with an open and fairly flexible mind because the unforeseen is almost certain to occur. The art of strategy is to deal with the unknown as well as the known. *The real measure of power advantage in the nuclear age is the degree to which physical power is adequate to sustain the confidence that one will prevail if war should come.* If this degree of power is provided, and this is not easy, then supremacy in the protracted conflict will be determined as much by the purposefulness and the quality of strategic thought as by military "hardware."

.   .   .

Novel as are the problems of the nuclear age, the moral equation of national security remains the same as it has been throughout history. Washington in his fifth annual address to the Congress of the United States in Philadelphia, December 3, 1793, said:

There is a rank due to the United States among nations, which will be withheld, if not absolutely lost, by the reputation of weakness. If we desire to avoid insult, we must be able to repel it; if we desire to secure peace, one of the most powerful instruments of our rising prosperity, it must be known that we are at all times ready for war.

PRINCIPLES OF FORWARD STRATEGY

The principles of a Forward Strategy for the United States must be derived from the following propositions:

1. The priority objective of any American grand strategy is, by a broad margin, the preservation and enhancement of our political system rather than the maintenance of peace. The attainment of this objective may or may not be predicated on the establishment of compatible systems all over the world, but it certainly is predicated on the maintenance or establishment of compatible free systems in some key parts of the world. All other objectives, such as increased social welfare and continuing economic progress, while interrelated with the primary objective, are of secondary importance. Historically, democracies have proved to be short-lived. In the light of the unprecedented dangers which now beset human freedom, it behooves us to think through the weaknesses of the democratic system and to overcome them. Perhaps the root weakness of democracy is reluctance to gauge the full measure of the perennial and ever-recurring threat to its very existence—the very precariousness of freedom. It is because of this deficiency of will that democracies cavil at taking the steps in time that will insure their defense in the moment of supreme peril. The very existence of so aggressive and dynamic a force as communism imperils the survival of democracy everywhere. Woodrow Wilson's celebrated dictum carries today a meaning far deeper than his generation could read into it: To make the world safe for democracy is to make it safe for the continuing growth of the individual and freedom. The American system, in particular, can survive and grow only in a world that is safe for the pursuits of peace. It is upon this premise that American strategy must rest.

2. Our philosophy of international relations must be based on the self-evident axiom that utopias are, by definition, unattainable. Societies will not conform to our vision of perfection, certainly not on a global basis, and most assuredly not in the near future. For we live in permanent crisis. . . . The argument that the permanent threat to our existence can be fought by limiting our initiatives to programs for better education, higher living standards and improved international co-operation for world economic develop-

ment is not only fallacious but also dangerously deceptive. It detracts attention from the hard solutions which our continuing survival demands.

3. Alliances are an integral part of our security system. But alliances will not lighten our burden. Unless our intrinsic strength improves, defection will inevitably thin the ranks of our allies. Our own strength is the most convincing pledge of our loyalty to friends and allies. Our military programs are the hard core of our alliance systems and Free World security. We do not hold with the comfortable assumption that economic assistance to the underdeveloped countries can be a satisfactory alternative to military and alliance programs. The idea that help to the underdeveloped countries will by itself insure Free World stability and security is a flagrant form of Fabianism applied on an international scale. Unless incorporated in a stronger security system, a policy hitched primarily to the idea of world economic growth will drain our own resources and, in the bargain, might strengthen the hands of those factions in the underdeveloped countries who look upon us with cupidity, if not with hatred. . . .

4. If strategy were just a matter of systematic procedures and orderly schemes for mastering predictable events, no campaign mounted by a resource-rich contender would ever have been lost. In the main, strategy, rather than being predetermined, is a more or less crude attempt at keeping one jump ahead of the contingent: *"On s'engage et puis on voit."* ("You join the issue and then you see.") Long-range plans provide the necessary frame for purposeful action. But in addition to devising long-range programs and concepts, strategy threads together numerous ad hoc responses to concrete situations. . . . Strategy is inseparable from the willingness to take risks and deny the enemy a guarantee of immunity in case he desists from a particular aggression. If it is our purpose to combat communism, then it follows that our overriding objective is not to preserve peace at all costs, but to destroy the aggressive power of communism. In approaching specific problems we should ask: Does the decision hurt the enemy or put him under pressure or at least compound his decision-making problems? Does it hasten his demise, or help to replenish his capabilities for waging international conflict? Firmness—hardness—of decision should not be mistaken for continuously rattling the saber. A sense of measure and moderation is the leaven of all constructive undertakings. But without the willingness to use force and without the sacrifice which the use of force as well as the prevention of war entails, no major international crisis ever has been settled short of appeasement or surrender.

5. We cannot concur with the interpretation of democracy as a system which is too flaccid to allow for the making of firm decisions. Vigorous public debate and high national morale, the spirit of sacrifice and the strength of motivations are all elements of our political system. Our political system is basically sound, but it must be stripped for action and, in part, reorganized so it is equal to its dangerous tasks in a dangerous environment. It would be foolish to pretend that, in a crisis in which societies are pitted

against societies, the collective will is not a decisive element. Our collective will is weak, partly because our grasp on the meaning of the challenge has been weak—and because we persist in emphasizing the products of our system to the detriment of the system itself. Well-being flows from freedom and order. But by fastening our attention on the good things of life we cannot preserve the political conditions under which we have prospered.

6. The fundamental decision before us is whether we should accept the communist concept of coexistence in one form or the other or bring about the final defeat of communism. If we choose the latter course, we must decide whether we should bank on the defeat of communism by such fortuitous circumstances as internal erosion or revolution or whether we should extend ourselves to achieve this objective. We must decide whether a passive, expectant strategy might actually delay the demise of communism while hastening our own. And, lastly, we should decide why we really want to defeat communism. Is it because we wish to replace one "economic order" with another? Or do we seek to disestablish a particular political system, raze the intellectual prison camp of communism and help the peoples within the communist bloc to obtain self-government? Or do we stake our policies on the belief that communism, despite its present hostility, might be a more tractable opponent than a possible successor system—assuming that we live long enough to see that successor?

Shorn of all ideological connotations, our policy must be based upon the premise that we cannot tolerate the survival of a political system which has both the growing capability and the ruthless will to destroy us. We have no choice but to adopt a Catonic strategy. Cato the Censor was not the most lovable of men.[4] No man who, in and out of season, chooses to propound a discomforting truth can gain popularity. If we are to triumph in the protracted conflict, we have to face what it means to have implacable enemies who, in turn, deem us to be *their* implacable enemies. We have to cultivate those dour virtues which alone sustain a people in mortal combat. To equate democracy with vapidity of spirit and the indulgence of the flesh is an unforgivable insult to democracy. Freedom is not a marginal luxury. Of all forms of government, democracy should be the one best fitted to inspire men with the sense of what they owe to one another and to themselves. But, if the communists prove to have more courage, a stronger will, a more steadfast spirit, a clearer intellectual insight into conflict in the nuclear age, they obviously are the better men and deserve to win—and probably will.

---

[4] Cato the Elder (234–149 B.C.) was the Roman senator who became famous for his insistence that Rome's security depended upon the complete destruction of its great rival Carthage. *Editor.*

3] A Choice of Evils

H. Stuart Hughes, a Harvard University historian, has been in recent years one of the most outspoken critics of American military and foreign policy. The position he takes here, in a selection from *An Approach to Peace*, has come to be called "nuclear pacifism." Urging that the United States rely for its protection upon conventional means of defense, Hughes appeals for a unilateral renunciation of nuclear weapons.*

The trouble with the phrase "unilateral disarmament" is that it suggests an all-or-nothing stance. It seems to convey the impression that we are going to strip right down to our underwear shorts without enticing hesitations along the way. Scarcely any unilateralist would advocate this; such a position is rather that of the doctrinaire pacifists, with whom people like myself work in harmony on specific issues but with whom they differ on the wider question of the role of force in human affairs. Unilateralism as I conceive it necessarily proceeds by stages—with pauses to give our potential adversaries the opportunity to respond in kind. Actually, the first moves might entail little risk at all.[5] The main point is that *something* must be done right away to prove that we are in earnest about disarmament.

Yet the logic of the unilateralist position lies ultimately in the complete renunciation of nuclear weapons. Nor will it do to hold on to these weapons while saying we will not use them—as President Eisenhower in effect did in the last five years of his presidency, following the Geneva summit meeting of 1955. This is too ambiguous; I quite agree with one of the most penetrating critics of "nuclear pacifism" that "the proposal to withdraw from the arms race while retaining the weapons already possessed, to accept relative weakness while nevertheless remaining dangerous, manages to embrace the worst of all possible worlds."[6] In short, I believe that we and our allies should eventually restrict our defense to conventional weapons alone.

I well know the awful risks that such a decision would involve. Every conscientious unilateralist has spent countless hours of worry over the implications of what he recommends: he can never be sure that he is right. We face a choice of evils—a choice of risks. All we can say is that to us the risks involved in depriving our country of nuclear weapons loom less threateningly than the dangers of going on with the arms race; we agree with Sir Charles Snow that if matters continue on their present course, there is al-

[5] The case for unilateral initiatives has been persuasively argued by Charles E. Osgood in "Suggestions for Winning the Real War with Communism," *Conflict Resolution,* III (December, 1959), 295–325.

[6] Robert W. Tucker, "Nuclear Pacifism: Some Reflections on the Community of Fear," *The New Republic,* CXLIV (February 6, 1961), 24.

* From *An Approach to Peace* by H. Stuart Hughes. Copyright © 1962 by H. Stuart Hughes. Reprinted by permission of Atheneum Publishers.

most a mathematical certainty that some of the bombs or missiles will sooner or later go off. In this world of ghastly insecurity, we would rather take our chances on nuclear defenselessness and trust to the more primitive devices by which free men in earlier ages have safeguarded their liberty. That is what next needs to be explained.

At this point of the argument people who think as I do are usually confronted with the now classic question, "Would you rather be red than dead?" I object strongly to such a formulation: it is one chosen by our adversaries to put us in the worst possible light; it eliminates all intermediate possibilities and shades of meaning. Yet I do not agree with certain of my friends that it is a question we should not answer: I believe in answering all questions, no matter how unfair and "loaded"; any other course may be interpreted as evasion or cowardice. If our adversaries want to phrase the issue that way, I see no alternative to accepting the challenge: the only possible answer is a thunderous "Yes." Certainly I would rather be red than dead— in the sense that I choose life over senseless slaughter. But should there be a chance of a meaningful death, then I might make the other choice. This is why I do not think an affirmative answer to this crude and primitive question is the same thing as "surrender."

.   .   .

When Patrick Henry said, "Give me liberty or give me death," he meant it quite literally. He meant that by sacrificing his life he might help set his people free; he could not have imagined a situation in which he (and tens of millions of others) would give up their lives, and liberty would still not be the result. Moreover, he meant that he and a few thousands of like-minded citizens were making a personal choice: the rest could stay on the sidelines if they so desired—as, in fact, during the Revolution, most Americans did. Patrick Henry and his friends were committing only themselves and those who felt as they did; they were not consigning to destruction, mutilation, or genetic degeneration uncounted millions among the neutrals, the unborn, and the animal world. They were not a small minority deciding the fate of vast assemblages of living beings who could never be consulted and could do no more than passively await their end. The proponents of the American Revolution were free men in a double sense—they were free to choose a freedom that was a real alternative.

Today none of this exists. Today a handful of men are indeed free to choose, in that they hold the power of decision over whether or not to push the fatal button. But they have only a vague idea of what will be the consequences of their act—even though they must be aware that these will extend far, far beyond anything they can possibly intend or imagine. War in this new sense has grown beyond the proportions of humanity. The problem for those of us who do not renounce force entirely is to return it to a human scale.

Does this mean "surrender"? Does it mean "to invite the conquest of the world" or to offer ourselves "on a platter" to our putative enemies? (I am quoting some of the phrases that have been thrown at me in debate.) I do not think so. I do not believe that a unilateral American renunciation of thermonuclear deterrence would make nearly so much of a difference as most of my countrymen suppose. It has yet to be proved that our "deterrent" has deterred anybody from anything. I do not think it has been the threat of thermonuclear retaliation that has kept the Soviet Union out of Western Europe. What has given the Russians second thoughts about occupying West Germany or France has been the conviction that they would find themselves most unwelcome there.

The point, then, is to make military occupation too expensive a matter —both physically and morally—to be worthwhile for the attacker. The prime need is to develop a pattern of defense by conventional weapons alone that would be "credible" (to use another arms control phrase) both to ourselves and to our potential enemies. George Kennan has delineated in imaginative fashion the character of such a defense. Although he has written simply of the Western European Continent, I think his principle can be extended to the West as a whole, including our own country. If the Continental nations were left to their own devices, he surmises, the problem of their defense

would be primarily one of the internal health and discipline of the respective national societies, and of the manner in which they were organized to prevent the conquest and subjugation of their national life by unscrupulous and foreign-inspired minorities in their midst. What they need is a strategic doctrine addressed to this reality. Under such a doctrine, armed forces would indeed be needed; but I would suggest that as a general rule these forces might better be paramilitary ones, of a territorial-militia type, somewhat on the Swiss example, rather than regular military units on the World War II pattern. . . . The training of such forces ought to be such as to prepare them not only to offer whatever overt resistance might be possible to a foreign invader but also to constitute the core of a civil resistance movement on any territory that might be overrun by the enemy; and every forethought should be exercised to facilitate their assumption and execution of this role in the case of necessity.[7]

It would be an understatement to say that such a proposal represents a radical departure from current American military thinking. (Moreover, I should not want to make Ambassador Kennan responsible for an enormous extension of a suggestion he advanced rather tentatively more than four years ago in quite a different context; he may well disagree completely with what I am now putting forward.) My proposal would involve a drastic reduction of our country's present overseas commitments. It would mean the liquidation of a number of our alliances. For it implies that we would come to the defense of *those nations alone which had sufficient social and political solidity* to organize and support a territorial-militia or guerrilla-resistance type of defense—that is, those nations which, without necessarily conforming to *our*

---

[7] *Russia, the Atom, and the West* (New York: Harper & Brothers, 1958), p. 63.

definition of democracy, were based on a bond of trust between government and people strong enough to hold out against trials and temptations of unprecedented magnitude.   .   .   .

If this "modest proposal" has far-reaching implications for our present alliance system, it has still wider consequences for our society at home. I am under no illusions as to the radical—indeed, utopian—character of my suggestions. They involve a wholesale rethinking of nearly all the assumptions, stated or tacit, of our current policy. In terms of the "sacrifices" that our leaders so often and so hollowly call on us to make, what I am proposing demands far more individual dedication than a mere raising of taxes or contraction of consumer goods—for it implies that every able-bodied American will have to equip himself to serve as a citizen-soldier in the old-fashioned sense of the term. It means something much more strenuous than the rather perfunctory part-time military training that only a small minority of young Americans are currently receiving. It entails a tangible and personal commitment to an ideal—not just passive assent to an abstract call to greatness. It means that every American will be obliged to consider war as something close at hand, rather than as an indistinct menace whose very magnitude and remoteness make for escapism or fatalistic acceptance or moral callousness; he will need to decide when and how and for what concrete and visible loyalties he is willing to lay down his life.

That is what I mean by returning war to a human scale. The militia or guerrilla type of defense I am proposing would close the gap between rhetoric and actuality in our national behavior. It would constitute a policy that both our allies and our potential enemies could understand and act on. It would tap the resourcefulness and the talent for improvised local action that have been so marked a feature of our national tradition—and that have survived, if only in scattered communities, the enormous changes in our society over the past generation. It would restore the honored practice of resistance to oppression on the part of voluntary collectivities and spontaneous self-sustaining groups. This tradition in earlier centuries ranked as the chief support of Western liberty; the Second World War revived it in militant form on the European Continent; today in our own South young Negroes have learned what a potent weapon it is in the hands of men and women who have a clear vision toward which they are struggling.[8]

If the colonial wars of liberation over the past decade and a half have taught us nothing else, they have at least demonstrated that in the contemporary world a superiority in arms does not necessarily mean final victory. First in Indochina, then in Algeria, small bodies of men, poorly armed but familiar with the countryside and supported by the local population, have tied up for years the regular army of a major power. The native people have known what they were fighting for; the Europeans have been disoriented, far from home, and uncertain of their cause. The relevance of this example

[8] See Michael Walzer, "The Idea of Resistance," *Dissent*, VII (Autumn, 1960), 369–73.

for a Western democracy facing Communist "conquest" should be apparent to all. It is a lesson that we Americans need to ponder.

. . .

The proposal I have made for the non-nuclear defense of our own country and our allies will, I hope, never have to be applied. I think of it as a final deterrent to aggression—a real deterrent, as opposed to the abstract deterrent of our hydrogen bombs, which is too gruesome to be fully credible.

4] An Ethic of Responsibility

The school of thought that has come to be called "political realism" rejects the Utopian quest for a politics that is morally pure. The relations of sovereign states, the realists contend, cannot be judged by the same ethical standards that govern the lives of individual men. Thus a responsible approach to foreign policy will recognize the relevance of military force to the protection of the national interest, without at the same time forsaking the search for a *modus vivendi*. Kenneth Thompson, a leading political realist, argues here, in a selection from "Ethical Aspects of the Nuclear Dilemma," for a balanced use of force and negotiation based on minimal deterrence and, where necessary, limited conventional or nuclear warfare.*

The problem of nuclear weapons is part and parcel of the international political power struggle today. The issues are incredibly complex; not even the wisest scientist or statesman can encompass them all. The citizen may be tempted to seek out a path of least resistance. He may denounce the whole terrifying process of building up deterrent force and call on his country unilaterally to renounce its defenses. Or alternatively, he may shut out from view events that are distasteful to moral consciousness and "leave the whole unhappy realm" to cynics, militarists and power politicians.

The historic conception of political ethics in western thought, at least in its more profound expressions, repudiates both these approaches. It must reject the nuclear pacifism that would leave America defenseless against Soviet tyranny for the same reason it rejected traditional pacifism as normative. It must also reject no less a posture of withdrawal from all the vital problems of politics, for this is a false alternative. A viable ethic must deal realistically with the problems of power and all the perennial issues they raise.

. . .

The United States has endeavored since World War II to build up western power so that the Soviet Union might not be tempted, as were the Nazis, to expand its empire through threats and aggression. In applying this prin-

* "Ethical Aspects of the Nuclear Dilemma" by Kenneth W. Thompson is reprinted with the permission of Charles Scribner's Sons from *Nuclear Weapons and the Conflict of Conscience*, edited by John C. Bennett. Copyright © 1962 Charles Scribner's Sons.

ciple which is theoretically sound, the West has confronted practical problems arising from the uniqueness of the present armaments problem. Military strength today requires both conventional and nuclear capacities but both economic considerations and the moral factor set restraints on arms programs.

Moral restraints may work to influence the course of an armaments race in two respects. They may generate the motive force for attempts at general disarmament or may prompt discriminate judgments on the limitation or channeling of armaments buildups. The literature of peace movements in the United States and Britain has concentrated primarily on the overall reduction and elimination of armaments. Such an approach is particularly congenial to the sensitive moral conscience. By and large, most proponents of general disarmament have favored a test ban with firm safeguards if possible but without if necessary. This school of thought has unquestionably induced western leaders to bend every effort to achieve disarmament. It has given a sense of urgency to disarmament programs and focussed the spotlight of public attention on the threat.

Yet the moral dignity of an alternative approach deserves mention. The ideas of restraint, proportionality and limitation have an important place in moral theory. Restraint in these terms might mean that nuclear weapons not be multiplied beyond the point where they serve a security function. The principle of proportionality assumes that the means employed are proportionate to the goal undertaken. For example, the United States seeks to deter the Soviet Union through its nuclear armaments program, but not to assure total military victory. This in itself sets limits to any armaments program, but moral considerations reinforce the limitation. A nation which says its objective is national and international security is obligated to pursue armaments programs that faithfully reflect this purpose. It can hardly engage in an unlimited buildup of weapons if these carry no clear implication for security purposes.

Restraint and proportionality may commend a renewed stress on conventional armaments as distinct from accelerating nuclear weapons programs. They may mean that hardening existing missile sites is more acceptable than adding to the missile stockpile. The development of mobile striking power may be politically more imperative and morally more defensible than unrestrained nuclear buildup. These various strategies may be both morally and politically preferable; earlier political theorists stressed the marriage of the ethical and the political in the virtue of prudence. Sometimes in politics restraint and prudence are the highest obtainable moral position. Political wisdom involves a weighing of moral and political considerations and a sound judgment, in Lincoln's phrase, "to do the best you can." It requires an estimate made in light of all the facts of what nations can do under existing circumstances.

Particularly the West, confronting a numerically superior rival, has been forced to turn its major efforts to the development of nuclear weapons. In so doing, its leaders face [two] crucial questions that weigh heavily on the minds of the citizenry: . . . What are the prospects of a limited atomic war and its effects on the human race? and . . . What are the chances of survival in all-out nuclear conflict? If national security is based on some degree of nuclear capacity, responsible leaders must seek answers to these questions.

. . .

Proponents of a limited nuclear war strategy argue . . . that their policies need not result in unusually heavy casualties in human lives. In both conventional and all-out nuclear war, cities and industrial centers become appropriate military targets. In limited war, however, armies with high mobility and self-sufficiency replace cities as prime targets. Missiles and vertical take-off aircraft can be widely dispersed and concealed so that the elimination of a few important airfields is no longer essential. Opposing military forces are more important than communication systems or industrial centers, for each unit to the extent it is self-contained is the depository of its own crucial weapons.

This trend of thought foresees built-in restrictions to widespread destruction. It envisages sanctuaries, including cities and strategic nuclear forces (e.g., SAC), that will be relatively immune to nuclear strikes by the enemy. It questions whether limited nuclear war would be as destructive as conventional warfare given this prospect of self-limitation. Finally it urges that military experts not be defeatist about limited nuclear war at a time when the entire planning and development of our military establishment is built around nuclear weapons. The West, because of its superior industrial potential and broader, more diversified technology stands to gain more than the antagonist from the development of limited nuclear capacities, provided it devotes itself to this task with real dedication. Our very qualities of personal initiative and mechanical aptitude favor the West if we are prepared to sacrifice personal comfort in the interest of public safety.

On the other hand, an equally responsible body of opinion has grave and serious doubts that a limited nuclear strategy is possible. It asks whether the terms themselves are not mutually contradictory. It points to the fact that modern war, whatever the state of technology, has not been limited in the past. Witness the bombing of civilian centers and merchant ships in World War II. It argues that tactical nuclear weapons are now available that exceed in destructiveness the bombs used at Hiroshima and Nagasaki. The use of limited nuclear weapons will set off a tragic cycle of increasing military commitments that will eventuate in all-out nuclear warfare. A conventional war has a clearly defined cut-off point but a war fought with low-yield nuclear weapons would tempt the losing side to redress the balance by introducing weapons of greater and greater power.

For the region that comprised the battlefield, a limited nuclear conflict would cause destruction that approximated an all-out thermonuclear war. Europe would scarcely applaud limited as against total war, for it could be laid waste by tactical no less than strategic nuclear weapons however preferable this might be for the peoples within Soviet or American territory. If the aim of American policy is to preserve the people and civilization of Western Europe, limited nuclear warfare is not the way to do it. Nor can our allies be expected to see such a policy as in their self-interest.

. . .

The issue between the proponents and the foes of a limited nuclear strategy can be resolved only if we clarify the purpose such capacities are intended to serve. There is at least reasonable doubt that such a strategy provides a short-cut to less painful military victory. However, agreement may be possible on another level. Specifically, NATO's capacity for limited nuclear warfare may be the sword to deter the Russians from using their nuclear weapons in a limited attack. Without such a deterrent, NATO countries might be more vulnerable to Soviet aggression. The Russians weighing the costs of introducing tactical nuclear weapons in a limited European war in which we lacked such capacity might conclude that the risks were negligible. They might determine that they could quickly overrun European land armies. Similarly if our sole deterrent rested in strategic all-out retaliation, they could conclude they would escape retaliation in kind. It is in these terms that a limited nuclear establishment probably has a rational basis as a deterrent even though it cannot be defended as the means of an easy victory in war.

Confronted with the specter of all-out war, President Dwight D. Eisenhower late in his second term summed up the dilemma in the phrase "there is no alternative to peace." The bombs dropped over Hiroshima and Nagasaki had an explosive equivalent of 20,000 tons TNT (20 kilotons). Thermonuclear devices are now available with an explosive equivalent of more than 50,000,000 tons TNT (50 megatons) and there is apparently no upper limit. A 20 megaton weapon possesses a lethal radius of 8 miles and its area of total destruction is 48 square miles. Within such an area, 75 per cent of the population would be killed and the remainder critically injured. The radioactive effects of such a device would spread over an area larger than the state of New Jersey. If the enemy launched a successful attack on fifty of our metropolitan centers, at least 40 per cent of the population, 50 per cent of key facilities and 60 per cent of industry would be critically damaged.

In the face of these appalling figures, many are tempted to throw up their hands in despair. It should be remembered, however, that even if as many as 90 million Americans were killed in the first strike of a pre-emptive attack, this would still leave 90 million people alive. Agencies like the RAND Corporation and the present Administration of the State of New York urge consideration of measures that might increase the number of survivors to 120 or 150 million people. Some evidence exists that non-military programs of civil defense could appreciably increase our capacity to survive an initial nuclear attack and restore the national economy and democratic institutions. Non-military defense measures would of course depend on the effectiveness of both strategic-offense and active-defense capabilities. The latter would involve the "hardening" and dispersal of U.S. nuclear resources. It would require the strengthening of polaris and intercontinental guided missile capabilities and the development of more effective anti-missile devices. Any responsible U.S. government must weigh and evaluate the costs and possible effectiveness of its strategic offensive, air defense and local-war forces.

.   .   .

In other fields, prior planning and organized efforts would serve at least to ease the catastrophe. Agricultural products in storage as a result of price-support operations would be sufficient to supply a diet of 2000 calories per day to 180 million people for more than a year. These stocks are sufficiently dispersed to make them largely invulnerable to a city attack and after appropriate milling any grain including crops close to harvesting could be made suitable as an emergency ration. The cost of 3 months' shelter rations for 180 million people would be $6–$7 billion plus storage and deterioration costs. Adjustment of crop patterns and land use after a 50-city attack should permit a safe recuperation of agricultural production.

Most observers assume that industry would be more vulnerable than agriculture at least under existing patterns of industrial concentration. The fifty largest American cities contain only one-third the total population but more than one-half of manufacturing capital. What could be produced outside the 50 destroyed cities in the first year after reorganization? One study suggests that surviving capital could permit a Gross National Product of 50–60 per cent of the pre-attack GNP. On a per capita basis, if 85 per cent of the population survived, this would mean a level comparable to that of 1929 or 1940. A further estimate suggests that the pre-attack GNP could be achieved in a decade. Industrial recovery would of course depend on such things as stockpiling in peace of construction materials for patching up partially damaged capital, sheltering normal inventories of metals, building materials and machinery, and sheltering complete plants or standby components of plants in the durable goods sector.

We have no intention of minimizing the disaster of a thermonuclear war nor of disparaging the importance of continuous efforts at arms control by suggesting that perhaps there exist more promising means of alleviating the tragedy than has been generally recognized. Nevertheless the areas we have mentioned are but a few of the important spheres within which responsible authorities advise that prospects of survival could be brighter than sometimes assumed. Reasonable men differ on many of these issues and a broad research, development and planning program would be necessary before more general and authoritative estimates could be made. In addition, experts in the government and the RAND Corporation tell us the means are at hand to limit the long-term biological damage to the population from total radiation and of enforcing counter-measures to contain the strontium 90 problem even after very large attacks. If we assume disaster could never strike or fatalistically rule out well-laid responses to catastrophe, the alleviation of the tragedy will be impossible.[9]

.   .   .

Many of us in the past, in lecturing American policy-makers on concessions that the United States should make, have failed to grasp the nature of the Soviet threat. When the Soviet Union sees that its relative power position can be strengthened through steps such as the resumption of tests, it will act irrespective of the judgment of world public opinion. An ethic of protest that admonishes western leaders alone without recognizing this fact, is in the end an ethic of irresponsibility. An ethic of responsibility by contrast must accept the fact that the contest with Soviet Russia will not end through a single dramatic act. It seems destined to continue throughout the present generation with the ebb and flow of successive intensifications and reductions of tensions. The struggle can perhaps be limited and contained, the means of violence restricted or reduced, the scale and temper of conflict checked and circumscribed, and deterrents be made more credible. We are doomed not to extinction but to living with dangers more terrifying than man has ever known, at least for the forseeable future. I am persuaded that the moralist must help prepare men to live under these circumstances, not merely beckon him to a happier if imaginary land. We need moral resources not alone to be firm or flexible but to be both in dealings with Soviet leaders. There will be times as in the autumn of 1961, when firmness must precede flexibility if the adversary is to resume serious negotiations. But there may also be moments in history when from a position of strength, the West must be ready to initiate new and more flexible proposals for peace. To sense these moments and seize them at their tide is the ultimate challenge of statesmanship. No one calling from the sidelines can solve the problem of timing: when to act and when to wait, when to be firm and when to be flexible, or when to resist and when to negotiate. Yet success or failure in this endlessly complicated and uncertain process, far more than exhortations or blueprints of utopia will bring peace or war to the tormented human race.

5] The Moral Equivalent of War

Mulford Sibley, a University of Minnesota political scientist, is an outstanding American pacifist. In this selection from *The Quiet Battle* he argues for the use of nonviolent resistance as a new source of power with which to support foreign policy. Working within the tradition of Gandhi, Sibley contends that pacifism need not require surrender or martyrdom, but can become the basis for strategies capable of defending justice.*

[9] The best recent discussion of the effects of thermonuclear weapons and the problems of civil defense is Tom Stonier, *Nuclear Disaster*, Meridian Books, 1964. Kenneth Thompson's conclusions here should be carefully compared with those of Stonier. *Editor.*

* From *The Quiet Battle*, edited by Mulford Q. Sibley. Copyright © 1963 by Mulford Q. Sibley. Reprinted by permission of Doubleday & Company, Inc.

Perhaps we can grasp the meaning of non-violence more fully if we first sketch out the general lines of a society based on ideals of non-violence and then turn to the problem of how it can be achieved. In the process, the role and place of non-violent resistance may become clearer.

The ideal of a non-violent society, while never spelled out very fully, would appear to imply one in which social and political organizations are not used to manipulate men for the glory and gain of other men; in which the employment of physical force is always discriminate and never deliberately injurious—or disappears altogether; and in which conflict, assuming its inevitability in the life of man, takes place without resort to violence and increasingly at the level of ideas.

A non-violent society would clearly recognize the necessity for ample social and political freedom for the person. Similarly, it would see associations and groups as entitled to a certain autonomy or right to self-government. "Nations" would be among these groups.

But the war-making, sovereign nation-State of modern times could have no place within a non-violent society. And because so much of our life today turns on the demands of the war-making nation-State, its destruction would constitute a revolution in man's thought and institutional life. One's imaginative powers are inadequate to describe a world without military bureaucracies, conscription, bemedaled generals, twenty-one gun salutes, budgets dominated by the call to mass violence, and the centralization of power engendered in considerable measure by the war-State. At the very least, the nature of the historical "State" would be radically transformed as one of its major functions ceased to be preparation for war.

In a non-violent society, gross disproportions of power and wealth would not exist and, where they threatened, would be corrected by disciplined withdrawal from co-operation of disadvantaged groups. This withdrawal would help restore a kind of balance and would make easier a restatement of the framework within which groups co-operate for the common good. Even were a world "State" to arise, the necessity for non-violent resistance would not be eliminated; for "power" relations of some kind would still exist and with them the possibility of dangerous imbalances in power.

A non-violent society, too, would elaborate the machinery necessary for resolution of intergroup conflict and would facilitate an understanding of conditions that might, if uncorrected, lead to violence. A hallmark of such a social order would be the continuous, positive effort to root out the social and psychological bases of violence through the development of education, mental health services, a non-violent policy system whose work would be primarily preventive, and conditions encouraging a measure of stability in family life. A non-violent ethic would have far-reaching ramifications for the treatment of criminals . . . and equally for the care of the mentally ill. It would not tolerate capital punishment, prisons, or treatment of mental patients that is merely custodial.

In a non-violent society, moreover, a very high proportion of all persons would be acutely conscious of the fact that violence and tyranny arise as much out of the inner attitudes of ordinary men as they do from acts of the ruler. An individual without self-respect is much more likely to become an instrument of a tyrant than one who, for whatever reason, has come to value himself. But tyranny and violence are both the root and the fruit of a lack of self-respect: the very exercise of tyranny and violence against the person threatens to reduce him to a mere thing; while at the same time his tendency to live at the level of the vegetable so much of the time will encourage tyranny and violence.

Respect for human personality would be one of its central characteristics. This would be reflected in a non-authoritarian educational system and in social guarantees of a basic minimum of material well being. There would also be a large measure of political, economic, and administrative decentralization in order that decision-making and implementation might be as close as possible to those who would be expected to conform to the decisions. And insofar as possible, an effort would be made to arrive at decisions by consensus.

.   .   .

The advocate of non-violent resistance as means will, of course, fully admit that many non-violent patterns are already established in modern society, far removed as it may still be from an ideally non-violent community. Thus wherever channels of discussion remain open; parliamentary bodies genuinely deliberate; courts adjudicate under specified rules of law; citizens are consulted about the formation of public policy; the police use physical force, if at all, only in a discriminating and non-injurious way; and problems of social justice occupy a central place in political discussion—wherever conditions of this kind obtain, fundamentals of non-violence, both as means and as ends, already exist. Naturally, the exponent of non-violence will seek to sustain and expand all such patterns. Indeed, characteristics of this kind may be said to be common to both "democracy" and non-violence.

.   .   .

It is difficult to see how anyone with a concern for morality can possibly defend modern war and policies based on its threat. From the viewpoint of the morality of the means—and accepting the fact that there are important distinctions between their economic and political systems—there would seem to be little difference between Communism and Western Democracy in practice: both of them resort to threats of mass annihilation and both seem to be willing to shatter the whole structure of civilized society in the name of some abstraction which neither can define with precision. Each claims it is "defending" itself when it resorts to the most horrible preparations for mass slaughter. How any civilized human being can support either side, in view of these considerations, is difficult to understand. If the world does somehow survive, men in a future generation will look back to our time with both amazement and loathing: amazement that so many millions, East and West, tamely submitted themselves to be slaughtered; loathing at the rank hypocrisy involved in the whole process, with each side proclaiming its devotion to the highest civilized values. Just as we inquire today how millions of Germans could have submitted their fates to the commands of an immoral dictatorship, so will our descendants ask how millions of human beings professing "Christian" moral ideals could with scarcely a murmur build up stock piles of bacteria, H-bombs, and missiles to kill their fellow men and women.

·   ·   ·

What else can we do? It is at this point that the advocate of non-violent power has most to say. For he is asserting, essentially, that the development of an organized movement against both war and invasion, together with widespread commitment to completely unarmed defense, would be most likely to accomplish such widely proclaimed objectives as the frustration of invasion and defense of basic freedoms.

Before turning to the implications of non-violence for war and invasion, it might be well to point out that the fear of invasion is in some measure a groundless one, particularly insofar as it refers to the possibility of the Soviet Union or China occupying the United States or the United States invading the Soviet Union or China. For the Soviet Union to "control" the vast territory of the United States would be a very difficult task, even without military or formally organized non-violent resistance. The center of control would be remote from those to be controlled. Even today the Soviet Union has difficulties with its Eastern European satellites who are relatively close to it and who, moreover, resemble it in many ways. Any attempted invasion of the United States with the purpose of control would magnify these difficulties enormously. As Ambassador Kennan puts it, Americans seem not to recognize how hard it is to operate "far-flung lines of power" or to see that there are definite "limits to the effective radius of political power from any center in the world." [10]

Despite this undoubted fact, however, the advocate of non-violence must deal with the possibility of invasion, since it conceivably could occur. He must, moreover, suggest what a thoroughgoing policy of unilateral disarmament might imply for domestic and international policy in general.

A turn toward non-violence by any major nation would . . . necessitate a fundamental change in outlook, not only with respect to defense, but also in reference to the economic and international orders. Unilateral disarmament, to be effective in any sense, would entail such measures as the deliberate construction of a system of non-violent resistance, with as much energy devoted to it as we devote today, for example, to space exploration; a considerable measure of public economic planning to make far better use of human and material resources than we do today; surrender of nationally ad-

---

[10] See George F. Kennan, *Russia and the West under Lenin and Stalin* (Boston: Little, Brown, 1961). A similar thesis is suggested in his earlier work, *Russia, the Atom, and the West* (New York: Harper & Brothers, 1958).

ministered international services (like the Panama Canal) to international administration; full acceptance of the rule of law in international affairs, including jurisdiction of the International Court of Justice; and commitment of a very substantial proportion of the national income (possibly 10 per cent or more—and in addition to sums now utilized) for an indefinite period to the economic, social, and educational development of the world, not excluding the United States. Within a context of this kind, we could far better defend the freedom of Americans than through the threat of military violence—no matter what the character of the "other side." We could revolutionize the whole pattern of international politics and help transform the power struggle into a non-violent one. This would happen because of internal pressures and because it would find that its own interests could best be preserved by such measures. Non-violent acts on a large scale could be expected to provoke "retaliation" of a non-violent character, just as violent measures call forth violent responses.

.   .   .

We should never forget, of course, that a policy of non-violent resistance to invasion would entail a price. Not only would there have to be rigorous training and discipline beforehand but there would and could be no guarantee of success or of immunity from suffering. At a minimum, the scheme would involve: a table of alternative leadership, so that leaders hanged or imprisoned would automatically be succeeded by their understudies; thousands of hard-core Satyagrahis [11] who would be in the forefront of non-cooperation and civil disobedience campaigns; thorough preparation for psychological resistance, so that the general population would respect the persons of the invaders while refusing, in concert, to cooperate with their acts; and careful planning for food supplies. Unarmed resistance, as a matter of fact, requires at least as much planning as military defense.

Whatever the practical advantages of non-violent opposition . . . the moral superiority of non-violence consists in the fact that while under it we might have to suffer injustice (disruption of ordinary ways of life, physical injury, torture, or even death), we do not commit it (we do not deliberately kill, we confine coercion to that which does not seriously injure, and we constantly seek avenues for negotiation). And in the last analysis the advocate of non-violent resistance believes, with Socrates, that it is always better to suffer injustice than to commit it.

.   .   .

It has often been asserted that there is a severe crisis in modern civilization. The nature of the crisis is variously described. Many profess to see it primarily in the struggle between East and West. Some talk as if it cen-

---

[11] "Satyagrahis" are practitioners of satyagraha, a word coined by Gandhi and meaning, as he defined it, "the Force that is born of Truth and Love." *Editor.*

tered in the conflict between the imperatives of technology and the means of controlling it for desirable ends. Yet others speak of the spontaneous life of society and the natural community as against the planned, bureaucratized, and rationalized political segment.

Without denying a certain validity in each of these diagnoses, it would seem appropriate here to suggest in conclusion that the major crisis may have to do with the question of whether civilization, which produced the ideals of non-violence, can in fact discard the means of violence before those means destroy it. Will the methods of large-scale violence, also the product of civilized ingenuity, tend so completely to dominate—indeed, fascinate—their creators that the ideals of non-violence, enshrined in both religious and secular thought, will be largely forgotten?

It is not certain that civilization will not use its violent instruments to destroy its non-violent achievements and frustrate its aspirations. In the name of protecting the values of non-violent ends, elaborate and sensitive social organization and technology may be employed to defeat those ends through the use of violence as means. If this is not to be the outcome of our contemporary madness, it will be because men discover in time that they can neither attain nor defend the ends of non-violence and democracy by the methods of violent power: any apparent success is more than counterbalanced by the evil ends set up by the means.

Once they make this discovery, human beings will turn to the doctrine of non-violence and to the discipline and practice of non-violent resistance. Without regarding non-violent resistance as the only key to an ideal society, they will see in it, nevertheless, a form of power somewhat compatible with the goals they profess.[12] Their means will have been brought measurably into harmony with their ends; and they will find that in repudiating the immorality of killing they will also have discovered a far more useful method than violence for the attainment of justice.

[12] The ramifications and implications of power, both violent and non-violent, are complex and far-reaching. See, for example, Bertrand Russell, *Power: A New Social Analysis* (New York: Norton, 1939), . . . and Bertrand de Jouvenel, *Power—The Natural History of Its Growth* (London: Hutchinson, 1948) and *Sovereignty: An Inquiry into the Political Good* (University of Chicago Press, 1957).

CONCLUSION

THERE HAS, of course, been no historical conclusion to the moral dilemma of nuclear warfare; the problem remains for our generation to solve. It is no exaggeration to state that upon its solution depends the whole future of human civilization.

But while a historical conclusion of the crisis we are in belongs to the future, none can escape the responsibility for drawing his own ethical conclusions now. For it is in the moral sensitivities of each of us that the fate of man and all his works is taking shape. Whatever dulls our moral awareness, whatever private or social deceptions we allow to cloud our conscience, whatever hatred, passion, ignorance, or bitterness we permit to blind our judgment and reduce our humanity endanger not only our own generation's survival, but the entire heritage of intellect, artistry, and social institutions we call civilization.

A firm grasp of the realities of power as it works in the affairs of nations is, of course, indispensible to the forging of expedient policy. So, too, is the courage to face the demands power and policy make upon us. But never before in man's history has courage needed to be so little an outburst of visceral fervor and so much a manifestation of moral wisdom. And never before have the times so severely required of ordinary men the patience, compassion, and long-suffering of saints.

STUDY QUESTIONS

1] What are the implicit moral assumptions of the five authors presented here? Which author strikes the best balance between ethical responsibility and resistance to totalitarianism?

2] Which of the five writers seems to have the most realistic grasp of the policies and purposes of the Soviet Union?

3] Would you agree with Walter Stein that the very practice of nuclear deterrence, even if the policy ensures peace, involves us nevertheless in "immoral risks—and in immoral hypothetical decisions"? If deterrence is not morally justifiable, what alternatives have we to surrender or martyrdom?

4] Kenneth Thompson and H. Stuart Hughes argue for limited war as a defense against aggression. How dependably can modern warfare be limited? What are the dangers of "escalation"?

5] At what points do the various writers introduce historical material to support their arguments and policy recommendations? Which of the writers seem to handle their historical evidence most cogently?

RECOMMENDED READINGS

BATCHELDER, ROBERT. *The Irreversible Decision: 1939–1950* (Boston, 1962). An ethical analysis of political decision-making in the area of military affairs; deals especially with building the atomic bomb.

BENNETT, JOHN, ed. *Nuclear Weapons and the Conflict of Conscience* (New York, 1962). Essays by leading American moralists, including Paul Ramsey and Kenneth Thompson.

BROWN, HARRISON AND JAMES REAL. *Community of Fear* (Santa Barbara, Cal., 1960). A vivid presentation of the destructive effects of thermonuclear weapons.

CLANCY, WILLIAM, ed. *The Moral Dilemma of Nuclear Weapons* (New York: The Church Peace Union, 1961). A pamphlet containing essays by leading religious thinkers of all faiths.

KAHN, HERMAN. *Thinking About the Unthinkable* (New York, 1962). A review of various thermonuclear strategies by a leading authority.

KENNAN, GEORGE. *Russia, the Atom, and the West* (New York, 1958). A thoughtful examination of United States foreign and military policy by a leading American diplomat.

KING-HALL, STEPHEN. *Defence in the Nuclear Age* (London, 1958). A plan for the nonviolent defense of Great Britain by a leading British military expert.

LEVINE, ROBERT A. *The Arms Debate* (Cambridge, Mass., 1963). An analytical presentation of alternative positions on disarmament and deterrence.

MERTON, THOMAS, ed. *Breakthrough to Peace* (New York, 1962). Essays on thermonuclear war by several American and British thinkers.

MILLER, WILLIAM ROBERT. *Nonviolence: A Christian Interpretation* (New York, 1964). The most comprehensive analysis available of nonviolence; includes a "casebook" of historical examples.

NOEL-BAKER, PHILIP. *The Arms Race* (New York, 1958). The most detailed account of the arms race and disarmament negotiations up to 1958; written by a Nobel Peace Prize winner.

RAMSEY, PAUL. *War and the Christian Conscience* (Durham, N.C., 1961). An excellent detailed analysis of the just-war doctrine in the thermonuclear age.

RUSSELL, BERTRAND. *Common Sense and Nuclear Warfare* (New York, 1959). A great twentieth century philosopher suggests some "basic changes in outlook" necessary on the part of East and West alike if the cold war is to be settled peacefully.

SIBLEY, MULFORD, ed. *The Quiet Battle* (New York, 1963). Historical accounts and theoretical essays on nonviolence.

SNYDER, GLENN. *Deterrence and Defense: Toward a Theory of National Security* (Princeton, 1961). Presents the concept of "graduated deterrence" as an alternative to massive retaliation.

STEIN, WALTER, ed. *Nuclear Weapons: A Catholic Response* (London, 1964). A collection of excellent and incisive essays on the just-war tradition by British Catholics.

STRAUSZ-HUPÉ, ROBERT. *Protracted Conflict* (New York, 1963). A sophisticated, hard-line analysis of cold-war problems.

THOMPSON, CHARLES, ed. *Morals and Missiles* (London, 1960). Moral analyses by leading British Catholic theologians.

TUCKER, ROBERT. *The Just War: A Study in Contemporary American Doctrine* (Baltimore, 1960). A critical examination of the American public philosophy of war.

WINDAS, STANLEY. *Christianity Versus Violence* (New York, 1964). A social and historical study of war and Christianity by a leading British Catholic.